At the
MASTER'S
FEET

A DAILY DEVOTIONAL

COMPILED BY

Audie G. Lewis

At the
MASTER'S
FEET

A DAILY DEVOTIONAL

SELECTIONS FROM THE

BEST OF CHARLES
SPURGEON

GRAND RAPIDS, MICHIGAN 49530 USA

At the Master's Feet
Copyright © 2005 by The Zondervan Corporation

Requests for information should be addressed to:
Zondervan, *Grand Rapids, Michigan 49530*

Library of Congress Cataloging-in-Publication Data

Spurgeon, C. H. (Charles Haddon), 1834–1892.
    At the Master's feet : a daily devotional from the best of Charles
Spurgeon / compiled by Audie G. Lewis.
       p. cm.
   ISBN-13: 978-0-310-25196-5 (hardcover)
   ISBN-10: 0-310-25196-6 (hardcover)
   1. Devotional calendars—Baptists. 2. Bible—Meditations.
I. Lewis, Audie G. II. Title.
BV4811.S65 2005
242'.2—dc22

                                          2005013743

This edition printed on acid-free paper.

All Scripture quotations, unless otherwise indicated, are taken from the *Holy Bible: New International Version*®. NIV®. Copyright © 1973, 1978, 1984 by International Bible Society. Used by permission of Zondervan. All rights reserved.

Scriptures marked KJV are taken from the King James Version of the Bible.

The material for this book has been excerpted from The New Library of Spurgeon's Sermons, a twenty-volume set of *The Best of Spurgeon for the First Time Available Arranged According to Subject*. Published by Zondervan, Grand Rapids, Michigan, 1958–1963.

This edition has been updated and Americanized.

Interior design by Beth Shagene

Printed in the United States of America

---

05 06 07 08 09 10 /❖ DCI/ 13 12 11 10 9 8 7 6 5 4 3 2 1

This devotional is dedicated to the men and women who have submitted their lives to Jesus Christ. Like Charles Spurgeon, they are happiest when seated at the Master's feet.

Foreword

❦

Charles H. Spurgeon preached to upwards of ten million people during his forty-plus years of ministry before joining his Lord in 1892. Thousands came to Christ under his evangelistic influence while he served as the pastor of the New Park Street Chapel and the Metropolitan Tabernacle in London, England. Without the aid of microphones or modern technologies, Charles Spurgeon pastored a flock of more than six thousand members, the largest single congregation known to exist prior to his ministry. During this same period he helped to start more than forty other churches and oversaw the Pastor's College and the Stockwell Orphanage. During his lifetime, he was a major influence on the lives of many great Christian leaders including Dwight Moody, Hudson Taylor, George Mueller, and Oswald Chambers. Spurgeon's writings have sold millions worldwide including a continual republication of more than two thousand of his best sermons. Although he is often referred to as the "Prince of Preachers," his words of God-given insight have blessed many more laypeople than pastors.

Our hope in putting this devotional together is that many, many more laypeople, pastors, and future Christians will be encouraged and strengthened by these spiritual insights that have been gathered from the best of the best of Charles Spurgeon's timeless sermons. Also included is an additional daily Scripture reference at the bottom of each page that corresponds to either an Old Testament or a New Testament book. If this additional reading is followed, it will allow the reader to completely read through the entire Bible in one year. May God continue to bless each and every reader as they sit with this great pastor at the Master's feet!

AUDIE AND HEATHER LEWIS

Introduction

❧

As I look back upon my own history, little did I dream when first I opened my mouth for Christ, in a very humble way, that I should have the honor of bringing thousands to Jesus. Blessed, blessed be his name! He has the glory of it. But I cannot help thinking that there must be some other lad here, such a one as I was, whom he may call by his grace to do service for him. When I had a letter sent to me by the deacons of the church at New Park Street to come up to London to preach, I sent it back by the next post, telling them that they had made a mistake, that I was a lad of nineteen years of age, happy among a very poor and lowly people in Cambridgeshire who loved me, and that I did not imagine they could mean that I was to preach in London. But they returned it to me and said that they knew all about it and that I must come. Ah, what a story it has been since then of the goodness and loving-kindness of the Lord!

CHARLES HADDON SPURGEON
FROM THE SERMON "THE LAD'S LOAVES"

Keep to the Word of God

❧

*Now the Bereans were of more noble character than the Thessalonians,
for they received the message with great eagerness and examined the
Scriptures every day to see if what Paul said was true.*
ACTS 17:11

I commend scrupulous obedience to all of you, and especially to those young people who have lately made a profession of their faith in Christ. Do not be as your fathers were, for the generation that is now going off the stage neither reads its Bible nor cares to know the Lord's will. If people searched the Scriptures, we should find them come together in union; but the least-read book in all the world, in proportion to its circulation, is the Word of God. It is distributed everywhere, but it is read scarcely anywhere with care and attention and with a sincere resolve to follow its precepts at all hazards. You come and listen to us, and we give you little bits taken from it here and there, but you do not get a fair notion of it as a whole. How can you? Ministers make mistakes, and you follow them without inquiry. One elects this leader and another that, to the creation of varieties of opinions and even of sects, which ought not to be, and would not be if all stood fast by the standard of inspired truth. If the Bible were but read and prayed over, many errors would die a speedy death, and others would be sorely crippled. Had that inspired Book been read in the past, many errors would never have arisen. Search you, then, the Book of God, I pray you; and whatever you find there, be sure to attend thereto. At all costs, keep to the Word of God.

Through the Bible in One Year: Matthew 1–2

He Will Supply All Your Needs

*And my God will meet all your needs according
to his glorious riches in Christ Jesus.*
PHILIPPIANS 4:19

If *he* will supply you, you will be supplied indeed, for God is infinite in capacity. He is infinitely wise as to the manner of his actions, and infinitely powerful as to the acts themselves. He never sleeps nor tires; he is never absent from any place but is always ready to help. Your needs come, perhaps, at very unexpected times; they may occur in the midnight of despondency or in the noonday of delight, but God is ever near to supply the surprising need. He is everywhere present and everywhere omnipotent, and he can supply all your needs, in every place, at every time, to the fullest degree. Remember that "omnipotence has servants everywhere" and that whenever God wishes to send you aid, he can do it without pausing to ask, "How shall it be done?" He has but to will it, and all the powers of heaven and earth are subservient to your necessity. With such a Helper, what case have you to doubt?

Through the Bible in One Year: Matthew 3–4

Priests unto the Most High

❧

But you are a chosen people, a royal priesthood, a holy nation,
a people belonging to God, that you may declare the praises of him
who called you out of darkness into his wonderful light.

1 PETER 2:9

Such a one as Jesus in such a one as I am! The King of Glory in a sinner's bosom! This is a miracle of grace, yet the manner of it is simple enough. A humble, repenting faith opens the door, and Jesus enters the heart at once. Love shuts the door with the hand of penitence, and holy watchfulness keeps out intruders. Thus is the promise made good, "If any man hear my voice, and open the door, I will come in to him, and will sup with him, and he with me" (Revelation 3:20 KJV). Meditation, contemplation, prayer, praise, and daily obedience keep the house in order for the Lord; and then follows the consecration of our entire nature to his use as a temple; the dedication of spirit, soul, and body, and all their powers, as holy vessels of the sanctuary; the writing of "Holiness unto the Lord" upon all that is about us, till our everyday garments become vestments, our meals sacraments, our life a ministry, and ourselves priests unto the Most High. Oh, the supreme condescension of this indwelling! He never dwelt in an angel, but he resides in a contrite spirit. There is a world of meaning in the Redeemer's words, "I in them." May we know them as Paul translates them, "Christ in you, the hope of glory."

Through the Bible in One Year: Matthew 5–6

The Disciple Whom Jesus Loved

This is how we know what love is: Jesus Christ laid down his life for us.
And we ought to lay down our lives for our brothers.
1 JOHN 3:16

If you wish to be "the disciple whom Jesus loved," begin soon. I suppose that John was between twenty and twenty-five when he was converted; at any rate, he was quite a young man. All the representations of him that have been handed down to us, though I attach no great value to them, yet unite in the fact of his youth. Youthful piety has the most profitable opportunity of becoming eminent piety. If you begin soon to walk with Christ, you will improve your pace, and the habit will grow upon you. He who is only made a Christian in the last few years of his life will scarcely reach to the first and highest degree, for lack of time, and from the hampering influence of old habits; but you who begin soon are planted in good soil, with a sunny aspect, and should come to maturity.

If you want to be the man whom Jesus loves, cultivate strong affection and let your nature be tender and kind. The man who is habitually cross and frequently angry cannot walk with God. A man of a quick, hot temper who never tries to check it, or a man in whom there is a malicious remembrance of injuries, like a fire smoldering amidst the embers, cannot be the companion and friend of Jesus, whose spirit is of an opposite character. A pitiful, compassionate, unselfish, generous heart is that which our Lord approves. Be willing to lay down, not only your comfort, but even your life for the brethren. Live in the joy of others, even as saints do in heaven. So shall you become a man greatly beloved.

Through the Bible in One Year: Matthew 7–8

Our Significance to God

When I consider your heavens, the work of your fingers,
the moon and the stars, which you have set in place,
what is man that you are mindful of him, the son of man
that you care for him?
PSALM 8:3–4

Lift up your eyes now to the heavens, and count the stars. Listen to the astronomer as he tells you those little specks of light are mighty worlds, some of them infinitely superior to this world of ours, and that there are millions upon millions of such worlds glittering in the sky, and that perhaps all these millions that we can see are only like one little corner, one little sand hill of the worlds that God has made, while throughout boundless space there may be long leagues of worlds, if I may use the expression, innumerable as the sands that belt the shore around the great and mighty deep. Now, one man in a world—how little! But one man in myriads of worlds, one man in the universe—how insignificant! And herein is love, that God should love so insignificant a creature. For what is God, compared with the worlds, their number, and their probable extent of space? God is infinitely greater than all the ideas we suggest by such comparisons. God himself is greater than all space. No conception of greatness that ever crossed a mind of the most enlarged faculties can enable us to apprehend the grandeur of God as he really is. Yet this great and glorious Being, who fills all things and sustains all things by the world of his power, condescends to rivet upon us, not his pity, mark you, not his thoughts, but the very love of his soul, which is the essence of himself, for he is love. "Herein is love!"

Through the Bible in One Year: Matthew 9–10

That Which Besets All Men

*"He causes his sun to rise on the evil and the good,
and sends rain on the righteous and the unrighteous."*
MATTHEW 5:45

Between us and other men there are many points of difference, but we share with them in the common infirmities, labors, sicknesses, bereavements, and necessities of our fallen race. We are outside of Eden's gate with the rest of Adam's family. We may be greatly beloved of God and yet be poor. God's love to Lazarus did not prevent his lying at the rich man's gate, nor hinder the dogs from licking his sores. Saints may be sick as well as other men; Job and David and Hezekiah felt sore diseases. Saints go into the hospital as well as sinners, for their bodies are liable to the same accidents and ailments. Such diseases as men bring upon themselves by vice, the godly escape, and therefore, as a rule, God's people have a great advantage over the reckless and reprobate in point of health. But still, in this respect the best of men are only men, and it will often be said, "Lord, he whom thou lovest is sick." Upon the bodies of the godly, the elements have the same power as upon others; upon them the hot sirocco blows, or through their garments the cold penetrates; the sun scorches them in the fierceness of his summer heat, or chilling damps threaten the flame of life. In this respect, one event happens unto all, though not without mysterious and blessed differences. No screen is set around the godly to protect them from physical suffering; they are not living in the land of Goshen so that light cheers their dwellings while the dense fog hangs over the rest of the land.

Through the Bible in One Year: Matthew 11–12

The Steadfast Friend of Truth

*He regarded disgrace for the sake of Christ
as of greater value than the treasures of Egypt,
because he was looking ahead to his reward.*
HEBREWS 11:26

Nowadays the truth that God has revealed seems of less account with men than their own thoughts and dreams, and they who still believe Christ's faithful word shall have it said of them, "I was a stranger, and ye took me in" (Matthew 25:35 KJV). When you see revealed truth, as it were, wandering about in sheepskins and goatskins, being destitute, afflicted, tormented, and no man saith a good word for it, then is the hour come to avow it because it is Christ's truth, and to prove your fidelity by counting the reproach of Christ greater riches than all the treasures of Egypt. Oh, scorn on those who only believe what everybody else believes, just because they must be in the swim with the majority. These are but dead fish borne on the current, and they will be washed away to a shameful end. As living fish swim against the stream, so do living Christians pursue Christ's truth against the set and current of the times, defying alike the ignorance and the culture of the age. It is the believer's honor, the chivalry of a Christian, to be the steadfast friend of truth when all other men have forsaken it.

Through the Bible in One Year: Matthew 13–14

Trust and Obey

May the God of hope fill you with all joy and peace as you trust in him,
so that you may overflow with hope by the power of the Holy Spirit.
ROMANS 15:13

The golden lesson is that you trust him. If all power is his, lean on him. We do not lean on Christ enough. He will never sink under your weight. All the burdens that men ever had to carry, Christ carried, and he certainly will carry yours. How often we weary ourselves with walking when we might ride—I mean, we carry our troubles when we might take them to Christ. We fret, and groan, and cry, and our difficulties do not get any the less, but when we leave them with him who cares for us and begin to trust, like a child trusts its father, how light of heart and how strong of spirit we become!

Heaven is the place of rest for us, not this world of temptation and sin. Still, stand ready to suffer or to serve. At the Master's gate watch and wait to do his bidding. Never on weekdays, and much less on Sabbath days, let your spirits be out of order for Christian service. We ought so to live that if called to die at any minute, we should not need to say a prayer—ready for heaven, ready for a life of service or for a death of glory. The true way for a Christian to live in this world is to be always as he would wish to be if Christ came at that moment, and there is a way of living in that style— simply depending upon the blood and righteousness of Jesus Christ, and then going out into daily service for him, moved by love to him, saying to him, "Lord, show me what you would have me to do."

Through the Bible in One Year: Matthew 15–16

Christt Died for Sinners

❧

This righteousness from God comes through faith in Jesus Christ
to all who believe. There is no difference, for all have sinned
and fall short of the glory of God.
ROMANS 3:22–23

The apostle here says that "there is no difference," yet he does not mean that all men are alike in all respects. There are many and important variations among men. It would be quite untrue and unjust to say that there are no differences of character even among unregenerate men, for there are certainly many varieties and gradations of sinners. There are some who have, as it were, sold themselves to work iniquity, and there are others who have, apparently, kept the commandments of God from their youth.

There are, then, differences of character among men; and there are, no doubt, differences of disposition that show themselves very early. Some children appear from the very first to be tender and docile, while others manifest a passionate and rebellious disposition. All of us probably know some friends who are not yet converted, but they are amiable, loving, considerate, kind; they have almost everything we could wish except the one thing needful; God grant that they may soon have that also! There are, alas, others whose dispositions are the very reverse of all this; they seem disposed to everything that is bad.

There is one point in which there is no difference, and that is that "all have sinned." All have forfeited every claim to personal righteousness, all must be made righteous by the imputation of the righteousness of Christ to them, and all who would have that righteousness must believe in the Lord Jesus Christ, for there is one way of salvation, and only one, and whatever other differences there may be, there is no difference about this matter; if we are saved at all, we must all be saved in one way.

Departing in Peace

❧

Lord, now lettest thou thy servant depart in peace,
according to thy word: For mine eyes have seen thy salvation.
LUKE 2:29–30 KJV

Simeon's basis of hope for a peaceful departure was "according to thy word," and surely no Scripture is of private interpretation or is to be reserved for one believer to the exclusion of the rest. The promises of God, which are "yes and amen in Christ Jesus," are sure to all the seed: not to some of the children is the promise made, but all the grace-born are heirs. If Simeon, as a believer in the Lord, had a promise that he should depart in peace, I have also a like promise if I am in Christ.

Every believer shall in death depart in the same sense as Simeon did. The word here used is suggestive and encouraging: it may be applied either to escape from confinement, or to deliverance from toil. The Christian man in the present state is like a bird in a cage: his body imprisons his soul. But the day comes when the great Master shall open the cage door and release his prisoners, singing all the way with a rapture beyond imagination. Simeon looked upon dying as a mode of being let loose—a deliverance out of durance vile, an escape from captivity, a release from bondage. The like redemption shall be dealt unto us. God, who gave us to aspire to holiness and spirituality and to likeness to himself, never implanted those aspirations in us out of mockery. He meant to gratify these holy longings, or else he would not have excited them.

Through the Bible in One Year: Matthew 19–20

Citizens of Heaven on Earth

❧

But our citizenship is in heaven.
PHILIPPIANS 3:20

What is meant by our being citizens in heaven? Why, first that we are under heaven's government. Christ the king of heaven reigns in our hearts; the laws of glory are the laws of our consciences; our daily prayer is, "Thy will be done on earth as it is in heaven." The proclamations issued from the throne of glory are freely received by us; the decrees of the Great King we cheerfully obey. We are not without law to Christ. The Spirit of God rules in our mortal bodies, grace reigns through righteousness, and we wear the easy yoke of Jesus. Oh, that he would sit as King in our hearts, like Solomon upon his throne of gold. Thine are we, Jesus, and all that we have; rule thou without a rival.

Let our lives be conformed to the glory of our citizenship. In heaven they are holy; so must we be—so are we if our citizenship is not a mere pretense. They are happy, so must we be rejoicing in the Lord always. In heaven they are obedient; so must we be, following the faintest monitions of the divine will. In heaven they are active; so should we be, both day and night praising and serving God. In heaven they are peaceful; so should we find a rest in Christ and be at peace even now. In heaven they rejoice to behold the face of Christ; so should we be always meditating upon him, studying his beauties, and desiring to look into the truths that he has taught. In heaven they are full of love; so should we love one another as brethren. In heaven they have sweet communion one with another; so should we—who though many, are one body— be everyone members one of the other.

Through the Bible in One Year: Matthew 21–22

Be Rich toward God

"Do not store up for yourselves treasures on earth,
where moth and rust destroy, and where thieves break in and steal.
But store up for yourselves treasures in heaven, where moth
and rust do not destroy, and where thieves do not break in and steal.
For where your treasure is, there your heart will be also."
MATTHEW 6:19–21

Christian men, you must never covet the world's esteem; the love of this world is not in keeping with the love of God. "If any man love the world, the love of the Father is not in him" (1 John 2:15 KJV). Treat its smiles as you treat its threats, with quiet contempt. Be willing rather to be sneered at than to be approved, counting the cross of Christ greater riches than all the treasures of Egypt. The men of this world were made to raise us to their seats of honor, for we are aliens and citizens of another country.

Furthermore, as aliens, it is not for us to hoard up this world's treasures. If we are aliens, the treasures of this world are like bits of paper, of little value in our esteem; and we should lay up our treasure in heaven, "where neither moth nor rust doth corrupt, and where thieves do not break through nor steal" (Matthew 6:20 KJV). The money of this world is not current in paradise; and when we reach its blissful shore, if regret can be known, we shall wish that we had laid up more treasure in the land of our fatherhood, in the dear fatherland beyond the skies. Transport your jewels to a safer country than this world; be rich toward God rather than before men.

Through the Bible in One Year: Matthew 23–24

Sacred Violence

The prayer of a righteous man is powerful and effective.
JAMES 5:16

Never cease your prayers. No time is ill for prayer. The glare of daylight should not tempt you to cease, and the gloom of midnight should not make you stop your cries. I know it is one of Satan's chief objects to make the Christian cease praying, for if he could but once put up the weapon of all-prayer, he would easily vanquish us and take us for his prey. But so long as we continue to cry to the Most High, Satan knows he cannot devour the very weakest lamb of the flock. Prayer, mighty prayer, will yet prevail if it hath but time.

And while you never cease from your trust, nor from your prayer, grow more earnest in both. Let your faith be still more resolved to give up all dependence anywhere but upon God, and let your cry grow more and more vehement. It is not every knock at mercy's gate that will open it; he who would prevail must handle the knocker well, and dash it down again, and again, and again. As the old Puritan saying goes, "Cold prayers ask for a denial, but it is red-hot prayers which prevail." Bring your prayers as some ancient battering ram against the gate of heaven, and force it open with a sacred violence, "for the kingdom of heaven suffereth violence, and the violent take it by storm." He who would prevail with God must take care that all his strength be thrust into his prayers.

Through the Bible in One Year: Matthew 25–26

In This World

*"I have told you these things, so that in me you may have peace.
In this world you will have trouble. But take heart!
I have overcome the world."*

JOHN 16:33

The believer is in two places, and he lives two lives. In the text are two places spoken of, "in me," and "in this world." The saint's noblest life is "hid with Christ in God"; this is his new life, his spiritual life, his incorruptible life, his everlasting life. Rejoice, beloved, if you are in Christ, and enjoy the privilege that belongs to that condition: "that in me you may have peace." Do not be satisfied without it; it is your right through your relationship to the Prince of Peace. Because you are in Christ, your life of lives is always safe and should be always restful. Your greatest interests are all secure, for they are guaranteed by the covenant of which Jesus is the surety. Your treasure, your eternal portion, is laid up with him in heaven where neither rust nor robber can enter. Therefore, be of good cheer.

You are sorrowfully conscious that you also live another life, for you dwell in the midst of evil men, or as the text puts it, you are "in the world." Even while you dwell in the sweet seclusion of domestic life, though your family has been graciously visited, and your dear ones are all believers, yet even there matters occur that make you feel that you are "in the world"—a world of sin and sorrow. You are not in heaven yet; do not dream that you are. It would be a pity for a sailor to expect the sea to be as stable as the land, for the sea will be the sea to the end; and the world will be the world to you as long as you are in it.

Through the Bible in One Year: Matthew 27–28

Labor for Him

❧

What good is it, my brothers, if a man claims to have faith
but has no deeds?
JAMES 2:14

Few of us can bear pain; perhaps fewer still of us can bear misrepresentation, slander, and ingratitude. These are horrible hornets that sting as with fire; men have been driven to madness by cruel scandals that have distilled from venomous tongues. Christ, throughout life, bore these and other sufferings. Let us love him as we think of how much he must have loved us. Will you try to get your souls saturated with the love of Christ? Admire the power of his love, and then pray that you may have a love somewhat akin to it in power.

We sometimes wonder why the church of God grows so slowly, but I do not wonder when I recollect what scant consecration to Christ there is in the church of God. Jesus was "a man of sorrows, and acquainted with grief"(Isaiah 53:3 KJV), but many of his disciples who profess to be altogether his are living for themselves. There are rich men who call themselves saints, and are thought to be so, whose treasures are hoarded for themselves and their families. Mayhap you have to confess you are doing nothing; do not let this day conclude till you have begun to do something for your Lord. We are talking about the church doing this and that—what is the church? The church is only the aggregation of individuals, and if any good is to be done, it must be performed by individuals, and if all individuals are idle, there is no church work done; there may be the semblance of it, but there is no real work done. Brother, sister, what are you doing for Jesus? I charge you by the nail prints of his hands, labor for him!

Through the Bible in One Year: Genesis 1–4

God Is Sovereign

❧

Then the LORD answered Job out of the storm.
He said: "Who is this that darkens my counsel with words without
knowledge? Brace yourself like a man; I will question you,
and you shall answer me. Where were you when I laid the earth's
foundation? Tell me, if you understand."
JOB 38:1–4

The God of Scripture is a sovereign God; that is, he is a God who has absolute authority and absolute power to do exactly as he pleases. Over the head of God there is no law; upon his arm there is no necessity; he knows no rule but his own free and mighty will. And though he cannot be unjust and cannot do anything but good, yet is his nature absolutely free; for goodness is the freedom of God's nature. God is not to be controlled by the will of man, nor the desires of man, nor by fate in which the superstitious believe; he is God, doing as he wills in the armies of heaven and in this lower world.

He is a God too, who gives no account of his matters; he makes his creatures just what he chooses to make them, and does with them just as he wills. And if any of them resent his acts, he says unto them: "Nay but, O man, who art thou that repliest against God? Shall the thing formed say to him that formed it, Why hast thou made me thus? Hath not the potter power over the clay, of the same lump to make one vessel unto honour, and another unto dishonour?" (Romans 9:20–21 KJV). God is good; but God is sovereign, absolute, knowing nothing that can control him. The monarchy of this world is no constitutional and limited monarchy; it is not tyrannical, but it is absolutely in the hands of an all-wise God.

Through the Bible in One Year: Genesis 5–8

Let Christ's Name Endure

You are still worldly. For since there is jealousy and quarreling among you, are you not worldly? Are you not acting like mere men? For when one says, "I follow Paul," and another, "I follow Apollos," are you not mere men?

What, after all, is Apollos? And what is Paul? Only servants, through whom you came to believe—as the Lord has assigned to each his task. I planted the seed, Apollos watered it, but God made it grow.

1 CORINTHIANS 3:3–6

Do you want to have your name put to everything that you do? Mind that God does not let you have your desire and then say to you, "There, you have done that unto yourself, so you can reward yourself for it." As far as ever you can, keep your own name out of all the work you do for the Lord. I used to notice in Paris that there was not a bridge or a public building without the letter *N* somewhere on it. Now, go through all the city, and find an *N* if you can. Napoleon hoped his fame would live in imperishable marble, but he had written his name in sand after all; and if any one of us shall, in our ministry, think it the all-important matter to make our own name prominent, we are on the wrong tack altogether. When George Whitefield was asked to start a new sect, he said, "I do not condemn my brother Wesley for what he has done, but I cannot do the same; let my name perish, but let Christ's name endure forever and ever."

Through the Bible in One Year: Genesis 9–12

Obedience in Little Things

"His master replied, 'Well done, good and faithful servant! You have been faithful with a few things; I will put you in charge of many things.'"
MATTHEW 25:21

Little things for Christ are often the best tests of the truth of our religion. Obedience in little things has much to do with the character of a servant. You engage a servant in your own house, and you know very well whether she be a good or bad servant that the main duties of the day are pretty sure to be attended to; the meals will be cooked, the beds will be prepared, the house will be swept, the door will be answered; but the difference between a servant who makes the house happy and another who is its plague lies in a number of small matters, which, peradventure, you could not put down on paper but which make up a very great deal of domestic comfort or discomfort, and so determine the value of a servant. So I believe it is in Christian life; I do not suppose that the most of us here would ever omit the weightier matters of the law; as Christian men we endeavor to maintain integrity and uprightness in our actions, and we try to order our households in the fear of God in great matters. But it is in the looking to the Lord upon minor details that the spirit of obedience is most displayed; it is seen in our keeping our eye up to the Lord. The really obedient spirit wishes to know the Lord's will about everything, and if there be any point which to the world seems trifling, for that very reason the obedient spirit says, "I will attend to it to prove to my Lord that even in the minutiae I desire to submit my soul to his good pleasure."

Through the Bible in One Year: Genesis 13–16

Persevere to Maturity

Consider it pure joy, my brothers, whenever you face trials of many kinds, because you know that the testing of your faith develops perseverance. Perseverance must finish its work so that you may be mature and complete, not lacking anything.

JAMES 1:2–4

Sometimes, if a mercy were to come to a believer immediately after he asked for it, it would come too soon, but God times it until it appears only at the right and best moment. Perhaps you are not yet ready for the blessing. You have asked for strong meat, but you are but as yet a babe, and therefore you are to be content with milk for a little while longer. You have asked for a man's trials, and a man's privileges, and a man's work, but you are as yet only a child growing up into manhood, and your good Father will give you what you ask for, but he will give it to you in such a way as to make it not a burden to you, but a boon. If it came now, it might involve responsibilities that you could not overtake, but, coming by and by, you shall be well prepared for it.

There are reasons too, I doubt not, that lie in our future, why our prayers are not answered. Delays in prayer may turn out to be a sort of training school for us. Take the apostle's instance. The "thorn in the flesh" was very painful, and though he was a chosen apostle, yet he had no answer. Thrice he cried, but still the "thorn in the flesh" was not removed. It was well that it was not, for Paul needed to be taught tenderness in order that he might write those loving epistles of his, and therefore he received an answer of another sort: "My grace is sufficient for thee."

Through the Bible in One Year: Genesis 17–20

The God of Scripture

Do not be deceived: God cannot be mocked. A man reaps what he sows.
The one who sows to please his sinful nature,
from that nature will reap destruction; the one who sows to please
the Spirit, from the Spirit will reap eternal life.

GALATIANS 6:7–8

And we now declare that the God of Holy Scripture is a God of inflexible justice; he is not the God whom some of you adore. You adore a god who winks at great sins; you believe in a god who calls your crimes peccadilloes and little faults. Some of you worship a god who does not punish sin but who is so weakly merciful, and mercilessly weak, that he passes by transgression and iniquity and never enacts a punishment. You believe in a god who, if man sins, does not demand punishment for his offense. You think that a few good works of your own will pacify him, that he is so weak a ruler that a few good words uttered before him in prayer will win sufficient merit to reverse the sentence, if indeed you think he ever passes a sentence at all. Your god is no God; he is as much a false god as the god of the Greeks or of ancient Nineveh. The God of Scripture is one who is inflexibly severe in justice and will by no means clear the guilty. "The LORD is slow to anger, and great in power, and will not at all acquit the wicked" (Nahum 1:3 KJV). The God of Scripture is a ruler who, when his subjects rebel, marks their crime and never forgives them until he has punished it, either upon them or upon their substitute.

Through the Bible in One Year: Genesis 21–24

Love One Another

Dear friends, since God so loved us, we also ought to love one another.
No one has ever seen God; but if we love one another,
God lives in us and his love is made complete in us.
1 JOHN 4:11–12

Christian, by the love that God has manifested to you, you are bound to love your fellow Christians. You are to love them though they have many infirmities. You have some yourself; and if you cannot love one because he has a crusty temper, perhaps he may reply that he cannot love you because you have a lethargic spirit. Jesus loved you with all your infirmities; then love your infirm brethren. You tell me you cannot love because you have been offended by such a brother; but you also offended Christ! What? Shall Christ forgive you all your myriad offenses, and you not forgive your brother? What was it, after all? "Well, he did not treat me respectfully." Ah, that is it—a poor worm wants to be treated respectfully! "But he spoke disparagingly of me; and there is a sister here—she may be a Christian woman, but she said a very unkind thing of me." Well, yes; but what does it matter? I have often thought, when people have spoken ill of me, and they have been very, very false in it, perhaps, if they had known me better, they might have found something true to say, and so I must be like we sometimes say of a boy when he is beaten and does not deserve it: "Well, he did deserve it, some time or other, for something else." Rather than get angry, smile over the offense. Who are we, that we should expect everybody to honor us when nobody honored our Lord? Oh, let us be ready at once to forgive even to seventy times seven.

Through the Bible in One Year: Genesis 25–28

How Can the Dead Work?

❧

As for you, you were dead in your transgressions and sins.
EPHESIANS 2:1

Spiritual life is not the result of working; how can the dead work for life? Must they not be quickened first, and then will they not rather work from life than for life? Life is a gift, and its bestowal upon any man must be the act of God. The gospel preaches life by Jesus Christ. Sinner, see where you must look! You are wholly dependent upon the quickening voice of him who is the resurrection and the life. "This," says one, "is very discouraging to us." It is intended so to be. It is kindness to discourage men when they are acting upon wrong principles. As long as you think that your salvation can be effected by your own efforts, or merits, or anything else that can arise out of yourself, you are on the wrong track, and it is our duty to discourage you. Remember that God's declaration is that "whosoever believeth in Jesus hath everlasting life." If, therefore, you are enabled to come and cast yourselves upon the blood and righteousness of Jesus Christ, you have immediately that eternal life which all your prayers, tears, repentance, church-goings, chapel-goings, and sacraments could never bring to you. Jesus can give it you freely at this moment, but you cannot work it in yourself.

You may imitate it and deceive yourself; you may garnish the corpse and make it seem as though it were alive, and you can galvanize it into a spasmodic motion, but life is a divine fire, and you cannot still the flame or kindle it for yourself; it belongs to God alone to make alive, and therefore I charge you, look alone to God in Christ Jesus.

Through the Bible in One Year: Genesis 29–32

Beware of Sin

For the wages of sin is death,
but the gift of God is eternal life in Christ Jesus our Lord.
ROMANS 6:23

Now this tendency is in every case the same, "the wages of sin is death" everywhere to everyone. It is so not only where you can see it operating upon the body, but where you cannot see it. I may perhaps startle you when I say that the wages of sin is death even in the man who has eternal life. Sin has the same deadly character to one as to the other; only an antidote is found. You, my Christian brother, cannot fall into sin without its being poison to you, as well as to anybody else; in fact, to you it is more evidently poison than to those hardened to it. If you sin, it destroys your joy, your power in prayer, your confidence toward God. If you have spent evenings in frivolity with worldlings, you have felt the deadening influence of their society. What about your prayers at night? You cannot draw nigh unto God. The operation of sin upon your spirit is most injurious to your communion with God. You are like a man who has taken a noxious drug, whose fumes are stupefying the brain and sending the heart into slumber. If you, being a child of God, fall into any of the sins that so easily beset you, I am sure you will never find that those sins quicken your grace or increase your faith; but on the contrary, they will work you evil, only evil, and that continually.

Through the Bible in One Year: Genesis 33–36

Living beyond Ourselves

*Therefore, as we have opportunity, let us do good to all people,
especially to those who belong to the family of believers.*
GALATIANS 6:10

By becoming doers of good, we are known as children of the good
God. "Blessed are the peacemakers; for they shall be called the
children of God" (Matthew 5:9 KJV). A man is a son of God
when he lives beyond himself by a thoughtful care for others;
when his soul is not confined within the narrow circle of his own
ribs, but goes abroad to bless those around him however unworthy they be. True children of God never see a lost one without
seeking to save him; never hear of misery without longing to
bestow comfort. "Ye know the heart of a stranger," said the Lord
to Israel (Exodus 23:9 KJV); and so do we, for we were once captives ourselves, and even now our choicest Friend is still a
Stranger, for whose sake we love all suffering men. When Christ
is in us, we search out opportunities of bringing prodigals,
strangers, and outcasts to the great Father's house. Our love goes
out to all mankind, and our hand is closed against none: if it be so,
we are made like to God, as little children are like their father. Oh,
sweet result of entertaining the Son of God by faith! He dwells in
us, and we gaze upon him in holy fellowship; so that "we all, with
open face beholding as in a glass the glory of the Lord, are
changed into the same image from glory to glory, even as by the
Spirit of the Lord" (2 Corinthians 3:18 KJV).

Through the Bible in One Year: Genesis 37–40

The God of Compassion

Jesus wept.
JOHN 11:35

We should weep, for Jesus wept. *Jesus wept for others.* I know not that he ever wept for himself. His were sympathetic tears. He embodied that command, "Weep with them that weep" (Romans 12:15 KJV). He has a narrow soul who can hold it all within the compass of his ribs. A true soul, a Christly soul, lives in other men's souls and bodies as well as in its own. A perfectly Christly soul finds all the world too narrow for its abode, for it lives and loves; it lives by loving and loves because it lives.

A flood of tears before the thrice Holy God will do far more than the hugest rolls of petition to our senators. "Jesus wept," and his tears were mighty weapons against sin and death. Please note that it is not written that Jesus thundered, but that "Jesus wept." You will do more good to offenders, more good to yourself, and more good to the best of causes if pity moistens all.

Lastly, when you have wept, *imitate your Savior—do something*! If the chapter before us had finished with "Jesus wept," it would have been a poor one. Suppose, after they had come to the grave, we had read, "Jesus wept, and went about his daily business." I should have felt small comfort in the passage. If nothing had come of it but tears, it would have been a great falling off from the usual ways of our blessed Lord. Tears! What are they alone? Salt water. A cup of them would be little worth to anybody. But, beloved, "Jesus wept," and then he commanded, "Roll away the stone." He cried, "Lazarus, come forth!"

Through the Bible in One Year: Genesis 41–44

Never Give Up

❧

"And will not God bring about justice for his chosen ones,
who cry out to him day and night?"
LUKE 18:7

As long as there is a place of prayer and a promise of an answer, no believer ought to give way to despair. "Go again," said Elijah to his servant seven times. It must have been weary work to the prophet to have to wait so long. He did not stand up once and pray to God as on Carmel, and then instantly came down the fire to continue the sacrifice; but again and again, and getting more humble in posture, with his face between his knees, he beseeches the Lord, not for fire, which was an unusual thing, but for water, which is the common boon of the skies. And yet, though he pleads for that which the Lord himself had promised, yet it did not at once come, and when his servant came back, four, five, six times, the answer was still the same; there was no sign of rain, but the brazen heavens looked down on an earth that was parched as if in an oven. "Go again!" said the prophet, and at the seventh time, lo, there appeared the cloud like unto a man's hand, and this cloud was the sure forerunner of the deluge and storm. Christian, go again seven times. Nay, I will venture to say seventy times seven, for God must keep his promise. Heaven and earth may pass away, but not one jot or tittle of Jehovah's Word can fail. "The grass withereth, the flower fadeth: but the word of our God shall stand for ever" (Isaiah 40:8 KJV). Do you plead that enduring Word? Let no dark thoughts drive you to despair. Continue to trust; continue to pray; increase in your fervency and in the hope that the blessing will yet come.

Through the Bible in One Year: Genesis 45–47

The Power of the Church

❦

The Son is the radiance of God's glory and the exact representation
of his being, sustaining all things by his powerful word.
HEBREWS 1:3

The true power of the church lies in Christ personally. You may
have all the stars that ever made bright the Milky Way with their
combined sheen, but there is no power in them to kill evil or conquer sin. The stars of the church shine because God makes them
shine. Their shining is not their own: it is borrowed light with
which they are radiant. But the power that overcomes evil,
wounds the hard heart, pierces the conscience, and kills reigning
sin is of the Lord alone. "Out of his mouth went a sharp two-
edged sword" (Revelation 1:16 KJV). Glory not, therefore, in
men; for power belongs unto God.

The power lies in Christ's Word: "Out of his mouth went a
sharp two-edged sword." "He that hath my word, let him speak
my word faithfully . . . saith the LORD" (Jeremiah 23:28 KJV).
People are disturbed and troubled by the real gospel: under the
false gospel they can sleep into destruction. Bring out the sword:
it is made to wound; let it exercise its salutary sharpness. The
gospel has two edges so that none may play with it. When they
think to run their fingers along the back of it, they will find themselves cut to the bone. Whether we regard its threats or its promises, it cuts at sin. Let us therefore know that the power of the
church does not lie anywhere but in the Word as Jesus himself
speaks it. Let us keep to his own pure, unadulterated, unblunted
Word, and let us pray him to send it forth with power out of his
own mouth into the hearts and consciences of men.

Through the Bible in One Year: Genesis 48–50

Battles in the War of Life

❧

We know that the law is spiritual; but I am unspiritual,
sold as a slave to sin. I do not understand what I do.
For what I want to do I do not do, but what I hate I do.
ROMANS 7:14–15

I did but look to Christ in the little chapel, and I received eternal life. I looked to Jesus, and he looked on me: and we were one forever. That moment my joy surpassed all bounds, just as my sorrow had aforetime driven me to an extreme of grief. I was perfectly at rest in Christ, satisfied with him, and my heart was glad; but I did not know that this grace was everlasting life till I began to read in the Scriptures and to know more fully the value of the jewel that God had given me. The next Sunday I went to the same chapel, as it was very natural that I should. But I never went afterwards, for this reason: that during my first week the new life that was in me had been compelled to fight for its existence, and a conflict with the old nature had been vigorously carried on. This I knew to be a special token of the indwelling of grace in my soul. But in that same chapel I heard a sermon upon "O wretched man that I am! who shall deliver me from the body of this death?" (Romans 7:24 KJV), and the preacher declared that Paul was not a Christian when he had that experience. Babe as I was, I knew better than to believe so absurd a statement. This conflict is one of the surest evidences of my new birth; the struggle becomes more and more intense; each victory over sin reveals another army of evil tendencies, and I am never able to sheathe my sword, nor cease from prayer and watchfulness.

Through the Bible in One Year: Mark 1–2

After We Are Called

*As he walked along, he saw Levi son of Alphaeus
sitting at the tax collector's booth.
"Follow me," Jesus told him, and Levi got up and followed him.*

*While Jesus was having dinner at Levi's house, many tax collectors
and "sinners" were eating with him and his disciples,
for there were many who followed him.*

MARK 2:14–15

No sooner was Matthew called and led to follow the Lord Jesus than he said to himself, "Now, what can I do for my new Master?" Levi made a great feast in his own house and said to the Lord Jesus, "You have bidden me follow you, and I am trying to do so; and one way in which I am following you is that I am going to have a great feast in my house tonight and to fetch in all my old companions. Will you come, and when they are all happy around my table, will you do for them what you have done for me?"

Now, has it been so with you, dear friend? Have you brought any others to Jesus? Have you brought your children to Jesus? Have your prayers brought your husband to Jesus? Have your entreaties brought your brethren to Jesus? If not, you have failed as yet in accomplishing that which should be your life work. Ask the Lord to help you now to begin with somebody or other of your own circle and your own standing, to whom you will be most likely to speak with the largest measure of influence and power of any man. Let each man, according to his calling, feel, "He who bade me follow him has bidden me do so that others may, through my instrumentality, be led to follow him too."

Through the Bible in One Year: Mark 3–4

Scoff Not at the Book

"Do not think that I have come to abolish the Law or the Prophets;
I have not come to abolish them but to fulfill them. I tell you the truth,
until heaven and earth disappear, not the smallest letter,
not the least stroke of a pen, will by any means disappear
from the Law until everything is accomplished."
MATTHEW 5:17–18

Let me call your attention to the fact that when Jesus had risen from the dead, he was just as tender of Scripture as he was before his decease. He told them that "all things must be fulfilled, which were written in the law of Moses, and in the prophets, and in the psalms, concerning me. Then opened he their understanding that they might understand the scriptures, and said unto them, Thus it is written, and thus it behoved Christ to suffer, and to rise from the dead'" (Luke 24:44–46 KJV). Find Jesus where you may, he is the antagonist of those who would lessen the authority of Holy Scripture. "It is written" is his weapon against Satan, his argument against wicked men. The learned at this hour scoff at the Book and accuse of Bibliolatry those of us who reverence the divine Word; but in this they derive no assistance from the teaching or example of Jesus. Not a word derogatory of Scripture ever fell from the lips of Jesus Christ; but evermore he manifested the most reverent regard for every jot and tittle of the inspired volume. Since our Savior, not only before his death, but after it, took care thus to commend the Scriptures to us, let us avoid with all our hearts all teaching in which Holy Scripture is put into the background.

Through the Bible in One Year: Mark 5–6

Drilled and Trained for War

Finally, be strong in the Lord and in his mighty power.
Put on the full armor of God so that you can take your stand against
the devil's schemes. For our struggle is not against flesh and blood,
but against the rulers, against the authorities, against the powers
of this dark world and against the spiritual forces of evil
in the heavenly realms.
EPHESIANS 6:10–12

We ought to regard the Christian church, not as a luxurious hostelry where Christian gentlemen may each one dwell at his ease in his own inn, but as a barracks in which soldiers are gathered together to be drilled and trained for war. We should regard the Christian church, not as an association for mutual admiration and comfort, but as an army with banners, marching to the fray to achieve victories for Christ, to storm the strongholds of the foe, and to add province after province to the Redeemer's kingdom.

We may view converted persons when gathered into church membership as so much wheat in the granary. God be thanked that it is there, and that so far the harvest has rewarded the sower; but far more soul-inspiring is the view when we regard those believers as each one likely to be made a living center for the extension of the kingdom of Jesus, for then we see them sowing the fertile valleys of our land and promising ere long to bring forth some thirty, some forty, some fifty, and some a hundredfold. The capacities of life are enormous; one becomes a thousand in a marvelously brief space. Within a short time a few grains of wheat would suffice to seed the whole world, and a few true saints might suffice for the conversion of all nations.

Through the Bible in One Year: Mark 7–8

Only One Payment Required

❧

But he was pierced for our transgressions, he was crushed
for our iniquities; the punishment that brought us peace was upon him,
and by his wounds we are healed. We all, like sheep, have gone astray,
each of us has turned to his own way; and the LORD has laid
on him the iniquity of us all.

ISAIAH 53:5–6

This is your comfort: that you cannot die. How can you perish if Jesus was put into your place? If your debt was paid of old by Christ, can it ever be demanded of you again? Once paid, it is fully discharged; the receipt we have gladly accepted; and now we can cry with the apostle, "Who shall lay any thing to the charge of God's elect? It is God that justifieth. Who is he that condemneth? It is Christ that died, yea rather, that is risen again, who is even at the right hand of God, who also maketh intercession for us" (Romans 8:33–34 KJV). See here the mainstay of every believer's confidence. He knows that Christ died for him because he has put his trust in his blessed mediation. If Jesus died for me, then I cannot be condemned for the sins that he expiated. God cannot punish twice for the one offense. He cannot demand two payments for one debt.

Through the Bible in One Year: Mark 9–10

Tutored by Affliction

❧

*Now I rejoice in what was suffered for you, and I fill up
in my flesh what is still lacking in regard to Christ's afflictions,
for the sake of his body, which is the church.*
COLOSSIANS 1:24

Affliction frequently opens truths to us and opens us to the truth—I know not which of these two is the more difficult. Experience unlocks truths that else were closed against us; many passages of Scripture will never be made clear by the commentator; they must be expounded by experience. Many a text is written in a secret ink that must be held to the fire of adversity to make it visible. I have heard that you see stars in a well when none are visible above ground, and I am sure you can discern many a starry truth when you are down in the deeps of trouble which would not be visible to you elsewhere. Besides, I said it opened us to the truth as well as the truth to us. We are superficial in our beliefs: we are often drenched with truth, and yet it runs off from us like water from a marble slab; but affliction, as it were, plows us and subsoils us, and opens up our hearts so that into our innermost nature the truth penetrates and soaks like rain into plowed land. Blessed is that man who receives the truth of God into his inmost self; he shall never lose it, but it shall be the life of his spirit. Affliction, when sanctified by the Holy Spirit, brings much glory to God out of Christians, through their experience of the Lord's faithfulness to them.

Through the Bible in One Year: Mark 11–12

The Believer's Garden

❧

Then Jesus asked, "What is the kingdom of God like?
What shall I compare it to? It is like a mustard seed,
which a man took and planted in his garden.
It grew and became a tree,
and the birds of the air perched in its branches."
LUKE 13:18–19

Some Christian people have no garden—no personal sphere of service. They belong to the whole clan of Christians, and they pine to see the entire band go out to cultivate the whole world; but they do not come to personal particulars. It is delightful to be warmed up by missionary addresses and to feel a zeal for the salvation of all the nations, but after all, the net result of a general theoretic earnestness for all the world does not amount to much.

It is the duty of every believer in Christ, like the first man, Adam, to have a garden to dress and to till. Children are in the Sunday schools by millions: thank God for that! But have you a class of your own? All the church at work for Christ! Glorious theory! Are you up and doing for your Lord? It will be a grand time when every believer has his allotment and is sowing it with the seed of truth. The wilderness and the solitary place will blossom as the rose when each Christian cultivates his own plot of roses. Teach your own children, speak to your neighbors, seek the conversion of those whom God has especially entrusted to you.

Through the Bible in One Year: Mark 13–14

Learn and Then Go

❧

"Even now the reaper draws his wages, even now he harvests the crop for eternal life, so that the sower and the reaper may be glad together."
JOHN 4:36

He came out from his solitude and began to sow. This is what I mean. At first, a Christian man very wisely lives indoors. There is a lot of cleaning and scrubbing to be done there. When the bees come out of their cells, they always spend the first few days of their life in the hive cleaning and getting everything tidy. They do not go out to gather honey till they have first of all done the housework at home. I wish that all Christian people would get their housework done as soon as they can. It needs to be done. I mean, acquaintance with experimental matters of indwelling sin, and overcoming grace. But after that, then the sower went forth to sow. He was not content with his own private experience, but he went forth to sow. There are numbers of people who are miserable because they are always at home. Go out, brother; go out, sister. Important as your experience is, it is only important as a platform for real usefulness. Get all right within, in order that you may get to work without.

Through the Bible in One Year: Mark 15–16

Cobwebs Swept Away

❧

I consider them rubbish, that I may gain Christ and be found in him,
not having a righteousness of my own that comes from the law,
but that which is through faith in Christ—
the righteousness that comes from God and is by faith.
PHILIPPIANS 3:8–9

There is self-righteousness up there as a crown upon your fore-head; it will have to come down. You are covered with the beautiful garments of your own good deeds; take them off, brother. They are all without merit in the sight of God until you have trusted his Son. All that you have done and all that you think you have done are only as so many cobwebs that must be swept away. There stands the gate through which the most fallen may enter, and you must go through the same gate. There is no private path made for a gentleman like you; there is no royal road to heaven, save only that one royal road that is opened for the very chief of sinners. Down, Mr. Pride! Here is a man who is born of Christian parents, and perhaps he has listened to the lying logic of the present age, which says, "Children born of godly parents do not need conversion; there is something good in them by nature." I tell you, sirs, that I begin to tremble for the children of pious parents, for I think that they are more likely to be deceived than any others; they often fancy that they are converted when they are not, and they get admitted into churches while they are unconverted. Instead of boasting of their godly ancestry, high privilege as it is, let them remember that regeneration is not of blood, nor of birth, nor of the will of man, but of God; and to them, as to all others, Christ's words apply: "Ye must be born again."

Through the Bible in One Year: Exodus 1–4

God's Mantle of Love

Know that the LORD has set apart the godly for himself;
the LORD will hear when I call to him.
PSALM 4:3

You see, then, that God discerns godliness in men. There is a great deal of dross in all of us, but God spies whatever gold there may be; if there be any gold in the ore, God preserves the lump because of the precious metal that is in it. I know that you are not perfect. Perhaps you are at this moment grieving over a great fault; if so, I am glad you have the godliness that makes you grieve over sin. I know that you are not what you want to be, or wish to be, or ought to be. Still, you do fear the Lord, and you do trust him, and you do love him. Now, the Lord can spy all that out, and he knows about the good that is in you. He casts your sin behind his back, but that which is of his own grace he sets apart for himself, and he sets you apart for himself because of the good that is in you. I do like to notice in Scripture that although God's people are described as a very faulty people, and although the Lord is never tender toward sin, yet he is always very gentle toward them. If there is any good point about them, he brings it out, and he is most gracious to them; and his love casts a mantle over a thousand of their mistakes and errors.

Through the Bible in One Year: Exodus 5 – 8

Victory through Jesus

❧

*No, in all these things we are more than conquerors
through him who loved us.*
ROMANS 8:37

Are you helpless? Are you hopeless? This is a day in which God will come to your relief. Do you need strength to break the chains of habit? Do you need power even to repent? Do you need help to feel your helplessness? Do you need everything? I know some who can trust Christ for pardon, but their chief difficulty is how they can be made holy. I greatly delight in seekers in whom this is the main thought; not so much to escape punishment as to avoid future sin. Well, if you are fighting against evil in the name of Jesus Christ, do not be discouraged; you will master it, because it is the day of salvation, and it is written, "They shall call his name Jesus, for he shall save his people from their sins." Do I address a drunkard? Has the intoxicating cup a strange fascination for you, and have you gone back to drinking after having often loathed yourself for it? You need not be a slave to it any longer, for this is a day of salvation from that sin: by faith in Christ you shall be delivered out of that deadly snare. Or have you been tempted to some other gross iniquity that holds you spellbound? Does a certain vice fix its basilisk eyes upon you and enchant you till you can no longer restrain yourself? Rejoice, then, for this is the day of salvation from sin. Neither saint nor sinner need sit down under the power of any sin, for in Christ Jesus' name we can overcome the power of evil.

Through the Bible in One Year: Exodus 9–12

Obedience in All Things

*But Joshua spared Rahab the prostitute, with her family
and all who belonged to her, because she hid the men Joshua had sent
as spies to Jericho—and she lives among the Israelites to this day.*
Joshua 6:25

Now, this is a question that I never intend to answer for anybody else, because I never intend to ask it on my own account. Whether or not a believer will perish because some known duty or scriptural ordinance is neglected, is a question that only selfishness would raise. Are we only to do that which will procure our progress or secure our salvation? Are we so grossly selfish as that? Does a loving child say, "If I refuse to do my father's will, shall I not still be my father's child? Shall I not still be fed and clothed by him?" Only an evil child would talk thus. The true son inquires, "What would my father have me do? I will do it cheerfully for his sake. What does my father forbid? For what he forbids shall be hateful to me." Rise above all questions concerning essential and nonessential, and learn to obey in all things; if it be only tying a scarlet thread in the window, or washing in water, do as you are bidden, and in nothing rebel against the Word of the Lord.

Through the Bible in One Year: Exodus 13–16

Precise Obedience

"Agreed," she replied. "Let it be as you say." So she sent them away and they departed. And she tied the scarlet cord in the window.
JOSHUA 2:21

She was told to tie the scarlet thread in the window, and she did it; there was exact obedience. It was not merely a thread, a line, but the scarlet line. She did not substitute a blue, or a green, or a white line. The order was this scarlet line, not another, and she took that particular one. Obedience to God will be very much seen in small matters. Love always delights to attend to the little things, and thereby makes the little things great. I have heard of a Puritan who was charged with being too precise, but his answer was excellent: "I serve a precise God." The Lord our God is a jealous God, and he is very jealous of his commands. It appeared a little mistake that Moses made when he struck the rock instead of speaking to it, and yet he could not enter into the promised rest because of his offense. A small action may involve a great principle, and it is for us to be very cautious and careful, searching out what the Master's will is, and then never halting or hesitating for any reason whatever, but doing his will as soon as ever we know it. Christian life should be a mosaic of minute obediences. The soldiers of Christ should be famous for their exact discipline.

Through the Bible in One Year: Exodus 17–20

Those Who Love Most

Then the disciple whom Jesus loved said to Peter, "It is the Lord!"
JOHN 21:7

What was the life of John? First, it was a life of intimate communion. John was wherever Christ was. Other disciples are put away, but Peter and James and John are present. When all the disciples sit at the table, even Peter is not nearest to the Lord Jesus, but John leans his head upon his bosom. Their relationship was very near and dear. Jesus and John were David and Jonathan over again. If you are a man greatly beloved, you will live in Jesus; your fellowship will be with him from day to day.

John's was a life of special instruction. He was taught things that no others knew, for they could not bear them. At the latter end of his life, he was favored with visions such as even Paul himself, though not a whit behind the chief of the apostles, had never seen. Because of the greatness of the Lord's love, he showed John future things and lifted up the veil so that he might see the kingdom and the glory. They shall see most who love most; they shall be taught most who most completely give up their hearts to the doctrine.

Through the Bible in One Year: Exodus 21–24

Throughout Eternity

I give them eternal life, and they shall never perish;
no one can snatch them out of my hand.
JOHN 10:28

I cannot advance an inch without praying my way, nor keep the inch I gain without watching and standing fast. Grace alone can preserve and perfect me. The old nature will kill the new nature if it can; and to this moment the only reason why my new nature is not dead is this: because it cannot die. If it could have died, it would have been slain long ago; but Jesus said, "I give unto my sheep eternal life" and "he that believeth on me hath everlasting life"; and therefore the believer cannot die. The only religion that will save you is one that you cannot leave, because it possesses you and will not leave you. To have Christ living in you, and the truth ingrained in your very nature—O sirs, this is the thing that saves the soul, and nothing short of it. It is written in the text, "God so loved the world, that he gave his only begotten Son, that whosoever believeth in him should not perish, but have everlasting life." What is this but a life that shall last through your threescore years and ten; a life that will outshine those stars and yon sun and moon; a life that shall coexist with the life of the Eternal Father? As long as there is a God, the believer shall not only exist, but live.

Through the Bible in One Year: Exodus 25–28

Divinely Commissioned

But you are a chosen people, a royal priesthood, a holy nation,
a people belonging to God, that you may declare the praises of him
who called you out of darkness into his wonderful light.

1 PETER 2:9

The ungodly cannot comprehend the godly; they scoff at them, they turn their glory into shame because they themselves love vanity and seek after lying. The godly man is not understood by the people among whom he dwells; God has made him to be a stranger and a foreigner in their midst. They who are born twice have a life that cannot be comprehended by those who are only born once. Those who have received the Spirit of God have a new spirit within them that is so singular that the carnal mind cannot perceive what it is. Spiritual things must be spiritually discerned. When a man has become a new creature in Christ Jesus, the old creatures round about him cannot make head or tail of him. They look at him, they see him actuated by motives they cannot understand, they see that he is kept in check by forces they do not acknowledge, that he is constrained by energies of which they are not partakers, and that he looks for something they do not desire; so the Christian becomes in a measure like to Christ himself, of whom the poet sings, "The Jewish world knew not their King, God's everlasting Son." "Therefore, the world knoweth us not, because it knew him not" (1 John 3:1 KJV).

Through the Bible in One Year: Exodus 29–32

Be Godly and Fear Not

⚜

Whatever happens, conduct yourselves in a manner worthy
of the gospel of Christ. Then, whether I come and see you or only hear
about you in my absence, I will know that you stand firm in one spirit,
contending as one man for the faith of the gospel
without being frightened in any way by those who oppose you.
PHILIPPIANS 1:27–28

God knows what godliness is, for he has created it, he sustains it, he is pledged to perfect it, and his delight is in it. What matters it whether you are understood by your fellow men or not, so long as you are understood by God? If that secret prayer of yours is known to him, seek not to have it known to anyone besides. If your conscientious motive be discerned in heaven, mind not though it be denounced on earth. If your designs—the great principles that sway you—are such as you dare plead in the great day of judgment, you need not stop to plead them before a jesting, jeering generation. Be godly, and fear not; and if you be misrepresented, remember that should your character be dead and buried among men, there will be "a resurrection of reputations" as well as of bodies. "Then shall the righteous shine forth as the sun in the kingdom of their Father" (Matthew 13:43 KJV).

Through the Bible in One Year: Exodus 33–36

Perfect in Christ Jesus

❧

What a wretched man I am!
Who will rescue me from this body of death?
Thanks be to God—through Jesus Christ our Lord!
ROMANS 7:24–25

Mourning Christian, dry up your tears. Are you weeping on account of sin? Why do you weep? Weep because of your sin, but weep not through any fear of punishment. Has the evil one told you that you shall be condemned? Tell him to his face that he lies. Ah, poor distressed believer, are you mourning over your own corruptions? Look to your perfect Lord, and remember, you are complete in him; you are in God's sight as perfect as if you had never sinned; nay, more than that, the Lord our righteousness has put a divine garment upon you, so that you have more than the righteousness of man—you have the righteousness of God. Oh, you who are mourning by reason of inbred sin and depravity, remember, none of your sins can condemn you. You have learned to hate sin, but have you learned to know that sin is not yours— it is put on Christ's head. Come, be of good cheer; your standing is not in yourself—it is in Christ; your acceptance is not in yourself, but in your Lord. With all your sin, you are as much accepted today as in your sanctification; you are as much accepted of God today, with all your iniquities, as you will be when you stand before his throne, rendered free from all corruption. Oh, I beseech you, lay hold on this precious thought, perfection in Christ! For you are perfect in Christ Jesus. Be of good cheer; do not fear to die; death has nothing terrible in it for you; Christ has extracted all the gall from the sting of death.

Through the Bible in One Year: Exodus 37–40

Sow No Regrets

❧

"About the eleventh hour he went out and found
still others standing around. He asked them, 'Why have
you been standing here all day long doing nothing?'

"'Because no one has hired us,' they answered.

"He said to them, 'You also go and work in my vineyard.'"
MATTHEW 20:6–7

I have waited quite long enough for favorable weather, but I remember that Solomon said, "He that observeth the wind shall not sow" (Ecclesiastes 11:4 KJV). Can I look upon some here, who have been members of the church for years, but who have never yet done anything for the Lord? If you have been a servant of God for many years and have never yet really worked for the salvation of souls, I want you now just to say to yourself, "Come now, I must really get at this work." You will be going home soon, and when your Master says to you, "Did you do any sowing for me?" you will have to reply, "No, Lord; I did plenty of eating. I went to the tabernacle, and I enjoyed the services." "But did you do any sowing?" "No, Lord; I did a great deal of hoarding; I laid up a large quantity of the good seed." "But did you do any sowing?" he will still ask, and that will be a terrible question for those who never went forth to sow.

I know not how far you may be going, but let it be written of you today, "The sowers went forth to sow"; they went forth with one resolve that by the power of the living Spirit of God, they who are redeemed with the precious blood of Jesus would make known his gospel to the sons of men, sowing that good seed in every place wherever they have the opportunity, trusting in God to make the seed increase and multiply.

Through the Bible in One Year: Luke 1–2

Saved to Serve

❧

"You call me 'Teacher' and 'Lord,' and rightly so, for that is what I am.
Now that I, your Lord and Teacher, have washed your feet,
you also should wash one another's feet."
JOHN 13:13–14

As he takes the basin, and the ewer, and the towel, and washes his disciples' feet, you can see the meekness of his disposition. And soon after this you see him giving up himself, his body, his soul, and his Spirit, in order that he might serve us. And what if I say that even at this very moment, as the Son of Man in heaven, he continues a kind of service of his people! For Zion's sake he does not hold his peace, and for Jerusalem's sake he does not rest but continues still to intercede for those whose names he bears upon his heart. Hear it, then, all you people, and let everyone who hears hail the gracious fact. Be you saints or sinners, be you saved already or athirst for the knowledge of salvation, the thought that Christ's errand was not to aggrandize himself, but to benefit us, must be welcome. He does not come to be served, but to serve. Does this not suit you, poor sinner—you who never did serve him, you who could not, as you are, minister to him? Well, he did not come to get your service; he came to give you his services; not that you might first do him honor, but that he might show you mercy. Oh, you need him so very much! And since he has come not to look for treasures, but to bestow unsearchable riches, not to find specimens of health, but to find instances of sickness upon which the healing art of his grace may operate, surely there is hope for you.

Through the Bible in One Year: Luke 3–4

May It Not Be

*"He answered, 'Then I beg you, father, send Lazarus
to my father's house, for I have five brothers. Let him warn them,
so that they will not also come to this place of torment.'"*
LUKE 16:27–28

In imagination—I pray that it may be only in imagination—I see some of you die unsaved; and I see you as you pass into the next world unpardoned, and your soul realizes, for the first time, what was the experience of the rich man, of whom our Savior said, "In hell he lifted up his eyes"—as though he had been asleep before and had only just awakened to his true condition. "He lifted up his eyes" and gazed all around, but he could see nothing except that which caused him dismay and horror; there was no trace of joy or hope, no track of ease or peace. Then, through the awful gloom, there came the sound of such questions as these: "Where are you, sinner? You were in a house of prayer a few weeks ago, and the preacher urged you to seek the Lord; but you procrastinated. Where are you now? You said that there was no such place as hell; but what do you say about it now? Where are you? You despised heaven and refused Christ; where are you now?" The Lord in mercy preserve all of you from that!

Through the Bible in One Year: Luke 5–6

A Hallowed Life

*Now it is God who has made us for this very purpose
and has given us the Spirit as a deposit,
guaranteeing what is to come.*

2 CORINTHIANS 5:5

When God gives a new nature to his people, the life that comes out of that new nature springs spontaneously from it. Fig trees do not bear figs on certain days and thorns at other times, but they are true to their nature at all seasons. He who has discovered what Christianity is knows that it is much more a life than an act, a form, or a profession. Much as I love the creed of Christendom, I am ready to say that true Christianity is far more a life than a creed. It is a creed, and it has its ceremonies, but it is mainly a life; it is a divine spark of heaven's own flame which falls into the human bosom and burns within, consuming much that lies hidden in the soul, and then at last, as a heavenly life, flaming forth, so as to be seen and felt by those around. Under the indwelling power of the Holy Spirit, a regenerate person becomes like that bush in Horeb, which was all aglow with Deity. The God within him makes him shine so that the place around him is holy ground, and those who look at him feel the power of his hallowed life.

Through the Bible in One Year: Luke 7–8

Apostles of Unbelief

※

But he said to them, "Unless I see the nail marks in his hands
and put my finger where the nails were, and put my hand into his side,
I will not believe it."

JOHN 20:25

Beloved, your risen Lord wants you to be happy. When he was here on earth, he said, "Let not your hearts be troubled": he says just the same to you today. He takes no delight in the distresses of his people. He loves you to believe in him and be at rest. Find if you can, beloved, one occasion in which Jesus inculcated doubt or bade men dwell in uncertainty. The apostles of unbelief are everywhere today, and they imagine that they are doing God service by spreading what they call "honest doubt." This is death to all joy! Poison to all peace! The Savior did not so. He would have them take extraordinary measures to get rid of their doubt. The removal of their doubt as to our Lord's resurrection needed that they should handle him, and therefore he bade them do so. O beloved, you who are troubled and vexed with thoughts and therefore get no comfort out of your religion because of your mistrust, your Lord would have you come very near to him and put his gospel to any test that will satisfy you. He cannot bear you to doubt. He appeals tenderly, saying, "O thou of little faith, wherefore didst thou doubt?" (Matthew 14:31 KJV). He would have you believe in the substantial reality of his religion, and handle him and see: trust him largely and simply, as a child trusts its mother and knows no fear.

Through the Bible in One Year: Luke 9–10

Love Unfathomable

Herein is love, not that we loved God, but that he loved us,
and sent his Son to be the propitiation for our sins.
1 JOHN 4:10 KJV

Are there not scenes and circumstances that now and then transpire before us and prompt an exclamation like that of the apostle, "Herein is love"? When we have seen the devotedness of a mother to her children, when we have marked the affection of friend for friend and caught a glimpse in different human relationships of the kindness that exists in human hearts, we have said, "Herein is love!" I shall ask you to look at and consider the wonder that the apostle discovered and that made him, with uplifted hands, exclaim, "Herein is love!"

When God loves those who love him, it seems to be according to the law of nature; but when he loves those who do not love him, this must be above even all laws—it is according, certainly, to the extraordinary rule of grace, and grace alone. There was not a man on earth who loved God. There was none who did good— no, not one; and yet the Lord fixed the eye of his electing love upon sinners in whom there was no thought of loving him. No more love to God is there in an unrenewed heart than there is life within a piece of granite. No more love to God is there within the soul who is unsaved than there is fire within the depths of the ocean's waves; and here forsooth is the wonder, that when we had no love to God, he should have loved us.

Through the Bible in One Year: Luke 11–12

Ready and Waiting

❧

"Therefore keep watch, because you do not know
on what day your Lord will come."
MATTHEW 24:42

In such an hour as they thought not, the Son of Man came. And now, though we have the words of the Scripture to assure us that he will come quickly, and that his reward is with him and his work before him, yet how few expect him! The coming of some foreign prince, the approach of some great event, is looked for and anticipated from the hour that the purpose is promulgated among the people. But your coming, Jesus, your glorious advent—where are they who strain their eyes to catch the first beams of the sun rising? There are a few of your followers who wait for your appearing. We meet with a few men who walk as though they know that time is short and that the Master may come at cock-crowing, or at midnight, or at the day-watch. We know a few beloved disciples who with longing hearts beguile the weary hours, while they prepare songs to greet you, O Immanuel! Lord, increase the number of those who look for you, and desire, and pray and wait, and watch through the dreary hours of the night for the morning that your coming shall usher in.

Through the Bible in One Year: Luke 13–14

Grateful Boasting

✒

It is because of him that you are in Christ Jesus,
who has become for us wisdom from God—
that is, our righteousness,
holiness and redemption. Therefore, as it is written:
"Let him who boasts boast in the Lord."
1 CORINTHIANS 1:30–31

When you thank God for the good things he has done for you,
thank him not only for keeping you out of sin, but also for
enabling you to do his will. No man has any right to take credit to
himself for his own integrity, for if he be a Christian, that integrity
is the gift of God's grace and the work of God's Spirit within him.
If you did in your youth form a candid, honest judgment of the
Word of God, and then, burning all bridges and boats and sever-
ing all connection with that which was behind you, if you did dare
to cast in your lot with the despised people of God, bless him for
it, and count it as a great favor he did you in that he enabled you
to act thus; and if, when tempted with heavy bribes, you have
hitherto been able to say, "Get thee behind me, Satan," and to follow close to the heels of Christ, give God all the glory of it, and
bless his holy name. In such a case as this, virtue is its own reward.
To have been obedient to Christ is one of the highest blessings
that God can have bestowed upon any man. There are some of us
who have to thank God that when there were pinching times, we
did not dare to yield; but when friends and enemies alike pointed
out another way, we saw what was our Master's way and followed
it by his grace. We shall have to thank him to all eternity for this.

Through the Bible in One Year: Luke 15–16

Manna from the Skies

How sweet are your words to my taste,
sweeter than honey to my mouth!
PSALM 119:103

The best of us need instruction. It is unwise for Christian people to be so busy about Christ's work that they cannot listen to Christ's words. We must be fed, or we cannot feed others. The synagogue must not be deserted if it be a synagogue where Christ is present. And oh, sometimes, when the Master is present, what a power there is in the Word: it is not the preacher's eloquence; it is neither the flow of language nor the novelty of thought; there is a secret, quiet influence that enters into the soul and subdues it to the majesty of divine love. You feel the vital energy of the divine Word, and it is not man's word to you, but the quickening voice of God sounding through the chambers of your spirit and making your whole being to live in his sight. At such times the sermon is as manna from the skies, or as the bread and wine with which Melchizedek met Abraham; you are cheered and strengthened by it and go away refreshed.

Through the Bible in One Year: Luke 17–18

A Lasting Business Perspective

Do not wear yourself out to get rich;
have the wisdom to show restraint.
PROVERBS 23:4

I knew your father well. He began life as you would have these young people begin, and he plodded on, and plodded on to the end of his allotted term, never having had time to think about religion. He was such a rare, sensible old gentleman, such a wise man! "What I want is facts and figures," said he, "none of your nonsense; do not tell me about your opinions; I cast my books up on a Sunday—that is the way to spend your Sabbath. I daresay when I have nothing else to do, I shall have time to think about my soul." He was a rare, "fine, old English gentleman," a very wise old man; howbeit, one night he lifted up his eyes in hell, and with all his accurate bookkeeping and balance of accounts, he had to sum it up: "No profits; I have gained my wealth but lost my soul." And oh, if he could come back again, he would say to his son, "My son, you had better begin business at the right end; make the soul sure, and then look after the body; hook yourself fast to eternity, and make that right, and then see after the slippery things of time as best you can in subservience to that." At any rate, let Mr. Worldly Wiseman say what he may; for God, who knows more about us than we do about ourselves, says, "Seek ye first the kingdom of God, and his righteousness; and all these things shall be added unto you."

Through the Bible in One Year: Luke 19–20

Deceive Not Our Youth

*"He was a murderer from the beginning,
not holding to the truth,
for there is no truth in him.
When he lies, he speaks his native language,
for he is a liar and the father of lies."*

JOHN 8:44

"Oh, stop a little longer; we should like these young people to know something about life." Well, but, base world, what do you mean by that? What have you to do with life? We too want the young people to know something about life. But what is life? Why, true life is to be found only in the followers of Christ, in whom is life. "Well," says the world, "but we mean the *life*." I know what you mean; you mean the death. You want the young people to know something about life, you say. I hear you; it is the voice of the same hissing serpent that said, "Ye shall be as gods, knowing good and evil"; and our mother Eve, in order to know evil as well as to know good, has destroyed this race. And many a young man and young woman, in trying to know good and to know evil, has come to know that which has made the head to ache, and the heart to palpitate, and the nerves to tingle with exquisite pain, that which has brought the frail body to an early grave and the doomed soul down to the lowest hell! I pray God that our young people may not know life in that aspect, but that they may know life in the true sense and search for it where only it is to be found.

Through the Bible in One Year: Luke 21–22

The Sin of Ignorance

※

How can a young man keep his way pure?
By living according to your word.
I seek you with all my heart;
do not let me stray from your commands.
PSALM 119:9–10

Time and again have we spoken to you about the precious blood of Christ that cleanses from all sin and about the blessings that Jesus brings to you when he becomes your Savior; but we are bound also to remind all of you, who profess to have believed on him and to have become his disciples, that you must not only own him as your Master and Lord, but that you must do whatsoever he bids you. Faith must obey the Savior's will, as well as trust his grace. The moment we become Christians, who are saved by Christ, we become his servants to obey all his commandments. Hence, it is incumbent upon us to search the Scriptures that we may know what our Master's will is. There he has written it out for us in plain letters, and it is an act of disobedience to neglect this search. By refusing to learn what the will of our Lord is, the sin of ignorance becomes willful, because we do not use the means by which we might receive instruction. Every servant of Christ is bound to know what he is to do; and then, when he knows it, he should at once do it. The Christian man's business is, first, to learn Christ's will and, second, to do it. Once learned, that will is the supreme law of the Christian whatever may seem to oppose it.

Through the Bible in One Year: Luke 23–24

Wives as Counselors

❧

"We are doomed to die!" he said to his wife. "We have seen God!"

*But his wife answered, "If the LORD had meant to kill us,
he would not have accepted a burnt offering and grain offering from
our hands, nor shown us all these things or now told us this."*
JUDGES 13:22–23

Manoah had married a capital wife. She was the better one of the two in sound judgment. She was the weaker vessel by nature, but she was the stronger believer, and probably that was why the angel was sent to her, for the angels are best pleased to speak with those who have faith, and if they have the pick of their company, and the wife has more faith than the husband, they will visit the wife sooner than her spouse, for they love to take God's messages to those who will receive them with confidence. She was full of faith, evidently, and so when her husband tremblingly said, "We shall surely die," she did not believe in such a mistrustful inference. Moreover, though they say that women cannot reason, yet here was a woman whose arguments were logical and overwhelming. Certain it is that women's perceptions are generally far clearer than men's reasonings: they look at once into a truth, while we are hunting for our spectacles. Their instincts are generally as safe as our reasonings, and therefore when they have in addition a clear, logical mind, they make the wisest of counselors.

Through the Bible in One Year: Leviticus 1–4

Unanswered Prayer

And the prayer offered in faith will make the sick person well;
the Lord will raise him up. If he has sinned, he will be forgiven.
Therefore confess your sins to each other
and pray for each other so that you may be healed.
The prayer of a righteous man is powerful and effective.
JAMES 5:15–16

It may possibly happen that the cause of unanswered prayer many times lies in something connected with sin. Do you not think that unanswered prayers are often a Fatherly chastisement for our offenses? The Savior, in that wonderful chapter where he tells out his love to us, says, "If ye keep my commandments, ye shall abide in my love," (John 15:10 KJV) and then he notes, as a special favor, if a man abide in his love, and keep his commandments, he "shall ask what he will, and it shall be done unto him." Now, it seems to me to be only reasonable that if I will not do what God wills, God will refuse to do what I will: that if he asks me a certain duty and I refuse it, when I ask him for a certain privilege or favor, it is not unkind, but on the other hand, most wise and kind, that he should say, "No, my child, no: if you will not listen to my tender command, it is kind to refuse you your desire until you repent and obey." It may be also temporal affliction, but probably this is one of the main ways in which the Master inflicts the stripes upon his children. They are negligent of his commands, and he says, "Then you shall tarry awhile; I will not yet grant you what you seek, but when you come to a better mind and are more scrupulous and tender in the fulfilling of my commands, then your longings shall be satisfied."

Through the Bible in One Year: Leviticus 5–8

Be Certain of God's Will

For God's gifts and his call are irrevocable.
ROMANS 11:29

I have a right to ask for anything that God has promised me, but if I go beyond the range of the divine promises, I also go beyond the range of assured and confident expectation. The promises are very large and very wide, but when one gets a fancy in his head, he must not suppose that God is there, in his fancy. I have known some fanatical persons who thought they could live by faith. They were going to preach the gospel, having no gifts whatever for preaching. They were going to be missionaries in a district, having no more gift to be missionaries than horses in a plow. But they thought they were destined to do it, and therefore they tried to live by faith, and when they had been nearly half-starved, then they complained against the goodness and abandoned the labor. Had God really inspired and sent them, he would have sustained and kept them, but if they go about it willfully and stubbornly on their own account, they must be driven back to realize their own ignorance of the divine will. And then oftentimes we pray in a way in which our prayers could not be heard consistent with the dignity of the Most High. I love a holy familiarity with God, and I believe it to be commendable; but still, man is but man, while God is God, and however familiar we may be with him in our hearts, still we must recollect the distance there is between the Most High and the most elevated and most beloved of his creatures, and we are not to speak as though it were in our power to do as we will and as we please.

Through the Bible in One Year: Leviticus 9–12

Sin and Its Results

For the wages of sin is death, but the gift of God is eternal life
in Christ Jesus our Lord.
ROMANS 6:23

Sin is that evil power that is in the world in rebellion against the good and gracious power of righteousness that sits upon the throne of God. This evil power of unholiness, untruth, sin, and contrariety to the mind of God, holds the great mass of our fellow men beneath its sway at this hour. The rations with which it rewards the most desperate valor of its champions is death.

Death is the natural result of all sin. When man acts according to God's order, he lives; but when he breaks his Maker's laws, he wrecks himself and does that which causes death. When any man commits sin, he dies to holiness and purity. The further a man goes in lust and iniquity, the more dead he becomes to purity and holiness: he loses the power to appreciate the beauties of virtue or to be disgusted with the abominations of vice. Our nature at the very outset has lost that delicacy of perception that comes of healthy life; and as men proceed in unchastity, or injustice, or unbelief, or sin of any kind, they enter deeper and deeper into that awful moral death which is the sure wage of sin. You can sin yourself into an utter deadness of conscience, and that is the first wage of your service of sin.

Through the Bible in One Year: Leviticus 13–16

Almost Saved

❧

But Lot's wife looked back, and she became a pillar of salt.
GENESIS 19:26

Remember Lot's wife, and recollect that she went some way toward being saved. Mistress Lot so far believed the message that came to her about the destruction of the city that she was aroused. She rose early as her husband did, and she prepared to leave the house. She ran down the streets, she passed the city gate, she reached the open plain along with her husband.

This woman was actually out of Sodom, and she was almost in Zoar, the refuge city, and yet she perished. Almost saved, but not quite. Let me repeat those words, for they describe some of you who are present at this hour, and they may be your epitaph if you do not mind what you are about: "Almost saved, but not quite." Escaped from the vilest form of sin, but not truly in Christ; the mind not weaned from its idols, iniquity not given up in the soul, though perhaps given up in outward deed.

To have lived with God's people, to have been numbered with them, to have been joined to them by ties of blood, and then after all to perish, will be horrible indeed! To have heard the gospel, to have felt the gospel too, in a measure, to have amended one's life because of it, to have escaped from the filthiest corruption of the world, and yet still not to have been weaned from the world, not to have been clean divorced from sin, and so to perish—the thought is intolerable. That same brine and brimstone that fell upon the inhabitants of the four cities overtook Lot's wife. She was on the margin of the shower, and as it fell she was salted with fire; she was turned into a pillar of salt where she stood. Dreadful doom!

Through the Bible in One Year: Leviticus 17–20

The Whole Gospel in a Single Verse

Here is a trustworthy saying that deserves full acceptance:
Christ Jesus came into the world to save sinners—
of whom I am the worst.
1 TIMOTHY 1:15

This text contains the gospel in brief, and yet I may say that it contains the gospel in full. If you get condensed notes of a sermon or a speech, you often miss the very soul and marrow of it; but here you get all the condensation possible, as if the great truths of the gospel were pressed together by a hydraulic ram, and yet there is not a particle of it left out.

Jesus Christ came to save sinners of all sorts. So long as you can come under the general description "sinners," it matters not what shape your sin has taken. All men have alike sinned, and yet all have not sinned in the same way. They have all wandered the downward road, and yet each one has gone a different way from all the rest. Christ Jesus came into the world to save respectable sinners and disreputable sinners. He came into the world to save proud sinners and despairing sinners. He came into the world to save drunkards, thieves, liars, whoremongers, adulterers, murderers, and such like. Whatever sort of sin there is, this word is wonderfully comprehensive and sweeping: "Christ Jesus came into the world to save sinners." A black lot, a horrible crew, they are, and hell is their due reward; but these are the people Jesus came to save.

Through the Bible in One Year: Leviticus 21–24

Evidence of Salvation

*Let us fix our eyes on Jesus, the author and perfecter of our faith,
who for the joy set before him endured the cross, scorning its shame,
and sat down at the right hand of the throne of God.*

<small>HEBREWS 12:2</small>

The moment the sinner believes, there is the ax laid at the root of the dominion of Satan. He no sooner learns to trust the appointed Savior than his cure has certainly commenced and will shortly be carried on to perfection. After faith comes gratitude. The sinner says, "I trust in the incarnate God to save me. I believe he has saved me." Well, what is the natural result? The soul being grateful, thankful, how can it help exclaiming, "Blessed be God for this unspeakable gift!" and "Blessed be this dear Son who so freely laid down his life for me!" It were not natural at all, it were something less even than humanity, if the sense of such favor did not beget gratitude. The next emotion to gratitude is love. Has he done all this for me? Am I under such obligations? Then will I love his name. The very next thought to love is obedience. What shall I do to please my Redeemer? How can I fulfill his commandments and bring honor to his name? See you not that the sinner is getting healed most rapidly? His disease was that he was altogether out of unison with God, and resisted the divine law, but now look at him! With tears in his eyes he is lamenting that he ever offended; he is groaning and grieving that he could have pierced so dear a Friend and put him to such sorrows, and he is asking, with love and earnestness, "What can I do to show that I loathe myself for the past, and that I love Jesus for the future?"

Through the Bible in One Year: Leviticus 25–27

Trust God's Promises

*"No longer will you be called Abram; your name will be Abraham,
for I have made you a father of many nations."*
GENESIS 17:5

I do not know that Abraham understood all the spiritual meaning of the covenant made with him; probably he did not, but he did understand that the Christ was to be born of him, in whom all nations should be blessed. Though there appeared to this man, old and withered, with a wife ninety years of age, no likelihood that he should ever become a father, yet did he fully believe that he would be the father of many nations, and that upon no ground whatever but that the living God had so promised him, and therefore so it must be.

Well, now, the faith of every man who is saved must be of this character. Every man who receives salvation receives it by a faith like that of Abraham, for, my brethren, when we are saved we too take the promise of God and depend upon it. Yea, and as we search the Word by faith, we take each promise as we find it, and we say, "This is true," and "This is true," and so we rest upon all of them. Is it not so with all of you who have peace with God? Did you not gain it by resting upon the promise of God as you found it in the Word and as it was opened up to you by the Holy Spirit? Have you any other ground of confidence but God's promise? The faith that saves the soul believes in the possibility of regeneration and sanctification; nay, more, it believes in Jesus and obtains for us power to become children of God and strength to conquer sin.

Through the Bible in One Year: John 1–2

Belief in Christ Alone

For the law was given through Moses;
grace and truth came through Jesus Christ.
JOHN 1:17

You may know a great deal about faith, but the only saving faith is belief concerning Christ. "I know whom I have believed." To believe doctrine will not save a man. You may hold all the creed, and be orthodox, and then be no better than the devil; for I suppose that the devil is a very sound theologian. He surely knows the truth. He believes and trembles; but you may know it and not tremble, and so you may fall short of one virtue that even the devil possesses. A firm belief in what is preached to you is well enough in its way, but to believe a doctrine as such cannot save you.

Some have a belief in their minister, and I suppose that is so flattering to us that you will hardly expect us to speak against it; but of all vices it is one most surely to be dreaded because it is so very dangerous. We charge you in the sight of God, always weigh what we have to say to you, and if it be not according to Scripture, cast it away as you cast away refuse.

Many persons believe thoroughly in themselves. The doctrine of self-reliance is preached in many quarters nowadays. Your belief must not be that you can force your way to heaven, but you must believe Christ, for anything else is an unsaving faith.

You see, then, that the knowledge that saves and the belief that saves both hang upon the cross; they both look to the wounds of that dear man, that blessed God, who was there the propitiation for our sins and who suffered in our room and stead.

Through the Bible in One Year: John 3–4

Celestial Love

The LORD appeared to us in the past, saying:
"I have loved you with an everlasting love;
I have drawn you with loving-kindness."

JEREMIAH 31:3

Between that great heart in heaven and this poor throbbing, aching heart on earth there is love established—love of the dearest, truest, sweetest, and most faithful kind. In fact, the love of woman, the mother's love, the love of the spouse—these are but the water, but the love of God is the wine; these are but the things of the earth, but the love of God is the celestial. The mother's love mirrors the love of God, as the dewdrop mirrors the sun; but as the dewdrop compasses not that mighty orb, so no love that beats in the human bosom can ever compass, as no words can express the height, depth, length, and breadth of the love of God, which is in Christ Jesus our Lord. "Yea, I have loved thee." Oh, come near then, Christian. Your Father, he who chastened you yesterday, loves you; he whom you forget so often, and against whom you have offended so constantly, yet loves you. You know what it is to love. Translate the love you bear to your dearest friend, and look at it and say, "God loves me better than this." He took your sins, your sorrows, your death, your grave, that you might be pardoned, accepted, and received into divine favor and so might live and be blessed forevermore.

Through the Bible in One Year: John 5–6

The Heart's Residence

"Do not store up for yourselves treasures on earth,
where moth and rust destroy, and where thieves break in and steal.
But store up for yourselves treasures in heaven,
where moth and rust do not destroy,
and where thieves do not break in and steal.
For where your treasure is, there your heart will be also."
MATTHEW 6:19–21

Are you, moreover, day by day being drawn from earth to heaven? Do you feel as if there were a magnet up there drawing your heart, so that when you are at work in your business, in your family with all its cares, you cannot help darting a prayer up to the Most High? Do you ever feel this onward impulse of something you do not understand, which impels you to have fellowship with God beyond the skies? Oh! If this be so, rest assured that it is Christ who draws. There is a link between you and heaven, and Christ is drawing that link and lifting your soul forward toward himself. If your heart is here below, then your treasure is here; but if your heart is up there—if your brightest hopes, your fondest wishes be in the heavenly places—your treasure is manifestly there, and the title deed of that treasure will be found in the eternal purpose of God, whereby he ordained you unto himself that you might show forth his praise.

Through the Bible in One Year: John 7–8

The Necessity of Life

*That is why, for Christ's sake, I delight in weaknesses,
in insults, in hardships, in persecutions, in difficulties.
For when I am weak, then I am strong.*

2 CORINTHIANS 12:10

There is a high and blessed duty and privilege—I will call it both—which is to every Christian the necessity of his life, and that is to pray. Can you pray, my brother? If you know how to pray, you can move heaven and earth. Can you pray, my brother? Then you can set almighty forces in operation. You can suffer no need, for everlasting supplies await the hand of prayer: "Ask, and it shall be given you." You cannot miss your way, for you shall be guided in answer to prayer. You shall hear a voice behind you, saying, "This is the way, walk ye in it" (Isaiah 30:21 KJV).

"O sir," you say, "I cannot pray prevailingly." Then you are not like Jacob, good at wrestling. Well, then, let me bring the text before you. Out of this weakness in prayer, you can only be made strong by faith. Believe in God, and you will prevail with God. Believe in his promise, and plead it. Believe in his Spirit, and pray by his help. Believe in Jesus, who makes intercession; for through him you may come boldly to the throne of grace. He who knows how to pray has his hand on a lever that moves the universe. But there is no praying without believing. Believe in prayer, and you will pray believingly. Some do not think that there is much in prayer. Poor souls! The Lord teach them better!

Through the Bible in One Year: John 9–10

A Spirit of Earnestness and Enterprise

"Behold, I am coming soon! My reward is with me,
and I will give to everyone according to what he has done.
I am the Alpha and the Omega, the First and the Last,
the Beginning and the End."
REVELATION 22:12–13

Christ has bought this world, and he will have it in possession from the river even to the ends of the earth. He has redeemed it, and he will claim it for his own. You may rest assured that whatever is contained in the scroll of prophecy shall be fulfilled according to the determinate counsel and foreknowledge of God. Do not be troubled by seers or soothsayers. Rest patiently. "Of the times and the seasons, brethren, ye have no need that I write unto you. For yourselves know perfectly that the day of the Lord so cometh as a thief in the night" (1 Thessalonians 5:1–2 KJV).

As for you, your business is to work for the spreading of his kingdom, to be continually scattering the light you have and praying for more, to be waiting upon God for more of the tongue of fire, for more of the baptism of the Eternal Spirit, for more vital, quickening power. When the whole church shall be wakened up to a spirit of earnestness and enterprise, the conversion of this world will be speedily accomplished; the idols will then be cast to the moles and the bats; antichrist shall sink like a millstone in the flood, and the glory of the Lord shall be revealed, and all flesh shall see it together, for the mouth of the Lord has spoken it.

Through the Bible in One Year: John 11–12

Outward Appearances

*"For John came neither eating nor drinking, and they say,
'He has a demon.' The Son of Man came eating and drinking,
and they say, 'Here is a glutton and a drunkard, a friend of tax collectors
and "sinners."' But wisdom is proved right by her actions."*
MATTHEW 11:18–19

Other prophets, when they came, were dressed in rough garments and were austere and solemn in manner. Christ came not so; he came to be a man amongst men, a feaster with those who feast, an eater of honey with eaters of honey. He differed from none, and hence he was called a gluttonous man and a wine-bibber. Why did Christ do so? Why did he so commit himself, as men said, though it was verily a slander? It was because he would have his disciples not regard meats and drinks, but despise these things and live as others do; because he would teach them that it is not that which goes into a man, but that which comes out that defiles him. It is not what a man eats, with temperance, that does him injury; it is what a man says and thinks. It is not abstaining from meat; it is not the carnal ordinance of "Touch not, taste not, handle not" that makes the fundamentals of our religion, albeit it may be good addenda thereunto. Butter and honey Christ ate, and butter and honey may his people eat; nay, whatsoever God in his providence gives unto them, that is to be the food of the child Christ.

Through the Bible in One Year: John 13–14

Light to All the World

*When Jesus spoke again to the people, he said,
"I am the light of the world. Whoever follows me will never walk
in darkness, but will have the light of life."*

JOHN 8:12

He says, "I am the light of the world." He does not merely say, "I am the light of the Jews," or "I am the light of the Gentiles." He is both. He is the light of all mankind. There is a little light in Mohammedanism. Indeed, considering the age in which Mohammed lived, he had a very great deal of light; the religion of the Koran is immeasurably superior to the religions of the age in which the prophet flourished. He even taught the unity of the Godhead most clearly. Yet the light in the Koran is borrowed from the Old and New Testament. It is borrowed light. The intelligence is pilfered.

The light of the Parsee, the light of Zoroaster, the light of Confucius came originally from the sacred books of the Jews. From one source they must have all come, for all light comes from the great Father of lights.

Christ is the light of the world, destined to shed his beams over the whole earth. The day comes when all mankind will see this light. They who dwell in the wilderness shall bow before him, and his enemies shall lick the dust. The isles shall bring him tribute; Sheba and Seba shall offer gifts, yea, all kings shall fall down before him. I cannot help believing that the gospel yet is to be triumphant. I look for the coming of Christ. Let him come when he may; our hearts will leap for joy to greet him.

Through the Bible in One Year: John 15–16

The Church

Once you were not a people, but now you are the people of God;
once you had not received mercy, but now you have received mercy.
1 PETER 2:10

The Word of God tells us that in the midst of the great mass of men, there are to be found a special people—a people who were chosen of God out of the common race before the stars began to shine, a people who were dear to God's heart before the foundation of the world, a people who were redeemed by the precious blood of Jesus beyond and above the rest of mankind, a people who are the especial property of Christ, the flock of his pasture, the sheep of his hand, a people over whom Providence watches, shaping their course amid the tangled maze of life, a people who are to be produced at the last, every one of them faultless before the eternal throne and fitted for the exalted destiny which, in the ages to come, he shall reveal.

All through Scripture you read about this particular and special people. Sometimes they are called "a seed," at other times "a garden," at other times "a treasure," and sometimes "a flock." The common name in the New Testament for them is "the church." Christ tells us that the only way to enter the church is through himself. He is the door, the only door. There is no other mode of admission into the church but through himself. If you believe in Christ, you are a member of his church. If your trust is stayed upon Christ, who is God's great way of salvation, you have evidence that you were chosen of him from before the foundation of the world; and that faith of yours entitles you to all the privileges that Christ has promised in his Word to believers.

Through the Bible in One Year: John 17–18

The Storm Within

He replied, "You of little faith, why are you so afraid?" Then he got up and rebuked the winds and the waves, and it was completely calm.

MATTHEW 8:26

The winds were howling, the waters were roaring, and the disciples thought that the little ship must surely be engulfed in the raging sea, so they aroused their Master from his sorely needed sleep and cried to him, "Lord, save us: we perish." Being aroused because there was danger, he dealt first with the chief cause of danger; what was that? Not the winds or the waves, but the disciples' unbelief. There is always more peril, to a Christian, in his own unbelief than in the most adverse circumstances by which he may be surrounded.

I think I may venture to say—though with the Omnipotent, all things are possible—that it was an easier task for Christ to calm the winds and the waves than to still the tumult raised by doubt in his disciples' minds; he could more swiftly cause a calm to fall upon the stormy surface of the Galilean lake than upon the perturbed spirits of his terrified apostles. The mental always excels the physical; the ruling of hearts is a greater thing than the governing of winds and waves. So when we have to battle with trouble, let us always begin with ourselves—our own fears, mistrusts, suspicions, selfishness, and self-will—for the chief danger lies there. All the trouble in the world cannot harm you so much as half a grain of unbelief. He who is, by the grace of God, enabled to master his own soul need not doubt that he shall also be master of everything that opposes him.

Through the Bible in One Year: John 19–21

Divine Sight

❧

And, behold, they brought to him a man sick of the palsy,
lying on a bed: and Jesus seeing their faith said unto the sick of the palsy;
Son, be of good cheer; thy sins be forgiven thee.
MATTHEW 9:2 KJV

You will notice that our Lord did not wait for a word to be spoken; he simply looked, and he saw their faith. Matthew writes, "Jesus, seeing their faith." Who can see faith? It is a thing whose effects can be seen; its signs and tokens are discoverable; and they were eminently so in this case, for breaking up the roof and putting the man down before Christ in so strange a way were evidences of their belief that Jesus would cure him. Still, Christ's eyes saw not only the proofs of their faith, but the faith itself. There stood the four men, speaking with their eyes and saying, "Master, see what we have done! We are persuaded that we have done the right thing and that thou wilt heal him." There was the man, lying on his bed, looking up, and wondering what the Lord would do, but evidently cheered by the belief that he was now in a position of hope, where in all probability he would become a man favored beyond everyone else. Christ not merely saw the looks of this man and his bearers, but he saw their faith.

Ah, friends, we cannot see one another's faith; we may see the fruit of it. Sometimes we think that we can discern the lack of it, but to see the faith itself, this needs divine sight; this needs the glance of the eye of the Son of Man. Jesus saw their faith, and now that same eye is looking upon all in this audience, and he sees your faith. Have you any that he can see?

Through the Bible in One Year: Numbers 1–4

Forgiveness and Obedience

But that ye may know that the Son of man hath power on earth
to forgive sins, (then saith he to the sick of the palsy,)
Arise, take up thy bed, and go unto thine house.
And he arose, and departed to his house.
MATTHEW 9:6–7 KJV

I think that the detailed obedience that the Savior required was the best evidence that he had forgiven the man's sin: "Arise, take up thy bed, and go unto thine house." Henceforth, to do everything that Christ bids you do, in the order in which he bids you do it, because he bids you do it, to do it at once, to do it joyfully, to do it constantly, to do it prayerfully, to do it thankfully—this shall be the token that he has indeed dealt with you as a pardoning God. I am afraid that there are some who profess to have been forgiven who are not as obedient to Christ as they ought to be! I have known them neglect certain duties; I even knew a man once who would not read some parts of the Word of God because they made him feel uneasy; but be you sure of this, that when you and the Word of God fall out, the Word of God has right on its side. There is something rotten in the state of Denmark when you cannot read a chapter without feeling that you wish it was not there. There is something wrong with you whenever you quarrel with the Word of God. I say again that detailed obedience is the surest evidence that the Lord has forgiven your sin. For instance, "He that believeth and is baptized shall be saved" (Mark 16:16 KJV). Do not you omit any part of that precept; and if Christ bids you come to his table and thus remember him, do not live in neglect of that command.

Through the Bible in One Year: Numbers 5–8

March 16

The Healing Touch

Jesus said to him, "I will go and heal him."
MATTHEW 8:7

For three years our Lord himself walked the hospitals: he lived all day long in an infirmary, for all around him at one time they laid the sick in the streets, and at all times physical evil in some form or other came in his way. He put forth his hand, or spake the word, and healed all sorts of maladies, for it was part of his life work. "I will come and heal him," said he, for he was a physician in constant practice and would be round at once to see the patient. "He went about doing good," and in all this he would let his people know that he intended not to bless one part of man alone, but the whole of our nature, taking upon himself not only our sins, but our sicknesses. Jesus means to bless the body as well as the soul, and though for the present he has left our body very much under the power of sickness, for still "the body is dead because of sin; but the Spirit is life because of righteousness" (Romans 8:10 KJV), yet every restored limb and opened eye and healed wound is a token that Jesus cares for our flesh and blood, and means that the body shall share the benefits of his death by a glorious resurrection.

The genius of Christianity is pity for the sinful and the suffering. Let the church be a healer like her Lord: at least if she cannot pour forth virtue from the hem of her garment, nor "say in a word" so that sickness may fly, let her be among the most prompt to help in everything that can assuage pain or assist poverty.

Through the Bible in One Year: Numbers 9–12

The Days of Preparation

*On the day he comes to be glorified in his holy people
and to be marveled at among all those who have believed.
This includes you, because you believed our testimony to you.*

2 THESSALONIANS 1:10

The full glorification of Christ in his saints will be when he shall come a second time, according to the sure word of prophecy. He is glorified in them now, for he says, "All mine are thine, and thine are mine; and I am glorified in them" (John 17:10 KJV); but as yet that glory is perceptible to himself rather than to the outer world. The lamps are being trimmed; they will shine ere long. These are the days of preparation before that Sabbath which is in an infinite sense a high day. As it was said of Esther, that for so many months she prepared herself with myrrh and sweet odors before she entered the king's palace, to be espoused of him, even so are we now being purified and made ready for that august day when the perfected church shall be presented unto Christ as a bride unto her husband. John says of her that she shall be "prepared as a bride adorned for her husband." This is our night, wherein we must watch, but behold the morning comes, a morning without clouds, and then shall we walk in a sevenfold light because our Well Beloved has come. That second advent of his will be his revelation: he was under a cloud here, and men perceived him not, save only a few who beheld his glory; but when he comes a second time, all veils will be removed and every eye shall see the glory of his countenance. For this he waits and his church waits with him.

Through the Bible in One Year: Numbers 13–16

God Is Not Mute

※

Then Samuel said, "Speak, for your servant is listening."
1 SAMUEL 3:10

He who would hear God speak needs not to wait long, for God speaks to men continually by the Scriptures, which are given to us by inspiration. Alas that we should be so deaf to its teachings! This wonderful volume, so full of wisdom, is so little read that few of us could dare to gaze upon its pages and say, "O Lord, in this Book I have heard your speech." At other times, the Lord speaks by providence. Both national providences and personal providences have a meaning; providences that are afflicting and providences that are comforting all have a voice. But alas, I fear that oftentimes to us providence is dumb because we are deaf. I am afraid few of you can say of it, "O Lord, in providence I have heard your speech." The God of heaven speaks to men by his Holy Spirit. He does this, at times, in those common operations of the Spirit upon the ungodly which they resist, as did also their fathers. The Spirit strives with men; he calls, and they refuse; he stretches out his hands, and they regard him not. Though we have ears to hear, we frequently quench the Spirit; we grieve him, we neglect his monitions, and if we do not despise his teachings, yet too often we forget them and listen to the follies of earth instead of regarding the wisdom of the skies.

Through the Bible in One Year: Numbers 17–20

Bringing Down the Blessing

❧

Blessings crown the head of the righteous,
but violence overwhelms the mouth of the wicked.
PROVERBS 10:6

Consider. If you reflect, you will see that God is able to give his church the largest blessing, and give it at any time. Keep silence and consider, and you will see that he can give the blessing by you or by me; he can make any one of us, weak as we are, mighty through God to the pulling down of strongholds; can make our feeble hands, though we have but a few loaves and fishes, capable of feeding myriads with the bread of life. Consider this, and ask yourselves in the quiet of your spirits, what can we do to get the blessing? Are we doing that? What is there in our temper, in our private prayer, in our acts for God that would be likely to bring down the blessing? Do we act as if we were sincere? Have we really a desire for these things, which we say we desire? Could we give up worldly engagements to attend to the work of God? Could we spare time to look after the Lord's vineyard? Are we willing to do the Lord's work, and are we in the state of heart in which we can do it efficiently and acceptably? Keep silence and consider. I would suggest to every Christian that he should sit awhile before God when he reaches his home, and worship with the silence of awe, with the silence of shame, and then with the silence of careful thought concerning these things.

Through the Bible in One Year: Numbers 21–24

To Sit at the Master's Feet

*As Jesus and his disciples were on their way, he came
to a village where a woman named Martha opened her home to him.
She had a sister called Mary, who sat at the Lord's feet
listening to what he said. But Martha was distracted
by all the preparations that had to be made.*

LUKE 10:38–40

Noise wears us; silence feeds us. To run upon the Master's errands is always well, but to sit at the Master's feet is quite as necessary; for like the angels that excel in strength, our power to do his commandments arises out of our hearkening to the voice of his Word. If even for a human controversy quiet thought is a fit preparation, how much more is it needful in solemn pleadings with the Eternal One? Now let the deep springs be unsealed; let the solemnities of eternity exercise their power while all is still within us.

But how happens it that such silence renews our strength? It does so, first, by giving space for the strengthening Word to come into the soul and for the energy of the Holy Spirit to be really felt. Words, words, words; we have so many words, and they are but chaff, but where is *the Word* that in the beginning was God and was with God? That Word is the living and incorruptible seed: "What is the chaff to the wheat? saith the LORD" (Jeremiah 23:28 KJV). We want less of the words of man and more of him who is the very Word of God. Be quiet, be quiet, and let Jesus speak.

Through the Bible in One Year: Numbers 25–28

Labor Not in Vain

If the ax is dull and its edge unsharpened,
more strength is needed but skill will bring success.
ECCLESIASTES 10:10

The source of our worst weakness is our home-born strength, and the source of our worst folly is our personal wisdom. Lord, help us to be still till we have abjured ourselves, till we have said, "Lord, our ways of working cannot be compared with your ways of working; teach us how to work. Lord, our judgments are weak compared with your perfect judgment; we are fools; be our teacher and guide in all things."

Jehovah works everywhere, and all things are his servants. He works in the light, and we see his glory; but he equally works in the darkness, where we cannot perceive him. His wisdom is too profound to be at all times understood of mortal men. Let us be patient and wait his time. With no more doubt of our Father's power than the child at its mother's breast has of its mother's love; with no more doubt than an angel before the throne can have of Jehovah's majesty, let us commit ourselves, each one after his own fashion, to suffering and to labor for the grand cause of God, feeling well assured that neither labor nor suffering can be in vain in the Lord.

Through the Bible in One Year: Numbers 29–32

Intercede Boldly

We are therefore Christ's ambassadors,
as though God were making his appeal through us.
2 CORINTHIANS 5:20

Beloved, you who know the Lord, I would urge upon you to *draw near*. You are silent; you have renewed your strength; now enjoy access with boldness. The condition in which to intercede for others is not that of distance from God, but that of great nearness to him. Even thus did Abraham draw nigh when he pleaded for Sodom and Gomorrah. Let us remember how near we really are. We have been washed from every sin in the precious blood of Jesus; we are covered from head to foot at this moment with the spotless righteousness of Immanuel, God with us; we are accepted in the Beloved; yea, we are at this moment one with Christ and members of his body. How could we be nearer? How near is Christ to God? So near are we! Come near, then, in your personal pleadings, for you are near in your covenant Representative. The Lord Jesus has taken manhood into union with the divine nature, and now between God and man there exists a special and unparalleled relationship, the like of which the universe cannot present. Come near, then, O sons of God; come near, for you are near. Stand where your sonship places you, where your Representative stands on your behalf.

Through the Bible in One Year: Numbers 33–36

A Prayer-Hearing God

So Peter was kept in prison,
but the church was earnestly praying to God for him.
ACTS 12:5

God has given to the church untold mercies in answer to intercession, for he delights to bless his people at the mercy seat. The church of God has never gained a victory but in answer to prayer. Her whole history is to the praise of the glory of a prayer-hearing God. Come, then, if we have sped so well before, and if God invites us now, yea, if he delights in our petitions, let us not be slack but enlarge our requests before him.

I would earnestly urge upon my brethren in Christ to expostulate thus with the Lord: "O Lord, your truth does not prosper in the land, yet you have said, 'My word shall not return unto me void.' Lord, you are every day blasphemed, and yet you have said that your glory shall be seen of all flesh. Lord, they set up the idols; even in this land, where your martyrs burned, they are setting up the graven images again. Lord, tear them down for your name's sake; for your honor's sake, we beseech thee, do it. Do you not hear the enemy triumph? They say the gospel is worn out. They tell us that we are the relics of an antiquated race, that modern progress has swept the old faith away. Will you have it so, good Lord? Shall the gospel be accounted a worn-out almanac, and shall they set up their new gospels in its stead? Souls are being lost, O God of mercy! Hell is being filled, O God of infinite compassion! Jesus sees but few brought to himself and washed in his precious blood. Time is flying, and every year increases the number of the lost! How long, O God, how long? Wherefore do you tarry?" In this manner, order your case before the Lord, and he will hearken unto you.

Through the Bible in One Year: Acts 1–3

Spiritual Multiplication

❧

So the word of God spread.
The number of disciples in Jerusalem increased rapidly,
and a large number of priests became obedient to the faith.
ACTS 6:7

Multiplication is a very ancient form of blessing. The benediction pronounced upon man was of this sort, for we first read in the first chapter of Genesis, "And God blessed them, and God said unto them, Be fruitful, and multiply, and replenish the earth." In a spiritual sense, this is the blessing of the church of God. When the church is visited by the power of the Holy Spirit, she is increased on every side. When a church in the midst of a vast population remains stationary in numbers, or even becomes smaller, no man can see in such a condition the marks of God's blessing. Certainly it would be a novel sort of benediction, for the first blessing, the blessing of Pentecost, resulted in three thousand being added to the church in one day, and we find afterwards that "the Lord added to the church daily such as should be saved" (Acts 2:47 KJV). It is plain that one of the blessings that we as a church should seek with all our hearts is that of continual increase.

Through the Bible in One Year: Acts 4–6

Good Reason to Pray

Let us then approach the throne of grace with confidence,
so that we may receive mercy
and find grace to help us in our time of need.

HEBREWS 4:16

Every true Christian desires to see the church increase; at any rate, I should pity the man who thinks himself a Christian and yet has no such wish. "Let the whole earth be filled with his glory" is the natural aspiration of every child of God, and if any man has persuaded himself into the idea that he is a child of God, and yet does not desire to see the glory of the Lord made manifest by the conversion of multitudes, I pity the condition of his heart and of his understanding. I trust we all feel the missionary spirit; we all long to see the kingdom of the Lord come and to see the converts in Zion multiplied. But God has appended to the granting of our desire that we should pray for it: we must plead and inquire, or else the increase will be withheld.

The Lord knows how beneficial it is to us to be much in prayer, and therefore he makes it easy for us to draw near to him. He affords us a multitude of reasons for approaching the mercy seat and gives us errands that may be used as arguments for frequent petitioning. Now, as the Lord loves to commune with his people, he takes care to give them errands upon which they must come to him. We need never be afraid that we shall be interrogated at the gate of mercy and this stern question put: "What are you doing here?" For we have always some reason for praying; indeed, every promise is turned into a reason for prayer, because the promise is not to be granted to us until we have pleaded it at the mercy seat.

Through the Bible in One Year: Acts 7–9

Our Channel of Blessing

In those days Hezekiah became ill and was at the point of death. . . .

Hezekiah turned his face to the wall and prayed to the LORD, "Remember, O LORD, how I have walked before you faithfully and with wholehearted devotion and have done what is good in your eyes." And Hezekiah wept bitterly.

. . . "Tell Hezekiah, the leader of my people, 'This is what the LORD, the God of your father David, says: I have heard your prayer and seen your tears; I will heal you.'"

2 KINGS 20:1–5

Shall there be no prayer in our hearts, when God has appointed prayer to be the channel of blessing to sinners as well as to ourselves? Then how can we say that we are Christians? You may say, "Well, I think I may be excused," but I must reply you cannot. "I am very sick," says one. Ah, then you can lie in bed and pray.

"I am so poor," says one. Well, you are not called upon to pay a shilling every time you pray to God. It does not matter how poor you are; your prayers are just as acceptable; only remember, if you are so poor, you ought to pray all the more, because you cannot give your offering in the shape of gold. I should like you to say with the apostle, "Silver and gold have I none; but such as I have give I thee. My Master, I will be much in prayer."

"Ah," says another, "but I have no talent." That is another reason why you should pray more, and not why you should be prayerless, because if you cannot contribute to the church's public service from lack of talent, you should the more zealously contribute to her strength by the private exercise of prayer and intercession, and thus make those strong who are better fitted to go to the front.

Through the Bible in One Year: Acts 10–12

Without Excuse

*And pray in the Spirit on all occasions with all kinds
of prayers and requests. With this in mind, be alert
and always keep on praying for all the saints.*
EPHESIANS 6:18

On what ground can anybody be excused from the duty of prayer? Answer: on no ground whatever. You cannot be excused on the ground of common humanity; for if it be so that God will save sinners in answer to prayer, and I do not pray, what am I? Souls dying, perishing, sinking to hell, while the ordained machinery for salvation is prayer and the preaching of the Word; and if I restrain prayer, what am I? Surely the milk of human kindness has been drained from my breast and I have ceased to be human, and if so, it is idle to talk of communion with the divine. He who has no pity on a wounded man and would not seek to relieve the hunger of one expiring of want is a monster. But he who has no pity on souls who are sinking into everlasting fire, what is he?

Next, can any excuse be found in Christianity for neglect of prayer? I answer, there is none to be found in Christianity any more than in humanity, for if Christ has saved us, he has given us of his Spirit: "If any man have not the Spirit of Christ, he is none of his" (Romans 8:9 KJV). And what was the Spirit of Christ? Did he look upon Jerusalem and say, "I believe that the city is given up, predestined to be destroyed," and then coolly go on his way? No, not he. He believed in predestination, but that truth never chilled his heart. He wept over Jerusalem and said, "O Jerusalem, Jerusalem, how often would I have gathered thy children together, even as a hen gathereth her chickens under her wings, and ye would not!"

Through the Bible in One Year: Acts 13–16

Compassion for Others

❧

Streams of tears flow from my eyes because my people are destroyed.
My eyes will flow unceasingly, without relief,
until the LORD looks down from heaven and sees.

LAMENTATIONS 3:48–50

The more we become what we shall be, the more will compassion rule our hearts. The Lord Jesus Christ, who is the pattern and mirror of perfect manhood, what said he concerning the sins and the woes of Jerusalem? He knew Jerusalem must perish; did he bury his pity beneath the fact of the divine decree, and steel his heart by the thought of the sovereignty or the justice that would be resplendent in the city's destruction? Nay, not he, but with eyes gushing like founts, he cried, "O Jerusalem, Jerusalem, how often would I have gathered thy children together, even as a hen gathereth her chickens under her wings, and ye would not!" If you would be like Jesus, you must be tender and very pitiful. You would be as unlike him as possible if you could sit down in grim content and, with a Stoic's philosophy, turn all the flesh within you into stone. If it be natural, then, and above all, if it be natural to the higher grace-given nature, I beseech you, let your hearts be moved with pity; do not endure to see the spiritual death of mankind. Be in agony as often as you contemplate the ruin of any soul of the seed of Adam.

Surely those who receive mercy should show mercy; those who owe all they have to the pity of God should not be pitiless to their brethren. You shall find everywhere throughout the gospel that it rings of brotherly love, tender mercy, and weeping pity. Let me beseech you to believe that it is needful as well as justifiable that you should feel compassion for the sons of men.

Through the Bible in One Year: Acts 17–19

A Divine Hunger

*I speak the truth in Christ—I am not lying,
my conscience confirms it in the Holy Spirit—
I have great sorrow and unceasing anguish in my heart.
For I could wish that I myself were cursed
and cut off from Christ for the sake of my brothers,
those of my own race, the people of Israel.*

ROMANS 9:1–4

Paul becomes a savior of many because his heart's desire and prayer to God are that they may be saved. Oh! I would to God there should come upon us a divine hunger that cannot stay itself except men yield themselves to Jesus; an intense, earnest longing, a panting desire that men should submit themselves to the gospel of Jesus. This will teach you better than the best college training how to deal with human hearts. This will give the stammering tongue the ready word; the hot heart shall burn the cords that held fast the tongue. You shall become wise to win souls, even though you never exhibit the brilliance of eloquence or the force of logic. Men shall wonder at your power—the secret shall be hidden from them, the fact being that the Holy Ghost shall overshadow you, and your heart shall teach you wisdom, God teaching your heart. Deep feelings on your part for others shall make others feel for themselves, and God shall bless you, and that right early.

Through the Bible in One Year: Acts 20–22

March 30

Forget Not

If I speak in the tongues of men and of angels, but have not love,
I am only a resounding gong or a clanging cymbal.
1 CORINTHIANS 13:1

There is a temptation with each one of us to try to forget that souls are being lost. I can go home to my house along respectable streets, and naturally should choose that way, for then I need not see the poverty of the lowest quarters of the city, but am I right if I try to forget that there are Bethnal Greens and Kent Streets, and suchlike abodes of poverty? The close courts, the cellars, the crowded garrets, the lodging houses—am I to forget that these exist? Surely the only way for a charitable mind to sleep comfortably in London is to forget how one-half of the population lives; but is it our object to live comfortably? Are we such brute beasts that comfort is all we care for, like swine in their sty? Nay, brethren, let us recall to our memories the sins of our great city, its sorrows and griefs, and let us remember also the sins and sorrows of the wide, wide world and the tens of thousands of our race who are passing constantly into eternity. Nay, look at them! Do not close those eyes! Does the horror of the vision make your eyeballs ache? Then look until your heart aches too, and your spirit breaks forth in vehement agony before the Lord.

Look down into hell a moment; open wide the door; listen, and listen yet again. You say you cannot, it sickens your soul; let it be sickened, and in its swooning let it fall back into the arms of Christ the Savior, and breathe out a cry that he would hasten to save men from the wrath to come. Do not ignore, I pray you, what does exist.

Through the Bible in One Year: Acts 23–25

Friends of God

❧

"I have told you these things, so that in me you may have peace.
In this world you will have trouble. But take heart!
I have overcome the world."

JOHN 16:33

Ishmael was not mocked, but Isaac was, for he was born after the promise. Esau's posterity never suffered bondage in Egypt, but Israel must be trained by hard service. Persecution is for the righteous; wicked men are in honor among their ungodly associates. Slander shoots her poisoned arrows, not at the vicious, but at the virtuous. Birds do not peck at sour fruit, but they wage war upon the sweet and ripe. Holy men must expect to be misrepresented, misinterpreted, and often willfully maligned, while hypocrites have their reward in undeserved homage. Carry what load you choose upon your shoulders, and no one will notice it, unless indeed they obey the good old rule and "respect the burden"; but if you take up Christ's cross and bravely bear it, few will respect the burden or praise the bearer. Graceless men will add weight to your load, for the offense of the cross has not ceased. It is the nature of the wicked to hate the righteous, even as the wolf rages against the sheep. This world cannot be the friend of the friend of God, unless indeed Belial can have concord with Christ, and this we know is impossible. In one form or another, the Egyptian will oppress the Israelite till the day of the bringing out with a high hand and an outstretched arm. If today the enmity is restrained in its manifestation, it is because the law of the land, by the good providence of God, does not now allow of the rack, the stake, or the dungeon.

Through the Bible in One Year: Acts 26–28

How Can We Not Love Him?

❧

*"Love the Lord your God with all your heart and with all your soul
and with all your mind and with all your strength."*
MARK 12:30

This love, to which God's saints are exhorted, is in every way deserved. Think of the excellence of his character whom you are bidden to love. God is such a perfect being that I feel now that, altogether apart from anything he has done for me, I love him because he is so good, so just, so holy, so faithful, so true. There is not one of his attributes that is not exactly what it ought to be. If I look at his dear Son, I see that his character is so gloriously balanced that I wonder why even those who deny his Godhead do not worship such a character as his, for it is absolutely unique. When I think of the character of the ever-blessed Spirit, his patience and his wisdom, his tenderness and his love to us, I cannot help loving him. Yes, beloved, we must love Father, Son, and Spirit, for never had human hearts such an object to love as the Divine Trinity in Unity.

What is God? "God is love." That short word comprehends all. He is a great God, but he is as gracious as he is great. He is as full of goodness as the sun is full of light, and as full of grace as the sea is full of water; and all that he has he delights to give out to others. God, my God, you are altogether lovely; and where the heart is in a right condition, it must love you.

Through the Bible in One Year: Deuteronomy 1–4

The Elementary Truth

❧

For this reason Christ is the mediator of a new covenant,
that those who are called may receive the promised eternal inheritance—
now that he has died as a ransom to set them free
from the sins committed under the first covenant.
HEBREWS 9:15

The heart of the gospel is redemption, and the essence of redemption is the substitutionary sacrifice of Christ. They who preach this truth preach the gospel in whatever else they may be mistaken; but they who preach not the atonement, whatever else they declare, have missed the soul and substance of the divine message. In these days I feel bound to go over and over again the elementary truths of the gospel. There have risen up in the church itself men who speak perverse things. There be many who trouble us with their philosophies and novel interpretations, whereby they deny the doctrines they profess to teach and undermine the faith they are pledged to maintain. I have no desire to be famous for anything but preaching the old gospel.

I have found, my brethren, by long experience, that nothing touches the heart like the cross of Christ; and when the heart is touched and wounded by the two-edged sword of the law, nothing heals its wounds like the balm that flows from the pierced heart of Jesus. When we see men quickened, converted, and sanctified by the doctrine of the substitutionary sacrifice, we may justly conclude that it is the true doctrine of atonement. I have not known men made to live unto God and holiness except by the doctrine of the death of Christ on man's behalf.

Through the Bible in One Year: Deuteronomy 5–8

Citizens of Heaven

But our citizenship is in heaven.
And we eagerly await a Savior from there, the Lord Jesus Christ.
PHILIPPIANS 3:20

We must do our utmost while we are here to bring men to Christ, to win them from their evil ways, to bring them to eternal life, and to make them, with us, citizens of another and better land.

Seeking the good of the country as aliens, we must also remember that it behooves aliens to keep themselves very quiet. What business have foreigners to plot against the government or to intermeddle with the politics of a country in which they have no citizenship? So in this land of ours, where you and I are strangers, we must be orderly sojourners, submitting ourselves constantly to those who are in authority, leading orderly and peaceable lives, and according to the command of the Holy Ghost through the apostle, "honoring all men, fearing God, honoring the king"; "submitting ourselves to every ordinance of man for the Lord's sake." We are simply passing through this earth, and should bless it in our transit but never yoke ourselves to its affairs. Christians, as men, love liberty and are not willing to lose it even in the lower sense; but spiritually, their politics are spiritual, and as citizens they look to the interest of that divine republic to which they belong, and they wait for the time when, having patiently borne with the laws of the land of their banishment, they shall come under the more beneficent sway of him who reigns in glory, the King of Kings and Lord of Lords. If it be possible, as much as lies in you, live peaceably with all men and serve your day and generation still, but build not your soul's dwelling place here, for all this earth must be destroyed at the coming of the fiery day.

Through the Bible in One Year: Deuteronomy 9–12

April 4

Heavenly Speech

✣

Command and teach these things. Don't let anyone look down
on you because you are young, but set an example
for the believers in speech, in life, in love, in faith and in purity.
1 TIMOTHY 4:11–12

Our very speech should be such that our citizenship should be
detected. We should not be able to live long in a house without
men finding out what we are. A friend of mine once went across
to America, and landing I think at Boston, he knew nobody, but
hearing a man say, when somebody had dropped a cask on the
quay, "Look out there, or else you will make a Coggeshall job of
it," he said, "You are an Essex man I know, for that is a proverb
never used anywhere but in Essex: give me your hand"; and they
were friends at once. So there should be a ring of true metal about
our speech and conversation, so that when a brother meets us, he
can say, "You are a Christian, I know, for none but Christians
speak like that, or act like that." "Thou also wast with Jesus of
Nazareth, for thy speech betrayeth thee." Our holiness should act
as a sort of freemasonry by which we know how to give the grip to
the stranger, who is not a real stranger, but a fellow citizen with us
and of the household of faith.

Oh, dear friends, wherever we wander, we should never forget our beloved land. Brethren, just as people in a foreign land
who love their country always are glad to have plenty of letters
from the country, I hope we have much communication with the
old fatherland. We send our prayers there as letters to our Father,
and we get his letters back in this blessed volume of his Word.

Through the Bible in One Year: Deuteronomy 13–16

Trained into a Hero

I know what it is to be in need, and I know what it is to have plenty.
I have learned the secret of being content in any and every situation,
whether well fed or hungry, whether living in plenty or in want.
I can do everything through him who gives me strength.
PHILIPPIANS 4:12–13

Those people who only sail in a little boat on a lake have no stories to tell of adventures at sea; but he who is to write a book describing long voyages must travel far out of sight of land and behold the sea in the time of storm as well as in a calm. You are to become perhaps an experienced Christian; you are to bring great honor to God by being the means of comforting others who will be tried in a similar way to yours; you are to be trained into a hero, and that cannot be done except by great and bitter griefs coming upon you. I believe that there are some of us whom God cannot trust with much joy. His head would turn dizzy if he were set upon a high pinnacle, and he would get proud and self-sufficient, and so be ruined. God will not kill his children with sweets any more than he will destroy them with bitters. They shall have a tonic when they need it; but when that tonic is so bitter that they seem as if they could not drink it and live, their Lord will either take the tonic away or give them some delicious sweetness to remove all the bitter taste.

Through the Bible in One Year: Deuteronomy 17–20

Our All in All

※

"When my life was ebbing away, I remembered you, LORD,
and my prayer rose to you, to your holy temple. Those who cling
to worthless idols forfeit the grace that could be theirs.
But I, with a song of thanksgiving, will sacrifice to you.
What I have vowed I will make good. Salvation comes from the LORD."
JONAH 2:7–9

The difficulty all along has been to get to the end of you, for when a man gets to the end of himself, he has reached the beginning of God's working. When you are cleaned right out and have not anything at all left, then all the mercy of the covenant of grace is yours. I may have doubts about whether God's grace will be exercised in certain cases; but I cannot raise any question about the freeness of divine grace to a soul who is empty, to a soul who is ready to perish, to a soul who is inquiring after God, and to a soul who is hungering and thirsting after righteousness. When once your soul is so conscious of your sin that every hope of salvation by your own works is entirely abandoned and you feel that you are utterly condemned, then is Jesus Christ yours, for he came to call, not the righteous, but sinners. So accept him as yours; take him, receive him now. He is made of God fullness to our emptiness, righteousness to our unrighteousness, life to our death, salvation to our condemnation, all in all to our poverty, our wretchedness, our sin.

Through the Bible in One Year: Deuteronomy 21–24

A Hopeful Sign

Therefore I will give him a portion among the great,
and he will divide the spoils with the strong,
because he poured out his life unto death,
and was numbered with the transgressors.
For he bore the sin of many,
and made intercession for the transgressors.
ISAIAH 53:12

The motions of God's Spirit in the souls of his people are the footfalls of God's eternal purposes about to be fulfilled. It is always a hopeful sign for a man that another man prays for him. There is a difficulty in getting a man to hell whom a child of God is drawing toward heaven by his intercessions. Satan is often defeated in his temptations by the intercession of the saints. Have hope then that your personal sense of compassion for souls is an indication that such souls God will bless. Ishmael, whom Hagar pitied, was a lad about whom promises had been made large and broad; he could not die; Hagar had forgotten that, but God had not. No thirst could possibly destroy him, for God had said he would make of Ishmael a great nation. Let us hope that those for whom you and I are praying and laboring are in God's eternal purpose secured from hell, because the blood of Christ has bought them, and they must be the Lord's. Our prayers are ensigns of the will of God. The Holy Ghost leads us to pray for those whom he intends effectually to call.

Through the Bible in One Year: Deuteronomy 25–28

Talk with the Master First

❧

Then he prayed, "O LORD, God of my master Abraham,
give me success today, and show kindness to my master Abraham.
See, I am standing beside this spring, and the daughters
of the townspeople are coming out to draw water.
May it be that when I say to a girl, 'Please let down your jar
that I may have a drink,' and she says, 'Drink, and I'll water
your camels too'—let her be the one you have chosen
for your servant Isaac. By this I will know that
you have shown kindness to my master."
GENESIS 24:12–14

The faithful servant of Abraham, before he started, communed with his master; and this is a lesson to us, who go on our Lord's errands. Let us, before we engage in actual service, see the Master's face, talk with him, and tell to him any difficulties that occur to our minds. Before we get to work, let us know what we are at and on what footing we stand. Let us hear from our Lord's own mouth what he expects us to do and how far he will help us in the doing of it. I charge you, my fellow servants, never to go forth to plead with men for God until you have first pleaded with God for men. Do not attempt to deliver a message that you have not first of all yourself received by his Holy Spirit. Come out of the chamber of fellowship with God into the pulpit of ministry among men, and there will be a freshness and a power about you that none shall be able to resist. Abraham's servant spoke and acted as one who felt bound to do exactly what his master bade him and to say what his master told him; hence, his one anxiety was to know the essence and measure of his commission.

Through the Bible in One Year: Deuteronomy 29–31

Shower of Mercy

And Manoah said unto his wife,
We shall surely die, because we have seen God.
JUDGES 13:22 KJV

It was to Manoah and to his wife the highest conceivable joy of life, the climax of their ambition, that they should be the parents of a son by whom the Lord should begin to deliver Israel. Joy filled them—inexpressible joy—at the thought of it; but at the time when the good news was first communicated, Manoah, at least, was made so heavy in spirit that he said, "We shall surely die, because we have seen God." Take it as a general rule that dull skies foretell a shower of mercy. Expect sweet favor when you experience sharp affliction. Do you not remember, concerning the apostles, that they feared as they entered into the cloud on Mount Tabor? And yet it was in that cloud that they saw their Master transfigured; and you and I have had many a fear about the cloud we were entering, although we were therein to see more of Christ and his glory than we had ever beheld before. The cloud that you fear makes the external wall of that secret chamber wherein the Lord reveals himself.

I do believe that whenever the Lord is about to use us in his household, he takes us like a dish and wipes us right out and sets us on the shelf, and then afterwards he takes us down and puts thereon his own heavenly meat, with which to fill the souls of others. There must as a rule be an emptying, a turning upside down, and a putting on one side before the very greatest blessing comes. Manoah felt that he must die, and yet die he could not, for he was to be the father of Samson, the deliverer of Israel and the terror of Philistia.

Through the Bible in One Year: Deuteronomy 32–34

The Divine Remedy

And I pray that you, being rooted and established in love,
may have power, together with all the saints,
to grasp how wide and long and high and deep is the love of Christ,
and to know this love that surpasses knowledge—
that you may be filled to the measure of all the fullness of God.
EPHESIANS 3:17–19

The fall of Adam and the destruction of mankind made ample room and verge enough for love almighty. Amid the ruins of humanity, there was space for showing how much Jehovah loved the sons of men; for the compass of his love was no less than the world, the object of it no less than to deliver men from going down to the pit, and the result of it no less than the finding of a ransom for them. The far-reaching purpose of that love was both negative and positive; that, believing in Jesus, men might not perish, but have eternal life. The desperate disease of man gave occasion for the introduction of that divine remedy which God alone could have devised and supplied. By the plan of mercy and the great gift that was needed for carrying it out, the Lord found means to display his boundless love to guilty men. Had there been no fall and no perishing, God might have shown his love to us as he does to the pure and perfect spirits that surround his throne; but he never could have commended his love to us to such an extent as he now does. In the gift of his only begotten Son, God commended his love to us, in that while we were yet sinners, in due time Christ died for the ungodly.

Through the Bible in One Year: Romans 1–2

Love the Lord

❧

Love the LORD, all his saints!
PSALM 31:23

Some passions of our nature may be exaggerated, and toward certain objects, they may be carried too far; but the heart, when it is turned toward God, can never be too warm, nor too excited, nor too firmly fixed on the divine object: "O love the LORD, all ye his saints."

Put the emphasis upon that sweet word *love—love the Lord as you cannot love anyone or anything else.* Husband, you love your wife; parent, you love your children; children, you love your parents; and all of you love your friends; and it is well that you do so. But you must spell all other love in little letters, but spell LOVE to God in the largest capitals you can find. Love him intensely; love the Lord, all ye his saints, without any limit to your love.

Next, love him with a deep, abiding principle of love. There is a certain kind of human love that burns very quickly, like brushwood, and then dies out. So there are some Christians who seem to love the Lord by fits and starts, when they get excited, or at certain special seasons; but I pray you, beloved, to let your love be a deep-seated and lasting fire. What if I compare it to the burning in the very heart of a volcano? It may not be always in eruption, but there is always a vehement heat within; and when it does burst forth, oh, what heavings there are, what seethings, what boilings, what flamings, and what torrents of lava all around! There must always be the fire at the heart, even when it is somewhat still and quiet.

Through the Bible in One Year: Romans 3–4

Anticipating Conflict

❧

Now the betrayer had arranged a signal with them:
"The one I kiss is the man; arrest him and lead him away under guard."
Going at once to Jesus, Judas said, "Rabbi!" and kissed him.
The men seized Jesus and arrested him.

MARK 14:44–46

Our Lord said to his disciples, "In the world ye shall have tribulation" (John 16:33 KJV), and he explained it to mean that men would put them out of the synagogues; yea, that the time would come when those who killed them would think that they did God service. "All that will live godly in Christ Jesus shall suffer persecution" (2 Timothy 3:12 KJV).

Nor is the opposition of the world confined to persecution, but it sometimes takes the far more dangerous form of flattery—pleasing baits are held out, and allurements are used to decoy the believer from his Lord. Many have been grievously wounded by the world when it has met them with the kiss of Judas on its lips and a dagger in its right hand wherewith to slay the soul. Woe unto those who are ignorant of its devices. This is a sore trouble under the sun, that men are false; their words are softer than butter, but inwardly they are drawn swords. This has often surprised young Christians. They imagined that since the godly were charmed at the sight of their early graces, all others would be equally pleased; they stumble when they find that their good is evil spoken of. Is any hearer of mine one of these raw recruits? Let him learn that to be a soldier of the cross means real war, and not a sham fight. He is in an enemy's country, and the time will yet come when, as a veteran warrior, he will be surprised if he lives a day without a conflict or is able for an hour to sheathe his sword.

Through the Bible in One Year: Romans 5–6

The Tenderhearted

While they were stoning him, Stephen prayed,
"Lord Jesus, receive my spirit." Then he fell on his knees and cried out,
"Lord, do not hold this sin against them."
When he had said this, he fell asleep.
ACTS 7:59–60

Certain tender hearts are not only surprised, but daunted and grieved by the world's opposition. Gentle, loving spirits, who would not oppose anybody if they could help it, keenly feel the wanton assaults of those whom they would rather please than provoke. The sensitiveness of love renders the choicest characters the most susceptible to pain under cruel opposition, especially when it comes from beloved kinsfolk. To those who love God and man, it is at times an agony to be compelled to appear as the cause of strife, even for Christ's sake.

He is most like God who loves most, and he has come nearest to the image of Christ whose heart is fullest of tenderness—the rougher spirits turn out to be rather dwarfs than giants in the kingdom of God. We must have backbone and must be prepared to contend earnestly for the faith; but yet, the more love we exhibit the better, and hence the more pain it will cost us to be continually at war with unloving spirits. This is a part of the tribulation we must endure; and the more bravely we face it, the more thoroughly shall we win the battles of peace and purity.

Through the Bible in One Year: Romans 7–8

The Standard-Bearer

For our light and momentary troubles are achieving
for us an eternal glory that far outweighs them all.
2 CORINTHIANS 4:17

We think ourselves overweighted and speak of life as though it were rendered too stern a conflict by the load of our cares and responsibilities; but what comparison is there between our load and that of Jesus? A pastor with a great flock is not without his hourly anxieties; but what are those to the cares of the Chief Shepherd? He watched over the great multitude that no man can number, who were committed to him by the Father, and for these he carried all their griefs; here was a burden such as you and I, dear friend, cannot even imagine; and yet, without laying aside the weight, he fought the world and overcame it.

When the whole host marches to the fight, we each one take our place in the ranks and the war goes on against us all; but where, think you, did the arrows fly most thickly? Where were the javelins hurled one after the other, thick as hail? "The standard-bearer among ten thousand" was the chief target. It seems to me as if the prince of darkness has said to his armies, "Fight neither with small nor great, save only with the King of Israel"; for he was tempted in all points as we are. You and I encounter some temptations, but he endures them all. I have mine and you have yours, but he had mine and yours, and such as are common to all his saints; and yet, standing in the thick of the fray, he remained unwounded and cried aloud, "I have overcome the world." Grace, then, can clothe us also with triumph, for against us no such supreme charges of hosts upon hosts will ever be led.

Through the Bible in One Year: Romans 9–10

Our Guide

❧

"All this I have spoken while still with you.
But the Counselor, the Holy Spirit, whom the Father
will send in my name, will teach you all things
and will remind you of everything I have said to you."
JOHN 14:25–26

The Holy Spirit within us is for guidance. He opens up to us one truth after another by his light and by his guidance, and thus we are "taught of the Lord." He is also our practical guide to heaven, helping and directing us on the upward journey. I wish Christian people more often inquired of the Holy Ghost as to guidance in their daily life. Know ye not that the Spirit of God dwells in you? You need not always be running to this friend and to that to get direction: wait upon the Lord in silence; sit still in quiet before the oracle of God. Use the judgment God has given you; but when that suffices not, resort to him whom Mr. Bunyan calls "the Lord High Secretary," who lives within, who is infinitely wise, and who can guide you by making you to hear a voice behind you saying, "This is the way, walk ye in it." The Holy Ghost will guide you in life, he will guide you in death, and he will guide you to glory. He will guard you from the modern error and from ancient error too. He will guide you in a way that you know not; and through the darkness he will lead you in a way you have not seen: these things will he do unto you, and not forsake you.

Through the Bible in One Year: Romans 11–12

The Comforter

Praise be to the God and Father of our Lord Jesus Christ,
the Father of compassion and the God of all comfort, who comforts
us in all our troubles, so that we can comfort those in any trouble
with the comfort we ourselves have received from God.
2 CORINTHIANS 1:3–4

Our God would not have his children unhappy, and therefore, he himself, in the third person of the blessed Trinity, has undertaken the office of Comforter. Why does your face such mournful colors wear? God can comfort you. You who are under the burden of sin, it is true no man can help you into peace, but the Holy Ghost can. O God, to every seeker here who has failed to find rest, grant your Holy Spirit! Put your Spirit within him, and he will rest in Jesus. And you dear people of God, who are worried, remember that worry and the Holy Ghost are very contradictory one to another. "I will put my Spirit within you" means that you shall become gentle, peaceful, resigned, and acquiescent in the divine will. Then you will have faith in God that all is well. Can you say, "My God, my God"? Do you want anything more? Can you conceive of anything beyond your God? Omnipotent to work all forever! Infinite to give! Faithful to remember! He is all that is good. Light only: "In him is no darkness at all." The Holy Spirit makes us apprehend this when he is put within us. In him our happiness sometimes rises into great waves of delight, as if it leaped up to the glory.

Through the Bible in One Year: Romans 13–14

God's Sustaining Power

In his great mercy he has given us new birth into a living hope
through the resurrection of Jesus Christ from the dead,
and into an inheritance that can never perish, spoil or fade—
kept in heaven for you.
1 PETER 1:3–4

"Reserved in heaven for you, who are kept by the power of God through faith unto salvation" (1 Peter 1:4–5 KJV). This perhaps will be one of the greatest cordials to a Christian in heaviness: that he is not kept by his own power, but is kept by the power of God, and that he is not left in his own keeping, but is kept by the Most High. "My flesh and my heart faileth: but God is the strength of my heart, and my portion for ever" (Psalm 73:26 KJV). "I know whom I have believed, and am persuaded that he is able to keep that which I have committed unto him against that day" (2 Timothy 1:12 KJV). But take away that doctrine of the Savior's keeping his people, and where is my hope? What is there in the gospel worth my preaching or worth your receiving? I know that he has said, "I give unto them eternal life; and they shall never perish, neither shall any man pluck them out of my hand" (John 10:28 KJV). What, Lord, but suppose they should grow faint—that they should begin to murmur in their affliction. Shall they not perish then? No, they shall never perish. But suppose the pain should grow so hot that their faith should fail. Shall they not perish then? No. "They shall never perish, neither shall any man pluck them out of my hand." Ah! This is the doctrine, the cheering assurance "wherein ye greatly rejoice, though now for a season, if need be, ye are in heaviness through manifold temptations" (1 Peter 1:6 KJV).

Through the Bible in One Year: Romans 15–16

Worship through Giving

Each man should give what he has decided in his heart to give, not reluctantly or under compulsion, for God loves a cheerful giver.
2 CORINTHIANS 9:7

Mark also, once more, concerning those gracious actions that are but little esteemed by the most of mankind, that we know God accepts our worship in little things. He allowed his people to bring their bullocks, others of them to bring their rams, and offer them to him, and these were persons of sufficient wealth to be able to afford a tribute from their herds and flocks; but he also permitted the poor to offer a pair of turtle doves or two young pigeons, and I have never found in God's Word that he cared less for the turtle dove offering than he did for the sacrifice of the bullock. I do know too that our ever-blessed Lord himself, when he was here, loved the praise of little children. They brought neither gold nor silver like the wise men from the East, but they cried, "Hosanna," and the Lord was not angry with their Hosannas but accepted their boyish praise. And we remember that a widow woman cast into the treasury two mites, which only made a farthing, but because it was all her living, he did not reject the gift, but rather recorded it to her honor. We are now quite familiar with the incident, but for all that, it is very wonderful. Two mites that make a farthing given to the infinite God! A farthing accepted by the King of Kings! Measure, therefore, not little actions by human scales and measures, but estimate them as God does, for the Lord has respect unto the hearts of his people; he regards not so much their deeds in themselves as the motives by which they are actuated.

Through the Bible in One Year: Joshua 1–4

Each One Especially Called

❧

As Jesus passed forth from thence, he saw a man, named Matthew,
sitting at the receipt of custom: and he saith unto him,
Follow me. And he arose, and followed him.
MATTHEW 9:9 KJV

The call of the man named Matthew seemed accidental and unlikely. "As Jesus passed forth from thence," just as he was going about some work or other, going away from Capernaum, perhaps, or merely going down one of its streets, it was as he "passed forth" that this event happened.

At that time, also, there were many other people in Capernaum, yet Christ did not call them. He saw them, but not in the particular way in which he saw the man named Matthew. And in like manner, on that day of mercy when you received the blessing of salvation, perhaps there was a crowded congregation, but as far as you know, the blessing did not reach anybody but yourself. Why, then, did it come to you? You do not know, unless you have learned to look behind the curtains in the Holy Place and to see by the light of the lamp within the veil. If you have looked there, you know that when Jesus Christ is passing by, what men call his accidents are all intentional, the glances of his eye are all ordained from eternity; and when he looks upon anyone, he does it according to the everlasting purpose and the foreknowledge of God. The Lord has looked long before on that man named Matthew, so in the fullness of time, Jesus Christ must pass that way, and he must look in love and mercy upon that man named Matthew. He saw him then because, long before, he foresaw him.

Through the Bible in One Year: Joshua 5 – 8

When the Lord Questions

Then the man and his wife heard the sound of the LORD God
as he was walking in the garden in the cool of the day,
and they hid from the LORD God among the trees of the garden.
But the LORD God called to the man, "Where are you?"
GENESIS 3:8–9

One of the most dreadful things in connection with this meeting of God with Adam was that Adam had to answer the Lord's questions. The Lord said to him, "Hast thou eaten of the tree, whereof I commanded thee that thou shouldest not eat?" (Genesis 3:11 KJV). In our courts of law, we do not require men to answer questions that would incriminate them, but God does; and at the last great day, the ungodly will be condemned on their own confession of guilt. While they are in this world, they put on a brazen face and declare that they have done no wrong to anybody—not even to God—they pay their way, and they are as good as their neighbors, and better than the most of them; but all their brag and bravado will be gone at the day of judgment, and they will either stand speechless before God—and by their speechlessness acknowledge their guiltiness in his sight—or if they do speak, their vain excuses and apologies will but convict themselves. They will, out of their own mouths, condemn themselves, like that wicked and slothful servant, who was cast into the outer darkness where there was weeping and gnashing of teeth. God grant that we may never know, from sad personal experience, what that expression means!

Through the Bible in One Year: Joshua 9–12

The Natural Set of the Soil

*Jesus said, "Father, forgive them,
for they do not know what they are doing."*
LUKE 23:34

When a man is ignorant and does not know what he ought to do, what should he do? Well, he should do nothing till he does know. But here is the mischief of it: that when we did not know, yet we chose to do the wrong thing. If we did not know, why did we not choose the right thing? But being in the dark, we never turned to the right but always blundered to the left, from sin to sin. Does not this show us how depraved our hearts are? Though we are seeking to be right, when we are let alone, we go wrong of ourselves. Leave a child alone; leave a man alone; leave a tribe alone without teaching and instruction; what comes of it? Why, the same as when you leave a field alone. It never, by any chance, produces wheat or barley. Leave it alone, and there are rank weeds and thorns and briars, showing that the natural set of the soil is toward producing that which is worthless.

You needed light, but you shut your eyes to the sun. You were thirsty, but you would not drink of the living spring; and so your ignorance, though it was there, was a criminal ignorance, which you must confess before the Lord. Oh, come to the cross, you who have been there before and have lost your burden there! Come and confess your guilt over again, and clasp that cross afresh, and look to him who bled upon it, and praise his dear name that he once prayed for you, "Father, forgive them; for they know not what they do."

Through the Bible in One Year: Joshua 13–16

Imitate Christ

Therefore, prepare your minds for action; be self-controlled;
set your hope fully on the grace to be given you when Jesus Christ
is revealed. As obedient children, do not conform to the evil desires
you had when you lived in ignorance.

1 PETER 1:13–14

Ignorance of Christ and eternal things shall be hateful to us. If, through ignorance, we have sinned, we will have done with that ignorance. We will be students of his Word. We will study that masterpiece of all the sciences, the knowledge of Christ crucified. We will ask the Holy Ghost to drive far from us the ignorance that genders sin. God grant that we may not fall into sins of ignorance anymore; but may we be able to say, "I know whom I have believed; and henceforth I will seek more knowledge, till I comprehend, with all saints, what are the heights, and depths, and lengths, and breadths of the love of Christ, and know the love of God, which passes knowledge!"

I put in a practical word here. If you rejoice that you are pardoned, show your gratitude by your imitation of Christ. There was never before such a plea as this: "Father, forgive them; for they know not what they do." Plead like that for others. Has anybody been injuring you? Are there persons who slander you? Pray tonight, "Father, forgive them; for they know not what they do." Let us always render good for evil, blessing for cursing; and when we are called to suffer through the wrongdoing of others, let us believe that they would not act as they do if it were not because of their ignorance. Let us pray for them and make their very ignorance the plea for their forgiveness: "Father, forgive them; for they know not what they do."

Through the Bible in One Year: Joshua 17–20

The Path to Mercy

But with you there is forgiveness;
therefore you are feared.
PSALM 130:4

Have you noticed the verse that comes before the text? It runs thus: "If thou, LORD, shouldest mark iniquities, O Lord, who shall stand?" (Psalm 130:3 KJV). That is a confession. Now, confession must always come before absolution. "If we confess our sins, he is faithful and just to forgive us our sins" (1 John 1:9 KJV). If we try to cloak our sin, "if we say that we have no sin, we deceive ourselves, and the truth is not in us" (1 John 1:8 KJV), and no pardon can come from God to us. Therefore, plead guilty, plead guilty. You ought to do it, for you are guilty. You will find it wisest to do it, for this is the only way to obtain mercy. Cast yourself upon the mercy of your Judge, and you shall find mercy; but first acknowledge that you need mercy. Be honest with your conscience and honest with your God, and confess your iniquity, and mourn over the righteousness to which you have not attained.

Through the Bible in One Year: Joshua 21–24

Second-Guessing God?

*Then the LORD said to Satan, "Have you considered my servant Job?
There is no one on earth like him; he is blameless and upright,
a man who fears God and shuns evil. And he still maintains his integrity,
though you incited me against him to ruin him without any reason."*

JOB 2:3

The Lord sends upon us the evil as well as the good of this mortal life; his is the sun that cheers and the frost that chills; his the deep calm and his the fierce tornado. To dwell on second causes is frequently frivolous, a sort of solemn trifling. Men say of each affliction, "It might have been prevented if so-and-so had occurred." Perhaps if another physician had been called in, the dear child's life would have been spared; possibly if I had moved in such a direction in business, I might not have been a loser. Who is to judge of what might have been? In endless conjectures we are lost, and cruel to ourselves, we gather material for unnecessary griefs. Matters happened not so; then why conjecture what would have been had things been different? It is folly. We grow indignant with the more immediate agent of our grief, and so fail to submit ourselves to God. As long as I trace my pain to accident, my bereavement to mistake, my loss to another's wrong, my discomfort to an enemy, and so on, I am of the earth, earthy; but when I rise to my God and see his hand at work, I grow calm; I have not a word of repining. "I opened not my mouth; because thou didst it" (Psalm 39:9 KJV). "Cast thy burden on the Lord" is a precept that will be easy to practice when you see that the burden came originally from God.

Through the Bible in One Year: 1 Corinthians 1–2

The Cause Lies Far Off

Why, O LORD, do you reject me and hide your face from me?
PSALM 88:14

I do not wonder that some Christians suffer: I should wonder if they did not. I have seen them, for instance, neglect family prayer and other household duties; and their sons have grown up to dishonor them. If they cry out, "What an affliction," we would not like to say, "Ah, but you might have expected it; you were the cause of it"; but such a saying would be true. When children have left the parental roof and gone into sin, we have not been surprised when the father has been harsh, sour, and crabbed in temper. We did not expect to gather figs of thorns, or grapes of thistles. We have seen men whose whole thought was "Get money, get money," and yet they have professed to be Christians. Such persons have been fretful and unhappy, but we have not been astonished. No, if they walk frowardly with Christ, he will show himself froward to them.

But sometimes the cause of chastisement lies further off. Every surgeon will tell you that there are diseases that become troublesome in the prime of life or in old age that may have been occasioned in youth by some wrongdoing or by accident, and the evil may have lain latent all those years. So may the sins of our youth bring upon us the sorrows of our riper years, and faults and omissions of twenty years ago may scourge us today. I know it is so. If the fault may be of so great an age, it should lead us to more thorough search and more frequent prayer.

Through the Bible in One Year: 1 Corinthians 3–4

Stirring the Waters

Remove the dross from the silver,
and out comes material for the silversmith.
PROVERBS 25:4

God will visit his children's transgressions. He will frequently let
common sinners go on throughout life unrebuked, but not so his
children. If you were going home today and saw a number of boys
throwing stones and breaking windows, you might not interfere
with them, but if you saw your own lad among them, I will be
bound you would fetch him out and make him repent of it.

Perhaps the chastisement may be sent by reason of a sin as yet
undeveloped, some latent proneness to evil. The grief may be
meant to unearth the sin, that you may hunt it down. Have you
any idea of what a devil you are by nature? None of us know what
we are capable of if left by grace. We think we have a sweet temper, an amiable disposition! We shall see! We fall into provoking
company, and are so teased and insulted, and so cleverly touched
in our raw places, that we become mad with wrath, and our fine,
amiable temper vanishes in smoke, not without leaving blacks
behind. Is it not a dreadful thing to be so stirred up? Yes, it is, but
if our hearts were pure, no sort of stirring would pollute them. Stir
pure water as long as you like and no mud will rise. The evil is bad
when seen, but it was quite as bad when not seen. It may be a great
gain to a man to know what sin is in him, for then he will humble
himself before his God and begin to combat his propensities.
Sometimes, therefore, trial may be sent that we may discern the
sin that dwells in us and may seek its destruction.

Through the Bible in One Year: 1 Corinthians 5–6

Fruit Comes Later

❧

"He cuts off every branch in me that bears no fruit,
while every branch that does bear fruit
he prunes so that it will be even more fruitful."
JOHN 15:2

Do not let us expect when we are in the trouble to perceive any immediate benefit resulting from it. I have tried myself when under sharp pain to see whether I have grown a bit more resigned or more earnest in prayer, or more rapt in fellowship with God, and I confess I have never been able to see the slightest trace of improvement at such times, for pain distracts and scatters the thoughts. Remember that word, "Nevertheless afterward it yieldeth the peaceable fruit of righteousness" (Hebrews 12:11 KJV). The gardener takes his knife and prunes the fruit trees to make them bring forth more fruit; his little child comes trudging at his heels and cries, "Father, I do not see that the fruit comes on the trees after you have cut them." No, dear child, it is not likely you would, but come round in a few months when the season of fruit has come, and then shall you see the golden apples that thank the knife. Graces that are meant to endure require time for their production and are not thrust forth and ripened in a night.

Severe trouble in a true believer has the effect of loosening the roots of his soul earthward and tightening the anchor-hold of his heart heavenward. Every mariner on the sea of life knows that when the soft zephyrs blow, men tempt the open sea with outspread sails, but when the black tempest comes howling from its den, they hurry with all speed to the haven.

Through the Bible in One Year: 1 Corinthians 7–8

The Power to Sympathize

※

"You said, 'Woe to me! The LORD has added sorrow to my pain;
I am worn out with groaning and find no rest.'"
JEREMIAH 45:3

Affliction gives us through grace the inestimable privilege of conformity to the Lord Jesus. We pray to be like Christ, but how can we be if we are not men of sorrows at all, and never become the acquaintance of grief? Like Christ, and yet never traverse through the vale of tears! Like Christ, and yet have all that the heart could wish, and never bear the contradiction of sinners against ourselves, and never say, "My soul is exceeding sorrowful, even unto death!" O sir, you know not what you ask. Have you said, "Let me sit on thy right hand in thy kingdom"? It cannot be granted to you unless you will also drink of his cup and be baptized with his baptism. A share of his sorrow must precede a share of his glory.

Once more, our sufferings are of great service to us when God blesses them, for they help us to be useful to others. It must be a terrible thing for a man never to have suffered physical pain. You say, "I should like to be the man." Ah, unless you had extraordinary grace, you would grow hard and cold; you would get to be a sort of cast-iron man, breaking other people with your touch. No; let my heart be tender, even be soft, if it must be softened by pain, for I would fain know how to bind up my fellow's wound. Let my eye have a tear ready for my brother's sorrows even if in order to do that, I should have to shed ten thousand for my own. An escape from suffering would be an escape from the power to sympathize, and that were to be deprecated beyond all things.

Through the Bible in One Year: 1 Corinthians 9–10

Forgiveness

*Bear with each other and forgive whatever grievances
you may have against one another. Forgive as the Lord forgave you.*
COLOSSIANS 3:13

Turn to the Old Testament, and you will see that it reveals sacrifice—lambs and bullocks and goats. What did they all mean? They meant that there was a way of pardon through the shedding of blood; they taught men this: that God would accept certain sacrifices on their behalf. Then turn to the New Testament, and there you will see it revealed more clearly still that God has accepted a sacrifice, the sacrifice he himself gave, for he "spared not his own Son, but delivered him up for us all" (Romans 8:32 KJV). In this Book you read how he can be "just, and the justifier of him which believeth in Jesus" (Romans 3:26 KJV); how he can be a just God and yet a Savior; how he can forgive and yet be just as righteous as if he punished and showed no mercy. This, in fact, is the revelation of the gospel; this is what this Book was written to teach, to tell you that "God was in Christ, reconciling the world unto himself, not imputing their trespasses unto them" (2 Corinthians 5:19 KJV). Therefore, we come to you, not merely with a hopeful whisper, but with a full, distinct, emphatic, unquestionable assurance, "There is forgiveness. There is forgiveness."

Through the Bible in One Year: 1 Corinthians 11–12

Thank God It Is So!

And it shall come to pass,
that whosoever shall call on the name
of the Lord shall be saved.
ACTS 2:21

There is here a wide word, a very wide word: "*Whosoever* shall call upon the name of the Lord shall be saved." "*Whosoever.*" I have heard that when a person is making his will, if he wishes to leave all he has to one person, say, to his wife, if he just says so, that is the best thing he can do; but he had better not go into detail and begin making a list of what he is leaving, because he will probably leave something or other out. Now, in order to make this will of God very distinct, he does not go into any detail, but he just says, "Whosoever." That means the black man, and the red man, and the yellow man, and the white man. It means the rich man and the poor man. It means everybody of every sort, and those who are of no sort at all, or of all sorts put together. "Whosoever." That includes me, I am sure; but I am equally certain that it includes you, you who are a stranger and a foreigner, whoever you may be. It is much better to have it put so, without going into detail, because otherwise somebody might be left out.

Through the Bible in One Year: 1 Corinthians 13 – 14

Do You Hear the Call?

How, then, can they call on the one they have not believed in?
And how can they believe in the one of whom they have not heard?
And how can they hear without someone preaching to them?
And how can they preach unless they are sent?
As it is written, "How beautiful are the feet of those
who bring good news!"
ROMANS 10:14–15

Who ought to preach, then? Everyone who can preach should do so. The gift of preaching is the responsibility for preaching. There are a great many persons who ought to preach the gospel but who do not. For this work, a high degree of gifts is not required. It does not say, "How shall they hear without a doctor of divinity?" It does not say, "How shall they hear without a popular preacher?" Oh dear! Some of us would have been lost if we could not have been saved without hearing a man of great abilities. I learned my theology, from which I have never swerved, from an old woman who was the cook in the house where I was an usher. She could talk about the deep things of God; and as I sat and heard what she had to say, as an aged Christian, of what the Lord had done for her, I learned more from her instruction than from anybody I have ever met with since. It does not require a college training to enable you to tell about Christ; some of the best workers in this church have little enough of education, but they bring many to Christ.

Through the Bible in One Year: 1 Corinthians 15–16

Look Up

❧

The next day John saw Jesus coming toward him and said,
"Look, the Lamb of God, who takes away the sin of the world!"
JOHN 1:29

I know many whose consciences are truly awakened and who see themselves as sinners in the sight of God; but instead of beholding the Lamb of God, they are continually beholding themselves. I do not think that they have any confidence in their own righteousness, but they are afraid that they do not feel their guilt as much as they ought. They think that they are not yet sufficiently awakened, sufficiently humbled, sufficiently penitent, and so on, and thus they fix their eyes upon themselves in the hope of getting peace with God. Suppose that yesterday or the day before, you had felt very cold, and therefore you had gone outside your house and fixed your gaze upon the ice and the snow. Do you think that sight would have warmed you? No; you know you would have been getting colder all the time. Suppose you are very poor, and you studiously fix your mind's eye upon your empty pocket. Do you think that will enrich you? Or imagine that you have had an accident and that one of your bones is broken. If you think very seriously of that broken bone, do you think that your consideration will mend it? Yet some sinners seem to imagine that salvation can come to them through their consideration of their lost and ruined condition. My dear unconverted hearers, you are lost whether you know it or not. Take that fact for granted. If you would be saved, look not at yourselves, but "behold the Lamb of God."

Through the Bible in One Year: Judges 1–4

Our True Light

***

In the beginning was the Word, and the Word was with God,
and the Word was God. He was with God in the beginning.

Through him all things were made; without him nothing was made
that has been made. In him was life, and that life was the light of men.
The light shines in the darkness, but the darkness has not understood it.

JOHN 1:1–5

Jesus Christ was the true Light in opposition to the smoking flax of tradition. Listen to those rabbis! They think themselves the light of the world. Their sophism is an endless strife of words; their research is not worth your study; their knowledge is not worth the knowing. They can tell you exactly which is the middle verse of the Bible and which is the middle letter of the middle word. They discussed their paradoxes till they became addleheaded. They refined their subtleties till doctrine dwindled down into doubt; simple truth was degraded into silly twaddle; their translations of Scripture were a travesty, and their commentaries an outrage upon commonsense. But Christ, the true, the heavenly Light, extinguishes all your earthly luminaries. The Jewish rabbi, the Greek philosopher, the ecclesiastical father, and the modern theological thinker are meteors that dissolve into mist. They make void the Word of God through their traditions or their conjectures. Believe what Jesus said, and what his apostles taught, and what you have had revealed to you in his own pure Word—Christ is the true Light.

Through the Bible in One Year: Judges 5–7

Bring Glory to God

"You are the light of the world. A city on a hill cannot be hidden.
Neither do people light a lamp and put it under a bowl.
Instead they put it on its stand, and it gives light to everyone in the house.
In the same way, let your light shine before men,
that they may see your good deeds and praise your Father in heaven."
MATTHEW 5:14–16

If you have received light from God, let your light so shine before men that they may see it and glorify God for it. I am afraid that this observation ought to trouble a great many professing Christians. They say that they have seen the Lord. I have no reason to doubt the truth of what they say; but having seen, why do they not testify? John writes, "I have seen and testify" (John 1:34); but in many cases nowadays, it might be written, "We have seen and do not testify," for some who profess to have seen Christ by faith do not even come forward to confess him in baptism, according to his Word; and many do not unite with the visible church and do not occupy themselves in the Sunday school or in any form of Christian usefulness. What will become of you who, having a talent, never put it out to interest? O slothful ones, who have wrapped your talent in a napkin, how will you answer for it in the day when the Master calls his servants to give their reckoning?

Through the Bible in One Year: Judges 8–10

Trophies of Christ

It is written: "I believed; therefore I have spoken."
With that same spirit of faith we also believe and therefore speak,
because we know that the one who raised the Lord Jesus from the dead
will also raise us with Jesus and present us with you in his presence.
All this is for your benefit, so that the grace that is reaching more and
more people may cause thanksgiving to overflow to the glory of God.
2 CORINTHIANS 4:13–15

I can speak about matters of fact that prove to me the power of my Lord and Master, for I have seen the triumphs of Christ. I have seen men who used to live in sin and drunkenness made honest and sober; and I have seen fallen women brought to Jesus' feet as penitents. All along, what is growing to be a long ministry, the chariot of the gospel, in which I have ridden, has had captives to grace Christ's triumphs. All along, multitudes have decided to quit the ways of sin and have turned to the living God, and I must believe in the power of divine grace; I cannot doubt it. The proof of what the tree is surely is found in the fruit, and the fruit is most abundant. Ask the missionaries what Christ has done in the Southern Seas, and they will tell you of islands, once inhabited by naked cannibals, where now men are clothed and in their right mind, sitting at the feet of Jesus. The whole world teems with trophies of Christ and shall yet more fully teem with them. "We have seen and do testify that the Father sent the Son to be the Saviour of the world" (1 John 4:14 KJV), and we preach with the full conviction that yet "the earth shall be full of the knowledge of the LORD, as the waters cover the sea" (Isaiah 11:9 KJV).

Through the Bible in One Year: Judges 11–13

Pray for the Power

On one occasion, while he was eating with them,
he gave them this command: "Do not leave Jerusalem,
but wait for the gift my Father promised,
which you have heard me speak about.
For John baptized with water,
but in a few days you will be baptized with the Holy Spirit."
ACTS 1:4–5

If you feel impelled to cry to God to give you the power to preach, the spiritual power, the power of the Holy Ghost; if you are impelled to teach in the Sunday school—and it is not worth doing unless you feel that you are impelled to it and sent to it—then pray for the power to win the souls of those dear children for Christ. If you feel called upon to write a letter to a friend tomorrow about his soul or her soul, do it because you feel called upon to do it; but pray to God to show you how to do it. Pray to him to put the power into the words that you utter, that you may say the right words, and put even the right tone into those words. There is a good deal even in the tone of the preacher. "How shall they preach, except they be sent?" (Romans 10:15 KJV). They must be clothed with divine power; but the Lord can clothe even a child with that power; he has often done it. He can clothe a humble Christian woman, who never spoke in public, with the power to win souls; he has often done it. First tarry at Jerusalem till you are endued with power from on high; and then go forth as Christ's witnesses; for how shall you preach, except you be sent?

Through the Bible in One Year: Judges 14–17

Our Reasonable Service

*What good is it, my brothers, if a man claims to have faith
but has no deeds? Can such faith save him? Suppose a brother
or sister is without clothes and daily food. If one of you says to him,
"Go, I wish you well; keep warm and well fed," but does nothing
about his physical needs, what good is it? In the same way,
faith by itself, if it is not accompanied by action, is dead.*
JAMES 2:14–17

There are some who seem willing to accept Christ as Savior who will not receive him as Lord. They will not state the case quite as plainly as that, but as actions speak more plainly than words, that is what their conduct practically says. How sad it is that some talk about their faith in Christ, yet their faith is not proved by their works! Some even speak as if they understood what we mean by the covenant of grace, yet alas, there is no good evidence of grace in their lives, but very clear proof of sin (not grace) abounding. I cannot conceive it possible for anyone truly to receive Christ as Savior and yet not to receive him as Lord. One of the first instincts of a redeemed soul is to fall at the feet of the Savior and gratefully and adoringly to cry, "Blessed Master, bought with your precious blood, I own that I am yours—yours only, wholly, yours forever. Lord, what will you have me to do?" A man who is really saved by grace does not need to be told that he is under solemn obligations to serve Christ; the new life within him tells him that. Instead of regarding it as a burden, he gladly surrenders himself—body, soul, and spirit, to the Lord who has redeemed him, reckoning this to be his reasonable service.

Through the Bible in One Year: Judges 18–21

Full and Free Grace

❧

My little children, these things write I unto you,
that ye sin not. And if any man sin,
we have an advocate with the Father,
Jesus Christ the righteous.
1 JOHN 2:1 KJV

The apostle John presents us with a very clear and emphatic testimony to the doctrine of full and free forgiveness of sin. He declares that the blood of Jesus Christ, God's dear Son, cleanses us from all sin, and that if any man sin, we have an Advocate. It is most evident that he is not afraid of doing mischief by stating this truth too broadly; on the contrary, he makes this statement with the view of promoting the sanctity of his "little children." The object of this bold declaration of the love of the Father to his sinning children is "that ye sin not." This is a triumphant answer to that grossly untruthful objection that is so often urged by the adversaries of the gospel against the doctrines of free grace—that they lead men to licentiousness. It does not appear that the apostle John so thought, for in order that these "little children" should not sin, he actually declares unto them the very doctrine that our opponents call licentious. Those men who think that God's grace, when fully, fairly, and plainly preached, will lead men into sin, know not what they say nor whereof they affirm. It is neither according to nature nor to grace for men to find an argument for sin in the goodness of God.

Through the Bible in One Year: 2 Corinthians 1–3

Armed with Holy Courage

The seventy-two returned with joy and said,
"Lord, even the demons submit to us in your name."

He replied, "I saw Satan fall like lightning from heaven.
I have given you authority to trample on snakes and scorpions
and to overcome all the power of the enemy; nothing will harm you.
However, do not rejoice that the spirits submit to you,
but rejoice that your names are written in heaven."

LUKE 10:17–20

In the presence of man, Satan is great and strong and crafty, but in the presence of the Christ of God, he shrinks into utter insignificance. He knows that he cannot resist even a word from Christ's lips or a glance from his eyes, so he says, "What have I to do with thee, Jesus, thou Son of the most high God?" (Mark 5:7 KJV). The question appears as if Satan pleaded with Christ not to put forth his power, not to touch him, but just to let him alone as too insignificant to be noticed. Such is the craft of Satan, that he will whine like a whipped cur, and crouch at the great Master's feet, and look up to his face, and entreat to be let alone, for he knows well enough the power of the Son of God. Yes, the name of Jesus has wondrous power over all the hosts of hell; so let us not be discomfited nor dismayed by all the armies of Satan, but let us, with holy courage, contend against all the powers of evil, for we shall be more than conquerors over them through Jesus Christ our Lord and Savior.

Through the Bible in One Year: 2 Corinthians 4–6

Serve with Joy

❧

*And the disciples were filled with joy
and with the Holy Spirit.*
ACTS 13:52

Many people seem to think that it is a very sorrowful thing to be a Christian, that believers in Christ are a miserable, unhappy lot of folk who never enjoy themselves. Well, I must admit that I do know some little communities of people who reckon themselves the very pick of Christians and who meet together on a Sunday to have a comfortable groan together; but I do not think that the bulk of us, who worship in this place, could be truthfully charged with anything like that. We serve a happy God, and we believe in a joyous gospel, and the love of Christ in our hearts has made us anticipate many of the joys of heaven even while we are here on earth. "The peace of God, which passeth all understanding," keeps our hearts and minds through Christ Jesus; and "the joy of the Lord is our strength." Perhaps, if we were to let the ungodly know more about this joy and peace, they would throw down the weapons of their rebellion and say, "We did not know that the religion of Jesus Christ was so blessed as this. We did not know that there was such music as this in the great Father's house. We did not know that there was a fatted calf waiting to be killed for us and that the whole household would begin to be merry over us. Now that we know what joy there is, we will enter and go no more out forever."

Through the Bible in One Year: 2 Corinthians 7–8

Caught in the Great Net

"Once again, the kingdom of heaven is like a net that was let down into the lake and caught all kinds of fish. When it was full, the fishermen pulled it up on the shore. Then they sat down and collected the good fish in baskets, but threw the bad away."
MATTHEW 13:47–48

Remember how the Lord Jesus Christ said, concerning those cities in which his mighty works had been wrought, that it would be more tolerable for Sodom and Gomorrah in the day of judgment than it would be for Capernaum and Bethsaida where he had so often been. Christ has been near to you, and you have heard his gospel, which many poor heathens have not heard. Now that you have heard the gospel—the gospel of the atoning sacrifice of Christ—his blood will cry out against you, as the blood of Abel cried out against Cain, if it is not applied to you to cleanse you from sin. You cannot escape from the Lord Jesus Christ. You are caught in the meshes of the great net that he has cast over all those who have heard the gospel. "He that believeth not is condemned already, because he hath not believed in the name of the only begotten Son of God. And this is the condemnation, that light is come into the world, and men loved darkness rather than light, because their deeds were evil" (John 3:18–19 KJV). If you do not believe on the Lord Jesus Christ, you resolve not to be saved by him, but to remain in the condition in which you now are, that is, "condemned already."

Through the Bible in One Year: 2 Corinthians 9–10

Remedies

❦

"Surely you will quote this proverb to me:
'Physician, heal yourself!'"
LUKE 4:23

Travel as fast as you may in a wrong direction, you will not reach the place you seek. Vain are all things save Jesus our Lord.

Have you been to Doctor Ceremony? He is, at this time, the fashionable doctor. Has he told you that you must attend to forms and rules? Has he prescribed you so many prayers and so many services? Ah! Many go to him, and they persevere in a round of religious observances, but these yield no lasting ease to the conscience. Have you tried Doctor Morality? He has a large practice and is a fine old Jewish physician. "Be good in outward character," says he, "and it will work inwardly and cleanse the heart." A great many persons are supposed to have been cured by him and by his assistant, Doctor Civility, who is nearly as clever as his master; but I have it on good evidence that neither of them apart, nor even the two together, could ever deal with an inward disease. Do what you may, your own doings will not stanch the wounds of a bleeding heart. Doctor Mortification has also a select practice, but men are not saved by denying themselves until they first deny their self-righteousness. Doctor Excitement has many patients, but his cures seldom outlive the set of sun. Doctor Feeling is much sought after by tender spirits; these try to feel sorrow and remorse, but indeed, the way of cure does not lie in that quarter. Let everything be done that can be done apart from our blessed Lord Jesus Christ, and the sick soul will be nothing bettered. You may try human remedies for the space of a lifetime, but sin will remain in power, guilt will cling to the conscience, and the heart will abide as hard as ever.

Through the Bible in One Year: 2 Corinthians 11–13

At Jesus' Feet

One of them, when he saw he was healed, came back,
praising God in a loud voice. He threw himself at Jesus' feet
and thanked him—and he was a Samaritan.
Luke 17:15–16

This man fell down at Jesus' feet: he did not feel perfectly in his place until he was lying there. "I am nobody, Lord," he seemed to say, and therefore he fell on his face. But the place for his prostration was "at Jesus' feet." I would rather be nobody at Christ's feet than everybody anywhere else! There is no place so honorable as down at the feet of Jesus. Ah, to lie there always, and just love him wholly, and let self die out! Oh, to have Christ standing over you as the one figure overshadowing your life henceforth and forever! True thankfulness lies low before the Lord.

Added to this there was worship. He fell down at Jesus' feet, glorifying God and giving thanks unto him. Let us worship our Savior. Let others think as they like about Jesus, but we will put our finger into the print of the nails and say, "My Lord and my God!" If there be a God, he is God in Christ Jesus to us. We shall never cease to adore him who has proved his Godhead by delivering us from the leprosy of sin. All worship be to his supreme majesty!

Through the Bible in One Year: Ruth 1–2

The Line of Demarcation

❦

*Now when Joshua was near Jericho, he looked up and saw a man
standing in front of him with a drawn sword in his hand. Joshua went up
to him and asked, "Are you for us or for our enemies?"*

*"Neither," he replied, "but as commander of the army of the LORD
I have now come." Then Joshua fell facedown to the ground in reverence.*
JOSHUA 5:13–14

A crimson line runs between the righteous and the wicked, the line of atoning sacrifice; faith crosses that line, but nothing else can. Faith in the precious blood is the great distinction at the root, and all those graces that spring out of faith go to make the righteous more and more separate from the ungodly world, who, having not the root, have not the fruit. Do you believe on Jesus Christ? On whose side are you? Are you for us or for our enemies? Do you rally at the cry of the cross? Does the uplifted banner of a dying Savior's love attract you? If not, then you remain still out of God, out of Christ, an alien to the commonwealth of Israel, and you will have your portion amongst the enemies of the Savior.

There is a sharp line of division between the righteous and the wicked, as clear as that which divides death from life. A man cannot be between death and life; he is either living or dead. A clear line of demarcation exists between life and death, and such a division is fixed by God between the righteous and the wicked. There are no *betweenities*; no amphibious dwellers in grace and out of grace; no monstrous nondescripts, who are neither sinners nor saints. You are this day alive by the quickening influences of the Holy Spirit, or else you are dead in trespasses and sins.

Through the Bible in One Year: Ruth 3–4

Calculate Omnipotence?

"Can you bring forth the constellations in their seasons or lead out
the Bear with its cubs? Do you know the laws of the heavens?
Can you set up God's dominion over the earth? Can you raise your voice
to the clouds and cover yourself with a flood of water?
Do you send the lightning bolts on their way? Do they report to you,
'Here we are'? Who endowed the heart with wisdom or gave
understanding to the mind? Who has the wisdom to count the clouds?"

Job 38:32–37

We too often want to see how the Lord will perform his Word. We
begin calculating, like the disciples, that two hundred pennies'
worth of bread will not be enough for the multitude, and as for a
few loaves and fishes, we cannot believe that they will be of any
avail among so many. Of course, if we have to engineer according
to the laws of mechanics, we must calculate our forces and
demand means proportionate to the results to be produced; but
why apply the slender line of mechanics to the omnipotent God?
Nay, I think we do worse, for we hardly carry out our calculations
correctly in reference to the Lord's working; if we did, we should
calculate that given omnipotence, difficulties exist no longer, and
impossibilities have disappeared. If the Lord be indeed almighty,
then how dare we question as to ways and means? Ways and
means are his business and none of ours, and with him no such
question can ever arise.

Through the Bible in One Year: Galatians 1 – 2

Do Not Put God in a Box!

Who are you to judge someone else's servant?
To his own master he stands or falls. And he will stand,
for the Lord is able to make him stand.

ROMANS 14:4

God has a thousand ways of accomplishing his purposes. He might have turned every stone in Samaria into a loaf and made the dust of its streets into flour, if so he willed. If he sent food in the wilderness without harvests, and water in the wilderness without wind and without rain, he can do as he wills and perform his own work in his own way. Do not let us think of limiting the Holy One of Israel to any special mode of action. When we hear of men being led to break out into new ways of going to work, do not let us feel, "This must be wrong"; rather, let us hope that it is very probably right, for we need to escape from these horrid ruts and wretched conventionalisms that are rather hindrances than helps. Some very stereotyped brethren judge it to be a crime for an evangelist to sing the gospel; and as to that American organ— dreadful! One of these days another set of conservative souls will hardly endure a service without such things, for the horror of one age is the idol of the next. Every man in his own order, and God using them all; and if there happens to be some peculiarity, some idiosyncrasy, so much the better. God does not make his servants by the score as men run iron into molds; he has a separate work for each man, and let each man do his own work in his own way, and may God bless him.

Through the Bible in One Year: Galatians 3–4

Reason with God

❧

"Come now, let us reason together," says the LORD.
"Though your sins are like scarlet, they shall be as white as snow;
though they are red as crimson, they shall be like wool.
If you are willing and obedient, you will eat the best from the land;
but if you resist and rebel, you will be devoured by the sword."

For the mouth of the LORD has spoken.
ISAIAH 1:18–20

I think it will be wisdom on our part, sinful creatures that we are, to accept the conference that God proposes. Anyhow, we cannot lose anything by it. If the Lord says, "Come now, let us reason together," he must have some design of love in it; therefore, let us come and return to our God and reason with him. I would invite any man here, who is at all desirous to be right with God, to begin to think about his God and about his own ways. Surely, it is high time with some of you that you should turn to him whom you have so long provoked. There is his Book, for instance; do you read it? Does not the dust upon it witness against you? You do not think it worthwhile to know what God has revealed in his Word. You treat your Maker and your Friend as if his letters were not worth even an hour's reading; you leave them utterly neglected. Is this as it should be? If you want to get right with God, would not the first step be to obey that command, "Thus saith the LORD of hosts; Consider your ways" (Haggai 1:5 KJV)? And should not the next step be obedience to that other word, "Acquaint now thyself with him, and be at peace: thereby good shall come unto thee" (Job 22:21 KJV)?

Through the Bible in One Year: Galatians 5–6

Not by Works

For it is by grace you have been saved, through faith—
and this not from yourselves, it is the gift of God—
not by works, so that no one can boast.
For we are God's workmanship,
created in Christ Jesus to do good works,
which God prepared in advance for us to do.

EPHESIANS 2:8–10

We have need to keep on repudiating this old lie of Satan's that men are to be saved by their works. Those fig leaves that Adam wove together to cover his nakedness are still in favor with his descendants. They will not take the robe of Christ's righteousness, but will rather go about to save themselves. A word or two with you, my friend. Do you say you will go to heaven by keeping the law? Ah, you have heard the old proverb about locking the stable when the horse is gone; I am afraid it is very applicable to you! So you are going to keep the stable shut now, and you are sure the horse shall never get out? If you will kindly go and look, you will find it is out already! Why, how can you keep the law that you have already broken? If you would be saved, the law of God is like a chaste alabaster vase that must be presented to God without crack or spot. But do you not see that you have broken the vase? Why, there is a crack there. "Ah!" you say, "that was a long time ago." Yes, I know it was, but still it is a crack; and there is the black mark of your thumb just underneath there. Why, man, the vase is broken already, and you cannot go to heaven by your good works when you have none.

Through the Bible in One Year: 1 Samuel 1–4

It Seemed Good in His Sight

❧

"Do two walk together unless they have agreed to do so?"
Amos 3:3

The devil dreads all contact with Christ, and he does so because, first, Christ's nature is so contrary to his own. And these two, so far from being agreed, are absolutely opposed to each other in every respect. There is a very ancient warfare between them; a warfare that, so far as this world is concerned, was proclaimed in the garden of Eden when God said to the serpent, "I will put enmity between thee and the woman, and between thy seed and her seed; it shall bruise thy head, and thou shalt bruise his heel" (Genesis 3:15 KJV). Christ loves light; Satan loves darkness. Christ works life; Satan works death. Christ is love; Satan is hate. Christ is goodness; Satan is evil. Christ is truth; Satan is falsehood.

Moreover, in the next place, Satan is well aware that the mission of our Lord Jesus Christ in this world is not for his good. He has no share in Christ's incarnation, nor in his atoning sacrifice. This is one of the wonderful results of the election of grace. Those persons who stumble at the election of some men rather than others ought equally to stumble at the fact that Christ did not redeem the fallen angels, but only fallen men; for why God chose to save men, and not to save angels, who among us can tell? The only answer I know to that question is this: "Even so, Father: for so it seemed good in thy sight" (Matthew 11:26 KJV). The mighty angels were passed by, and we, who are but worms of the dust, were looked upon with eyes of favor and love; and Satan, knowing this and being jealous of the love that lights upon men, cannot endure the presence of Christ.

Through the Bible in One Year: 1 Samuel 5–8

Brass with Gold?

❦

"No one can serve two masters. Either he will hate the one and love the other, or he will be devoted to the one and despise the other. You cannot serve both God and Money."

MATTHEW 6:24

Let every believer regard the life of God within him as being his most precious possession, more valuable by far than the natural life. Is not the spirit infinitely more precious than the body? Brethren, if we starve at all, let us starve our bodies and not our spirits. If anything must be stunted, let it be the baser nature. Let us not live eagerly for this world and languidly for the world to come. Having the divine life within us, let us not neglect to feed it and supply its wants. Here is a man who gives up attendance upon religious services in the week because he hungers to increase his business: he buys brass with gold. Another quits the place where he enjoys a gospel ministry to go at a larger salary to a place where his soul will be famished: he barters fine flour for husks. Another goes into all sorts of evil company, where he knows that his character is injured and his soul imperiled, and his excuse is that it pays. O sirs, is it so after all, that this eternal life that you profess to possess is of trifling value in your eyes? Then I protest before you that you do not possess it at all. How could you thus play the fool if the Lord had made you wise unto salvation? "Lay hold on eternal life," for this is the chief good, for the sake of which you may quit inferior things. "Seek ye first the kingdom of God, and his righteousness; and all these things shall be added unto you."

Through the Bible in One Year: 1 Samuel 9–12

Live for Life Everlasting

※

"Everything is permissible"—but not everything is beneficial.
"Everything is permissible"—but not everything is constructive.
Nobody should seek his own good, but the good of others.
1 CORINTHIANS 10:23–24

I would that all men at this hour abounded in almsgiving, but specially those who are followers of the loving Jesus. Regard your transactions from the standpoint of eternity. Weigh what you do, not as it may be thought of by men of the world, but as it will be judged by yourself when you behold in the heavenly country the face of him you love. I do not want you to have to say when you come to die, "I have had large possessions, but I have been a bad steward. I have had a competence, and I have wasted my Master's goods. All I have done with my wealth was to furnish my house well, perhaps to buy expensive pictures, and to allow myself luxuries that did me more harm than good." I hope, on the contrary, you will have to say, "I am saved by grace alone, but that grace enabled me to consecrate my substance and put it to the best uses. I can render up my stewardship without fear. I did not live for the fleeting life that is now over, but for the life everlasting." Brethren, some men spend so much upon themselves and so little for the Lord that they seem to me to eat the apple and give Christ the parings: they hoard up the flour and give the Lord a little of the bran. Live not as insects that die in a day, but as men who live forever.

Through the Bible in One Year: 1 Samuel 13–16

Examine Yourselves

*Examine yourselves to see whether
you are in the faith; test yourselves.
Do you not realize that Christ Jesus is in you—
unless, of course, you fail the test?
And I trust that you will discover
that we have not failed the test.*

2 CORINTHIANS 13:5–6

I have known many a true believer much troubled for fear he should be a hypocrite, while many a hypocrite has never asked a question. Thousands who have gone safely to heaven have, on the road, stopped many times and put their fingers to their brow and said, "Am I a true believer? What strange perplexities arise! Have I really passed from death to life, or is it a fancy and a dream?" And yet I say unto you that the hypocrite has gone singing on his way, secure, as he thought, of passing through the gate of pearl, until he found himself at last dragged back to the hole in the side of the hill, which is the secret gate of hell. Many, who were fair to look upon, have been rotten to the core, such fruit as the King could not accept at his table. O you who never ask whether you are Christians, begin to question yourselves; examine yourselves whether you be in the faith; let not presumption hold you in its deadly embrace.

Through the Bible in One Year: 1 Samuel 17–20

Safeguard against Self-Conceit

✣

So, if you think you are standing firm,
be careful that you don't fall!
1 CORINTHIANS 10:12

The danger I am to warn you of, I will now endeavor to describe. A Christian man finds himself for a long time without any remarkable trouble: his children are spared to him, his home is happy, his business extremely prosperous—he has, in fact, all that heart can wish: when he looks round about him, he can say with David, "The lines are fallen unto me in pleasant places; yea, I have a goodly heritage" (Psalm 16:6 KJV). Now, the danger is that he should think too highly of these secondary things and should say to himself, "My mountain stands firm; I shall never be moved." And then, though the man would never dare to put it in words, yet an indistinct feeling creeps over him that there is no need for him to be so watchful as other people; he would be sure not to fall if he were tempted. In fact, he wonders how some of his brethren can live as they do live; he is sure he could not do so. He feels that he could fight with any temptation and come back more than a conqueror. He has grown so strong that he feels himself a Samson. He knows much more now than he used to and thinks himself too old a bird to be caught with chaff, as he might have been some years ago. "Ah!" thinks he, "I am a model Christian." He does not say as much, but that lurks in his mind. His heart is much hampered with earthly things, and his mind much bloated with self-conceit.

Through the Bible in One Year: 1 Samuel 21–24

Slackened by Degrees

Who can say, "I have kept my heart pure;
I am clean and without sin"?
PROVERBS 20:9

What heartbreaking news is sometimes brought to us who are set over the Christian church. Such and such a man, whom we knew as a high professor and who has sat with us at the table of fellowship and seemed to be greatly advanced in spiritual things, has fallen into some act of vice that is positively disgusting, from which the soul revolts; and this is the very man with whom we took sweet counsel and went up to the house of God in company. If the history of these great offenders could be traced, it would be very much like this: they began well, but they slackened by degrees, till at last they were ripe for foul sin. Ah! We do not know to what we may descend when we begin to go downhill; down, where it would end, we should pray God that we might sooner die than live to plunge into the terrors of that descent. Who would think that David, the man after God's own heart, should come to be the murderer of his friend Uriah, to rob him of his wife? O David, are you so near to heaven and yet so near to hell? There is a David in every one of our hearts, and if we begin to backslide from God, we do not know to what extent we may slip. The great secret danger coming out of all this is that when a man reaches the state of carnal security, he is ready for any evil.

Through the Bible in One Year: 1 Samuel 25–28

May 25

What Gifts Do You Bring?

Araunah said to David, "Let my lord the king
take whatever pleases him and offer it up. . . .
But the king replied to Araunah,
"No, I insist on paying you for it.
I will not sacrifice to the LORD my God
burnt offerings that cost me nothing."
2 SAMUEL 24:22, 24

There are hundreds of professors who never gave God anything that cost them a self-denial; no, not so much as going without a dish on the table, or a picture on the wall, or a ring on the finger. There are numbers of professing Christians who spend a deal more on the soles of their boots than on Christ, and many women who spend more on the feathers and the flowers that deck their bonnets than on their Savior. Yes, and I have heard of men who said they were perfect, and yet they were worth half a million of money and were hoarding up more! Sinners dying and being damned and missionaries without support, and yet these absolutely perfect men are piling up gold and letting the cause of Christ stop for means. It is not my theory of perfection; nay, it does not seem to me to come up to the idea of a common Christian who says he is not his own. If you are really saved, brethren, not a hair of your heads belongs to yourselves; Christ's blood has either bought you or it has not, and if it has, then you are altogether Christ's, every bit of you, and you are neither to eat nor drink nor sleep, but for Christ. "Whatsoever ye do, do all to the glory of God" (1 Corinthians 10:31 KJV). Have you ever got ahold of that?

Through the Bible in One Year: 1 Samuel 29–31

First-Rate Service

And now, brothers, we want you to know about the grace that God has given the Macedonian churches. Out of the most severe trial, their overflowing joy and their extreme poverty welled up in rich generosity. For I testify that they gave as much as they were able, and even beyond their ability. Entirely on their own, they urgently pleaded with us for the privilege of sharing in this service to the saints.

2 CORINTHIANS 8:1–4

Brethren, be just as hot to honor Christ as you once were to dishonor him. As you have given the devil first-rate service, let Christ have the same. You recollect in the days of your sin, some of you who went in for it thoroughly, that you never stood at any expense—did you? Oh no, if you wanted pleasure in sin, away went the five pounds, and the hundreds. How often do I meet with men, particularly those given to drink, who get pounds in their pockets and never know how much they go; but they will never leave off till all is spent, be it little or much. Poor fools, poor fools. Yet I wish we could serve Jesus Christ thus unstintedly. No expense should be reckoned so long as we can honor him and bless his name. Bring forth the alabaster box; break it, never minding the chips and pieces; pour out the oil; and let Jesus have it all. It was thus I served Satan and thus would I serve Christ.

Through the Bible in One Year: Ephesians 1–2

Consecrated Enlistees

I am not commanding you, but I want to test the sincerity of your love
by comparing it with the earnestness of others. For you know the grace
of our Lord Jesus Christ, that though he was rich, yet for your sakes
he became poor, so that you through his poverty might become rich.
2 CORINTHIANS 8:8–9

Oh, who will be my Master's servant? Here he comes! Do you not see him? He wears upon his head no diadem but the crown of thorns, adown his cheeks you see the spittle flowing, his feet are still rubied with their wounds, and his hands are still bejeweled with the marks of the nails. This is your Master, and these are the insignia of his love for you. What service will you render him? That of a mere professor, who names his name but loves him not? That of a cold religionist, who renders unwilling service out of fear? I pray you do not so dishonor him. I lift the standard to enlist beneath the banner of Christ those who will henceforth be Christ's men from head to foot; and happy shall the church be, and happy the entire Israel of God if a chosen number shall enlist and remain true to their colors. We need no more of your nominal Christians, your lukewarm Christians, whom my Master spews out of his mouth: we need men on fire with love, all over consecrated, intensely devoted, who, by the slavery from which they have escaped and by the liberty into which they have entered, are under bond to spend and be spent for the name of Jesus, till they have filled the earth with his glory and made all heaven ring with his praise.

Through the Bible in One Year: Ephesians 3–4

Sealed Continuously

❧

Having believed, you were marked in him with a seal,
the promised Holy Spirit, who is a deposit guaranteeing
our inheritance until the redemption of those who are God's possession—
to the praise of his glory.
EPHESIANS 1:13–14

Some have supposed that there is a separate act of the Spirit of God in which he seals believers. It may be so—I will not raise the question—but I should be very sorry if any man here, living in sin, should nevertheless look back upon some time of religious excitement or enjoyment and say, "I am safe, for on that occasion I was sealed"; and I should be very sorry to have any brother take as the sure reason why he is saved some remarkable experience that he underwent on a certain day long past. A seal is for the present and is not a mere memory, but an object palpable *now*, and before the eyes. I am afraid many have been deceived into carelessness by the notion of a sealing received long ago. Let us seek out the truth. According to the text, as far as I can read it, here is a man who has believed in Jesus, and he desires a seal that God loves him: God gives him the Spirit, and that is all he can wish for or expect. Nothing more is wanted; nothing else would be so good. The very fact that the Spirit of God works in you to will and to do according to God's good pleasure is your seal; you do not require anything beyond. I do not say that any one operation of the Holy Spirit is to be regarded as the seal, but the whole of them together, as they prove his being within us, make up that seal.

Through the Bible in One Year: Ephesians 5–6

Christ Must Make a Stir

❧

*When he saw Jesus from a distance, he ran and fell on his knees
in front of him. He shouted at the top of his voice,
"What do you want with me, Jesus, Son of the Most High God?
Swear to God that you won't torture me!"*

MARK 5:6–7

Wherever Jesus comes, there is a commotion. No sooner does he set his foot on the shore at Gadara than he is at once assailed by the powers of darkness, and it is not long before the whole population of the district is affected by his presence. However uninfluential other people may be, Jesus is never so. He is ever either "the savour of death unto death" or "the savour of life unto life" (2 Corinthians 2:16 KJV). He is never a savorless Christ. Virtue is always going out of him, and that virtue stirs up the opposition of evildoers so that, straightway, they come forth to fight against him.

You remember that when Paul and Silas preached at Thessalonica, the unbelieving Jews cried out, "These that have turned the world upside down are come hither also" (Acts 17:6 KJV). Was that a wonderful thing? Nay, rather, was it not exactly what the Lord Jesus Christ had prophesied when he said, "I came not to send peace, but a sword" (Matthew 10:34 KJV)? He said that because of him, there would be division even in families, so that a man would be at variance against his father, and a daughter against her mother, and a man's foes would be those of his own household. Christ must make a stir wherever he comes, and his gospel must cause a commotion wherever it is preached. Stagnation is inconsistent with life. Deathlike slumber is the condition of those who are dead in sin, but to be aroused to action is the sure consequence of the gospel coming with power to anyone.

Through the Bible in One Year: 2 Samuel 1–4

Under Construction

It was he who gave some to be apostles, some to be prophets,
some to be evangelists, and some to be pastors and teachers,
to prepare God's people for works of service, so that the body of Christ
may be built up until we all reach unity in the faith
and in the knowledge of the Son of God and become mature,
attaining to the whole measure of the fullness of Christ.
EPHESIANS 4:11–13

Are you not conscious, believers, that you are being built up unto a divinely glorious form, after a high and noble model? It does not yet appear what we shall be, but you must be conscious that course upon course of precious stones has been built upon the foundation of your faith in Christ. Since you have known the Lord, you have made a distinct advance. At times you are afraid you have only grown downwards, but you have grown; there is a something about you now that was not there ten years ago. I am distinctly conscious, somehow, that twenty years ago I was not what I now am. I want the life in me to be developed and set free. Do you never feel the same? Have you not felt as if you yourself were big with a far more glorious nature and longed for deliverance from flesh and frailty? These groanings, aspirations, hopes, and desires are all seals of salvation; you will never find the ungodly thus moved. These pangs are peculiar to life. You are not a finished structure, but a house in process of erection, and you may be sure that one of these days the top stone shall be brought forth with shoutings of "Grace, grace unto it."

Through the Bible in One Year: 2 Samuel 5–8

Ties of Grace

This is how we know what love is: Jesus Christ laid down his life
for us. And we ought to lay down our lives for our brothers.
If anyone has material possessions and sees his brother in need
but has no pity on him, how can the love of God be in him?
Dear children, let us not love with words or tongue but with actions
and in truth.
1 John 3:16–18

The ties of blood ought to be recognized by us far more than they are. We are too apt to forget that God "hath made of one blood all nations of men for to dwell on all the face of the earth" (Acts 17:26 KJV), so that by the common tie of blood, we are all brethren. But, beloved, the ties of grace are far stronger than the ties of blood. If you are really born of God, you are brothers by a brotherhood that is stronger even than the natural brotherhood that enabled you to lie in the same cradle and to hang at the same breast, for brothers according to the flesh may be separated eternally. The right hand of the King may be the position accorded to the one, and his left hand may be the position assigned to the other; but brothers who are truly born of God share a brotherhood that must last forever.

If we are of the world, the world will love its own, so is it true that if we are of the Spirit, the Spirit will love his own. The whole redeemed family of Christ is firmly bound together. Born of God ourselves, we keep looking out to see others who have been "born again, not of corruptible seed, but of incorruptible" (1 Peter 1:23 KJV), and when we do see them, we cannot help loving them. There is a bond of union between us at once.

Through the Bible in One Year: 2 Samuel 9–12

Cling to One Another

*Keep watch over yourselves and all the flock of which the Holy Spirit
has made you overseers. Be shepherds of the church of God,
which he bought with his own blood. I know that after I leave,
savage wolves will come in among you and will not spare the flock.*
Acts 20:28–29

Christians ought to love one another because they are the subjects
of one King, who is also their Savior. We are a little band of brothers in the midst of a vast multitude of enemies. "Behold," said
Christ to his disciples, "I send you forth as sheep in the midst of
wolves" (Matthew 10:16 KJV). If you are true Christians, you will
not have the love of worldlings; you cannot have it. They will be
sure to ridicule you and call you fools or hypocrites or something
equally uncomplimentary. Well, then, cling the more closely to
one another. We are like a small company of soldiers in an enemy's
country, strongly garrisoned by the vast battalions of the foe, so
we must hold together; we must be as one man, banded together
in closest fellowship, as our great Captain bids us. God grant that
the very fact that we are found in an enemy's country may result
in making us more completely one than we have ever been before!
When I hear a Christian man finding fault with his minister, I
always wish that the devil had found somebody else to do his dirty
work. I hope that none of you will ever be found complaining of
God's servants who are doing their best to help on their Lord's
cause. There are plenty who are ready to find fault with them, and
it is much better that their faults—if they have faults—should be
pointed out by an enemy rather than by you who belong to the
same family as they do.

Through the Bible in One Year: 2 Samuel 13–16

Our Holy Prompter

"When you are brought before synagogues, rulers and authorities,
do not worry about how you will defend yourselves or what you will say,
for the Holy Spirit will teach you at that time what you should say."
LUKE 12:11–12

The Holy Spirit acts to his people somewhat as a prompter to a reciter. A man has to deliver a piece that he has learned, but his memory is treacherous, and therefore somewhere out of sight there is a prompter, so that when the speaker is at a loss and might use a wrong word, a whisper is heard that suggests the right one. When the speaker has almost lost the thread of his discourse, he turns his ear, and the prompter gives him the catchword and aids his memory. If I may be allowed the simile, I would say that this represents in part the work of the Spirit of God in us—suggesting to us the right desire and bringing all things to our remembrance whatsoever Christ has told us. In prayer we should often come to a dead stand, but he incites, suggests, and inspires, and so we go onward. In prayer we might grow weary, but the Comforter encourages and refreshes us with cheering thoughts. When indeed we are in our bewilderment almost driven to give up prayer, the whisper of his love drops a live coal from off the altar into our soul, and our hearts glow with greater ardor than before. Regard the Holy Spirit as your prompter, and let your ear be opened to his voice.

Through the Bible in One Year: 2 Samuel 17–20

Set Apart

*And of this gospel I was appointed a herald and an apostle and a teacher.
That is why I am suffering as I am. Yet I am not ashamed,
because I know whom I have believed, and am convinced that he is
able to guard what I have entrusted to him for that day.*

*What you heard from me, keep as the pattern of sound teaching, with
faith and love in Christ Jesus. Guard the good deposit that was entrusted
to you—guard it with the help of the Holy Spirit who lives in us.*
2 TIMOTHY 1:11–14

Every man is called to do all the good he can, but some men are set
apart to labor in peculiar departments of Christian work, and they
should be doubly careful to do all in their Master's name. If a ship
were stranded and breaking up, and the crew were ready to perish, we are all of us authorized to do all we can to save the ship-
wrecked, but the men who belong to the lifeboat's appointed crew
have a right to come to the fore and take the oars and put out to
sea. They are authorized to lead the way in daring and danger. So,
my brethren, those of you who have felt the divine call within you,
the sacred impulse that compels you to devote yourself to the salvation of your fellow men, you may do it boldly and without apology. Your authority is from Christ, for the Holy Spirit has set you
apart for the work. Let no man hinder or dispirit you. Press forward to the front rank in self-denying labor.

Through the Bible in One Year: 2 Samuel 21–24

Abide Always

❦

*"Remain in me, and I will remain in you.
No branch can bear fruit by itself; it must remain in the vine.
Neither can you bear fruit unless you remain in me."*
JOHN 15:4

"Without me ye can do nothing," said our Lord (John 15:5 KJV), and we know the truth of that saying by unwise attempts that have ended in mournful failures; but let us in future remember this truth practically. Never let us commence a work without seeking strength from on high. We go about Christian service very often as though we felt ourselves quite up to the mark for it; we pray without asking the preparation of the heart from God; we sing—ah, my brethren, how universally it is so—without at all entreating the Holy Spirit to quicken our praises; and I fear some of us must confess sorrowfully that we preach at times as though the preaching were to be our work and not the work of the Holy Ghost through us.

Do all in the Master's strength, and how differently everything will be done! Acknowledge all the time you are at your work that your strength comes from the Lord alone. Never let the thought cross your mind that you as an experienced Christian have a fitness for the work peculiarly your own, so that you can dispense with prayers for divine aid, so necessary to the young; never imagine that because through long years you have performed a service with acceptance, you can therefore now do it without renewed help. This is the way in which the power of God and the vitality of godliness are rendered so rare in the churches. If we do not feel conscious day by day of abiding weakness and consequent need of fresh strength from the Most High, we shall soon cease to be full of grace.

Through the Bible in One Year: Philippians 1–2

Buried Talent

*"And now, compelled by the Spirit, I am going to Jerusalem,
not knowing what will happen to me there. I only know that in every city
the Holy Spirit warns me that prison and hardships are facing me.
However, I consider my life worth nothing to me,
if only I may finish the race and complete the task the Lord Jesus
has given me—the task of testifying to the gospel of God's grace."*
ACTS 20:22–24

We have thus seen what it is to do all in the name of the Lord
Jesus; let us stop a moment to remind you that this text administers a severe rebuke to many professed Christians. Too many
church members do nothing in Christ's name. Since the day when
they were baptized into the name of the Father, and of the Son,
and of the Holy Ghost, they have done nothing else in that name.
Ah, hypocrites! God have mercy upon you! Alas, how many others do but very little in Christ's name! I noted in a letter by a certain pastor, not I think given to speak severely, this remark—that
he did not think in his own church one in three of the members
were doing anything for Christ. I could not speak so sorrowfully
as that concerning you; but I much fear that a large proportion of
the strength of this church is not used for the Lord. I believe that
there is more used here than in almost any other church, but still
there is a great deal of waste steam, a great deal of buried talent,
and thereby Jesus is defrauded.

Through the Bible in One Year: Philippians 3–4

A Wonder of Grace

Do you not know that the wicked will not inherit the kingdom of God?
Do not be deceived: Neither the sexually immoral nor idolaters nor
adulterers nor male prostitutes nor homosexual offenders nor thieves
nor the greedy nor drunkards nor slanderers nor swindlers will
inherit the kingdom of God. And that is what some of you were.
But you were washed, you were sanctified, you were justified in the name
of the Lord Jesus Christ and by the Spirit of our God.

1 CORINTHIANS 6:9–11

Do you see that man who once was in the habit of going in and out of the tavern? His speech, in those evil days, was foul, filthy, abominable; his poor wife was bruised and battered by his cruelty; his children were starved and shoeless. He is now with us in this house of prayer, and he is a member of Christ's mystical body. If I were to ask him to stand up and tell us about the great change that has been wrought in him, we should all rejoice to hear him testify that the Lord has forgiven him, washed him, cleansed him, and renewed his heart. Did that man, in his unregenerate state, ever think that the life of Christ would be in him, quickening his mortal body and changing his whole nature? Such a thought never occurred to him. Is he not a wonder of grace? Why, I do verily believe that if the devil were to be converted and become a holy angel again, it would not be more wonderful than the conversion of some who are now present. The Lord has done strange things, marvelous things for them, whereof our hearts are glad as we think of what he has done.

Through the Bible in One Year: 1 Kings 1–4

He Meets Our Need

But because Jesus lives forever, he has a permanent priesthood.
Therefore he is able to save completely those who come to God through
him, because he always lives to intercede for them.

Such a high priest meets our need—one who is holy, blameless, pure,
set apart from sinners, exalted above the heavens.
HEBREWS 7:24–26

Is not this a wonderful partnership, that Christ should take upon himself all that appertained to us, even to sorrow and broken-heartedness and, at last, death itself? That blessed body, though it saw no corruption, yet was as truly dead as that of anyone else who ever died. Christ took everything that belonged to us into that wonderful partnership.

Now see the result of this union; thus Christ meets all our needs. For instance, I bring my sin, but against that he sets his atonement. I bring my bondage, but against that he sets his redemption. I bring him death, but he brings his resurrection. I bring him weakness, and he meets it with his strength. I bring my wickedness, and he is made of God unto me righteousness. I bring him my evil nature, and he is made of God unto me sanctification. Whatever there is of ill that I have to contribute to the partnership, he covers it all with a splendor of goodness that blots it out and makes my soul much richer than it was before. Oh, what a wonderful thing it is to be brought into the fellowship of his Son, Jesus Christ our Lord!

Through the Bible in One Year: 1 Kings 5–8

Covet Humble Work

"The greatest among you will be your servant.
For whoever exalts himself will be humbled,
and whoever humbles himself will be exalted."
MATTHEW 23:11–12

If there is a position in the church where the worker will have to toil hard and get no thanks for it, take it and be pleased with it. If you can perform a service that few will ever seek to do themselves, or appreciate when performed by others, yet occupy it with holy delight. Covet humble work, and when you get it be content to continue in it. There is no great rush after the lowest places; you will rob no one by seeking them. The first place we must have an election for and poll the whole community, but for the very lowest there is no great ambition; therefore, select such a place, and while you will escape envy, you will also gain a quiet conscience. If we were Christ's more thoroughly, we should cheerfully and voluntarily push ourselves into the places of self-sacrifice, counting it our chief honor to serve God and the church in ways that are obscure and despised, because in so doing we shall be saved from the pharisaic spirit that desires the praise of man.

Through the Bible in One Year: 1 Kings 9–12

The Day Shall Yet Dawn

❧

Then I saw a new heaven and a new earth,
for the first heaven and the first earth had passed away,
and there was no longer any sea.
REVELATION 21:1

"For this purpose the Son of God was manifested, that he might destroy the works of the devil" (1 John 3:8 KJV). What horrible work the devil has already done in the world! Behold how the garden of Eden is withered and blighted and turned into a desert. See the fertile earth bringing forth thorns and thistles; and see man, who was made in the image of God, reduced to the position of a toiling sinner, earning his bread by the sweat of his face. See war and famine and pestilence and all kinds of evil and woe thickly spread over the whole earth, and remember that all this has come as the result of that one disobedience into which man was led by the temptation of the evil one. But the evil one has little room to glory in the mischief that he has wrought, for Christ has come to undo it. In the person of the second Adam, the Lord from heaven, man is lifted up from all the sin into which he fell through the first Adam; and as to this poor world itself, sin-blighted as it now is, it travails in anticipation of the new birth that yet awaits it, and the day shall yet dawn when new heavens and a new earth shall prove how completely Christ has canceled the curse and made the earth fragrant with blessing. It is for this reason that Satan hates the presence of Christ, because Christ is to destroy his evil work, and therefore he dreads that Christ should come near to him.

Through the Bible in One Year: 1 Kings 13–16

Grace Combats "If"

My little children, these things write I unto you, that ye sin not.
And if any man sin, we have an advocate with the Father,
Jesus Christ the righteous.
1 JOHN 2:1 KJV

The apostle says, "If any man sin." The "if" may be written in as small letters as you will, for the supposition is a matter of certainty. "If any man sin?" Although the gentle hand of the beloved disciple uses such mild and tender terms, putting it as a supposition, as though it were an astonishing thing after so much love and mercy and kindness that we should sin, yet John very well knew that all the saints do sin, for he has himself declared that if any man says he does not sin, he is a liar, and the truth is not in him. Saints are, without exception, sinners still. Far be it from us that divine grace has wrought a wondrous change; it would have been no grace at all if it had not. It will be well to note this change. The Christian no longer loves sin; it is the object of his sternest horror; he no longer regards it as a mere trifle, plays with it, or talks of it with unconcern. He looks upon it as a deadly serpent, whose very shadow is to be avoided. He would no more venture voluntarily to put its cup to his lip than a man would drink poison who had once almost lost his life through it. Sin is dejected in the Christian's heart, though it is not ejected. Sin may enter the heart and fight for dominion, but it cannot sit upon the throne.

Through the Bible in One Year: 1 Kings 17–19

Mournful and Vexed

*If we claim to be without sin, we deceive ourselves and the truth
is not in us. If we confess our sins, he is faithful and just
and will forgive us our sins and purify us from all unrighteousness.
If we claim we have not sinned, we make him out to be a liar
and his word has no place in our lives.*

1 JOHN 1:8–10

The Christian never sins with that enormity of boasting of which the unregenerate are guilty. Others wallow in transgressions and make their shame their glory, but if the believer falls, he is very quiet, mournful, and vexed. Sinners go to their sins as children to their own father's orchard, but believers slink away like thieves when they have been stealing forbidden fruit. Shame and sin are always in close company in a Christian. If he be drunken with evil, he will be ashamed of himself and go to his bed like a whipped cur. He cannot proclaim his transgressions as some do in the midst of a ribald crowd, boasting of their exploits of evil. His heart is broken within him, and when he has sinned he goes with sore bones for many and many a day.

Nor does he win with the fullness of deliberation that belongs to other men. The sinner can sit down by the month together and think over the iniquity that he means to perpetrate, till he gets his plans well organized and has matured his project, but the Christian cannot do this. He may put the sin into his mouth and swallow it in a moment, but he cannot continue to roll it under his tongue. He who can carefully arrange and plot a transgression is still a true child of the old serpent.

Through the Bible in One Year: 1 Kings 20–22

Strong in Love

Jesus turned and said to them,
"Daughters of Jerusalem, do not weep for me;
weep for yourselves and for your children."
Luke 23:28

Too many people are so wrapped up in their own grief that they have no room in their souls for sympathy. Do you not know them? The first thing when they rise in the morning is the dreadful story of the night they have passed. Ah, dear! And they have not quite eaten a hearty breakfast before their usual pain is somewhere or other coming over them. They must have the special care and pity of the whole household. All the day long the one great business is to keep everybody aware of how much the great sufferer is enduring. It is this person's patent right to monopolize all the sympathy that the market can supply, and then there will be none to spare for the rest of the afflicted. If you are greatly taken up with self, there is not enough of you to run over to anybody else. How different this from our Lord, who never cried, "Have pity upon me! Have pity upon me, O my friends!" He is described as "enduring the cross, despising the shame." So strong was he in love that though he saved others, himself he could not save; though he succored the afflicted, none succored him.

Through the Bible in One Year: Colossians 1–2

Our Marching Orders

*Then Jesus came to them and said, "All authority in heaven
and on earth has been given to me. Therefore go and make disciples
of all nations, baptizing them in the name of the Father and
of the Son and of the Holy Spirit, and teaching them to obey everything
I have commanded you. And surely I am with you always,
to the very end of the age."*
MATTHEW 28:18–20

While I was meditating in private upon this text, I felt myself carried away by its power. I was quite unable calmly to consider its terms or to investigate its argument. The command with which the text concludes repeated itself again and again and again in my ears, till I found it impossible to study, for my thoughts were running hither and thither, asking a thousand questions, all of them intended to help me in answering for myself the solemn inquiry, "How am *I* to go and teach *all* nations, baptizing them in the name of the Father, and of the Son, and of the Holy Ghost?"

Oh! I would that the church could hear the Savior addressing these words to her now; for the words of Christ are living words, not having power in them yesterday alone, but today also. The injunctions of the Savior are perpetual in their obligation; they were not binding upon apostles merely, but upon us also, and upon every Christian does this yoke fall. We are not exempt today from the service of the first followers of the Lamb; our marching orders are the same as theirs, and our Captain requires from us obedience as prompt and perfect as from them.

Through the Bible in One Year: Colossians 3 – 4

Prove the Promise of God

*He said to them, "Go into all the world
and preach the good news to all creation.
Whoever believes and is baptized will be saved,
but whoever does not believe will be condemned."*

MARK 16:15–16

Brethren, the heathen are perishing; shall we let them perish? *His* name is blasphemed; shall we be quiet and still? The honor of Christ is cast into the dust, and his foes revile his person and resist his throne; shall we his soldiers suffer this and not find our hands feeling for the hilt of our sword, the sword of the Spirit, which is the Word of God? Our Lord delays his coming; shall we begin to sleep or to eat or to be drunken? Shall we not rather gird up the loins of our mind and cry unto him, "Come, Lord Jesus, come quickly"? The scoffing skeptics of these last days have said that the anticipated conquest of the world for Christ is but a dream or an ambitious thought that crossed our leader's mind but is never to be accomplished. It is asserted by some that the superstitions of the heathen are too strong to be battered down by our teachings and that the strongholds of Satan are utterly impregnable against our attacks. Shall it be so? Shall we be content foolishly to sit still? Nay, rather let us work out the problem; let us prove the promise of God to be true; let us prove the words of Jesus to be words of soberness; let us show the efficacy of his blood and the invincibility of his Spirit by going in the spirit of faith, teaching all nations, and winning them to the obedience of Christ our Lord.

Through the Bible in One Year: 2 Kings 1–4

Will You Go?

Therefore I glory in Christ Jesus in my service to God.
I will not venture to speak of anything except what Christ
has accomplished through me in leading the Gentiles to obey God
by what I have said and done—by the power of signs and miracles,
through the power of the Spirit. So from Jerusalem all the way around
to Illyricum, I have fully proclaimed the gospel of Christ.
It has always been my ambition to preach the gospel where Christ was not
known, so that I would not be building on someone else's foundation.

ROMANS 15:17–20

My soul sometimes pants and longs for the liberty to preach Christ where he was never preached before; not to build upon another man's foundation, but to go to some untrodden land, some waste where the foot of Christ's minister was never seen, that there "the solitary place might be glad for [us], and the wilderness rejoice and blossom as the rose" (Isaiah 35:1 KJV). I have made it a solemn question whether I might not testify in China or India the grace of Jesus, and in the sight of God I have answered it. I solemnly feel that my position in England will not permit my leaving the sphere in which I now am, or else tomorrow I would offer myself as a missionary. You who are free from so great a work as that which is cast upon me—you who have talents as yet undevoted to any special end, and powers of being as yet unconsecrated to any given purpose, and unconfined to any one sphere; do you not hear my Master saying, in tones of plaintive sorrow, blended with an authority that is not to be denied, "Go ye therefore, and teach all nations, baptizing them in the name of the Father, and of the Son, and of the Holy Ghost" (Matthew 28:19 KJV)?

Through the Bible in One Year: 2 Kings 5–8

Unleash the Power

The king's heart is in the hand of the LORD;
he directs it like a watercourse wherever he pleases.
PROVERBS 21:1

All power is given to Christ—power over the wills of men as well as over the waves of the sea. But political occurrences prevent your landing on a certain country; through treaties or a want of treaties, there is no room for the missionary in such and such an empire. *Pray*, and the gates shall be opened; *plead*, and the bars of brass shall be cut in twain. Christ has power over politics. He can change the hearts of princes and preside in the counsels of senates; he can cause nations that have long been shut up to be opened to the truth.

Truly God has opened up the world and brought it to our threshhold; if he has not made a smaller world, at least he has made it more convenient and nearer to our hand. Countries that once could not be reached have been opened to us. And there are other lands and other places that once seemed to be environed by impassable mountains, into which we have now a road. Oh, for the will to dash through that road riding upon the white horses of salvation! Oh, for the heart, the spirit, and the soul to avail ourselves of the golden opportunity and to preach Christ where he has never been preached before! All power, then, we can clearly see, over everything in this world has been given to Christ and has been used for the propagation of his truth.

Through the Bible in One Year: 2 Kings 9–12

Send the Best

*On coming to the house, they saw the child with his mother Mary,
and they bowed down and worshiped him.
Then they opened their treasures and presented him
with gifts of gold and of incense and of myrrh.*

MATTHEW 2:11

Now, I would that the divine call would come to some gifted men. You who have, perhaps, some wealth of your own, what could be a better object in life than to devote yourself and your substance to the Redeemer's cause? You, young men, who have brilliant prospects before you but who as yet have not the anxieties of a family to maintain, why, would it not be a noble thing to surrender your brilliant prospects, that you may become a humble preacher of Christ? The greater the sacrifice, the more honor to yourself and the more acceptable to him.

I long that we may see young men out of the universities and students in our grammar schools—that we may see our physicians, advocates, tradesmen, and educated mechanics, when God has touched their hearts, giving up all they have, that they may teach and preach Christ. It will never do to send out to the heathen men who are of no use at home. We cannot send men of third- and tenth-class abilities; we must send the highest and best. The bravest men must lead the van. O God, anoint your servants, we beseech you; put the fire into their hearts that never can be quenched; make it so hot within their bones that they must die or preach, that they must lie down with broken hearts or else be free to preach where Christ never has been heard.

Through the Bible in One Year: 2 Kings 13–15

Lord of Truth

Jesus said, "My kingdom is not of this world.
If it were, my servants would fight to prevent my arrest by the Jews.
But now my kingdom is from another place."

"You are a king, then!" said Pilate.

Jesus answered, "You are right in saying I am a king.
In fact, for this reason I was born, and for this I came into the world,
to testify to the truth. Everyone on the side of truth listens to me."
JOHN 18:36–37

You remember Napoleon's saying: "I have founded an empire by force, and it has melted away; Jesus Christ established his kingdom by love, and it stands to this day, and will stand." That is the kingdom to which our Lord's Word refers, the kingdom of spiritual truth in which Jesus reigns as Lord over those who are of the truth. He claimed to be a king, and the truth which he revealed, and of which he was the personification, is therefore the scepter of his empire. He rules by the force of truth over those hearts that feel the power of right and truth and therefore willingly yield themselves to his guidance, believe his Word, and are governed by his will. It is as a spiritual Lord that Christ claims sovereignty among men; he is King over minds that love him, trust him, and obey him, because they see in him the truth that their souls pine for. Other kings rule our bodies, but Christ our souls; they govern by force, but he by the attractions of righteousness; theirs is, to a great extent, a fictitious royalty, but his is true and finds its force in truth.

Through the Bible in One Year: 2 Kings 16–18

Bear Witness to the Truth

❧

Therefore put on the full armor of God, so that when the day
of evil comes, you may be able to stand your ground,
and after you have done everything, to stand. Stand firm then,
with the belt of truth buckled around your waist, with the breastplate
of righteousness in place, and with your feet fitted
with the readiness that comes from the gospel of peace.
EPHESIANS 6:13–15

If you love the Lord, bear witness to the truth. You must do it personally; you must also do it collectively. Never join any church whose creed you do not entirely and unfeignedly believe, for if you do, you act a lie and are moreover a partaker in the error of other men's testimonies. I would not for a moment say anything to retard Christian unity, but there is something before unity, and that is "truth in the inward parts" and honesty before God. I dare not be a member of a church whose teaching I knew to be false in vital points. I would sooner go to heaven alone than belie my conscience for the sake of company.

Are you willing to walk with the truth through the mire and through the slough? Have you the courage to profess unfashionable truth? Are you willing to believe the truth against which science, falsely so-called, has vented her spleen? Are you willing to accept the truth although it is said that only the poor and uneducated will receive it? Are you willing to be the disciple of the Galilean, whose apostles were fishermen? Verily, verily, I say unto you, in that day in which the truth in the person of Christ shall come forth in all its glory, it shall go ill with those who were ashamed to own it and its Master.

Through the Bible in One Year: 2 Kings 19–21

Offended by Christ

He said: "A man of noble birth went to a distant country
to have himself appointed king and then to return.
So he called ten of his servants and gave them ten minas.
'Put this money to work,' he said, 'until I come back.'

"But his subjects hated him and sent a delegation after him to say,
'We don't want this man to be our king.'"

LUKE 19:12–14

You remember that the writer of the second psalm says, "The kings of the earth set themselves, and the rulers take counsel together, against the LORD, and against his anointed, saying, Let us break their bands asunder, and cast away their cords from us" (Psalm 2:2–3 KJV). The resolve of human nature until it is renewed is always this: "We will not have this Man to reign over us." Men might be willing for Christ to save them, but not for him to reign them. Such laws as these—"Thou shalt love thy neighbour as thyself," "Thou shalt forgive till seventy times seven," the law of love, the law of gentleness, the law of kindness—man says that he admires them, but when these laws come home to him and lay hold of the reins of his ambition, cramp his covetousness, and condemn his self-righteousness, straightway he is offended; and when Christ says, "Heaven and earth shall pass away, but my words shall not pass away"; when he begins to teach the necessity of absolute purity and to say that even a lascivious glance of the eye is a sin, then men reply, "His rule will never do for us," and they hang him up to die because they will not submit to his authority.

Through the Bible in One Year: 2 Kings 22–25

Such Are We

❧

Here is a trustworthy saying that deserves full acceptance:
Christ Jesus came into the world to save sinners—
of whom I am the worst. But for that very reason I was shown mercy
so that in me, the worst of sinners, Christ Jesus might display his
unlimited patience as an example for those who would believe on him
and receive eternal life.
1 TIMOTHY 1:15–16

Yes, beloved, when we beseech you to be reconciled to God, we give to ourselves no airs, as though we were superior to you by nature or had been superior in our former conduct before conversion. Nay, rather, we are bone of your bone and flesh of your flesh. Are you sinful? Such were we. Are you rebellious against God? Such were we. Are your hearts hard? Such were ours. We do not look down upon you from an elevated platform of affected dignity, for we recognize our own nature in yours; therefore, we come to you as to fellow sinners, and albeit it is a sorrowful thing ever to have sinned, we are glad to think that we can speak to you of an evil that has vexed us, the power of which we have painfully felt and penitently mourned, as you must yet do. We hope that our former condition as sinners and unbelievers will make us speak to you more tenderly and will enable us to reach your hearts the better. God might have sent angels to you, and you would, perhaps, at first, have been awed by their glory; but their sermons must have been cold and unsympathetic compared with ours, for they could not know your misery and degradation as we do.

Through the Bible in One Year: 1 Thessalonians 1–2

The Badge of Discipleship

*Peter replied, "Repent and be baptized, every one of you,
in the name of Jesus Christ for the forgiveness of your sins.
And you will receive the gift of the Holy Spirit.
The promise is for you and your children and for all who are far off—
for all whom the Lord our God will call."*

ACTS 2:38–39

"He that believeth and is baptized shall be saved" (Mark 16:16 KJV). That is to say, if a man would participate in the bounteous salvation that Christ has wrought, he must believe in Christ; he must trust Christ; he must believe Christ to be God's appointed Savior and to be able to save him. He must act on that belief and trust himself in the hands of Jesus, and if he does that, he shall be saved.

Further, the text says *he must be baptized*. Not that there is any virtue whatsoever in baptism, but it is a small thing for Christ to expect that the man trusting to be saved by him should own and avow his attachment to him. He who wishes to have Christ as his Savior should be prepared openly to acknowledge that he is on Christ's side. Baptism thus becomes the badge of discipleship, the outward token of inward faith, by which a man says to all who look on, "I confess myself dead to the world; I confess myself buried with Christ; I declare myself risen to newness of life in him; make what you will of it, and laugh at it as much as you like, yet in the faith of Jesus as my Lord, I have taken leave of all else to follow him."

Through the Bible in One Year: 1 Thessalonians 3–5

Bonds of Love

*Husbands, love your wives, just as Christ loved the church
and gave himself up for her to make her holy, cleansing her
by the washing with water through the word, and to present her
to himself as a radiant church, without stain or wrinkle
or any other blemish, but holy and blameless.*

EPHESIANS 5:25–27

A mysterious union has been established between Christ and his church, which is constantly compared to that of marriage: "For the husband is the head of the wife, even as Christ is the head of the church: and he is the saviour of the body" (Ephesians 5:23 KJV). Jesus is the bridegroom; his church is his bride. They are espoused one to another; in bonds of love they are bound forever to each other; and they are alike with sacred expectation waiting for the marriage day, when shall be accomplished the eternal purpose of God and the desire of the Redeemer. As the husband exercises a headship in the house, not at all (when the relationship is rightly carried out) tyrannical or magisterial, but a government founded upon the rule of nature and endorsed by the consent of love, even so Jesus Christ rules in his church, not as a despotic lord, compelling and constraining his subject bride against her will, but as a husband well beloved, obtaining obedience voluntarily from the heart of the beloved one, being in all things so admired and held in esteem as to win an undisputed preeminence.

Jesus Christ's kingdom is no tyranny; his scepter is not made of iron; he rules not with blows and curses and threats; but his scepter is of silver and his rule is love. The only chains he uses are the chains of his constraining grace; his dominion is spiritual and extends over willing hearts who delight to bow before him and to give him the honor due unto his name.

Christt Is the Head

❧

And he is the head of the body, the church;
he is the beginning and the firstborn from among the dead,
so that in everything he might have the supremacy.
COLOSSIANS 1:18

Since Christ is the head of his body, the church, he alone can determine doctrines for her. Nothing is to be received as divinely warranted except it comes with his stamp upon it. It is nothing to the faithful servant of Jesus Christ that a certain dogma comes down to him with the gray antiquity of the ages to make it venerable. Like a sensible man, the Christian respects antiquity, but like a loyal subject of his King, he does not so bow before antiquity as to let it become ruler in Zion instead of the living Christ. A multitude of good men may meet together, and they may, in their judgment, propound a dogma and assert it to be essential and undoubted, and they may even threaten perils most abundant to those who receive not their verdict; but if the dogma was not authorized long before they decided it—if it was not written in the Book, the decision of the learned council amounts to nothing. All the fathers and doctors and divines and confessors put together cannot add a word to the faith once delivered unto the saints; yea, I venture to say that the unanimous assent of all the saints in heaven and earth would not suffice to make a single doctrine binding upon conscience unless Jesus had so determined.

Through the Bible in One Year: 1 Chronicles 5–8

Christ's Authority

*He must hold firmly to the trustworthy message
as it has been taught, so that he can encourage others
by sound doctrine and refute those who oppose it.*
TITUS 1:9

The sole authority of Jesus Christ in all respects must be maintained rigorously, but churches are very apt to be guided by something else. Some would have us guided by results. We have heard a discussion upon the question whether or not we should continue missionary operations, since there are so few converted! How can the question ever be raised while the Master's order runs thus— "Go ye into all the world, and preach the gospel to every creature" (Mark 16:15 KJV)? Spoken by the mouth of Jesus our ruler, that command stands good, and the results of missions can have no effect upon loyal minds either one way or the other as to their prosecution. If from this day for the next ten thousand years not a single soul should be converted to God by foreign missions, if there still remained a church of Christ, it would be her duty with increasing vigor to thrust her sons forward into the mission field; because her duty is not measured by the result, but by the imperial authority of Christ.

But the discoveries of science, we are told, have materially affected belief, and therefore we should change our ways according as philosophy changes. We have the same King still, the same laws still, the same teaching of the Word still, and we are to deliver this teaching after the same sort and in the same spirit. If we shall do this, if any church shall do this, namely, take its truth from Jesus' lips, live according to Jesus' Word, and go forward in his name, such a church cannot by any possibility fail, for the failure of such a church would be the failure of the Master's own authority.

Through the Bible in One Year: 1 Chronicles 9–12

No Joy Excels It

❧

The fruit of the righteous is a tree of life,
and he who wins souls is wise.
PROVERBS 11:30

Brethren and sisters, I do pray you preach the gospel of Jesus Christ, for your own sakes, if there were no other reason. Depend upon it—your own spiritual vigor will be very much enhanced by your labors of love and your zeal for the service of Christ. I have remarked it as an invariable thermometer by which to gauge the spirituality of a man's heart. Whether he is either doing or not doing something for Christ will tell upon his life and conversation. Did you ever feel the joy of winning a soul for Christ? If so, you will need no other argument for attempting to spread the knowledge of his name among every creature. I tell you, there is no joy out of heaven that excels it—the grasp of the hand of one who says, "By your means I was turned from darkness to light, rescued from drunkenness, or reclaimed perhaps from the grossest vices, to love and serve my Savior"; to see your spiritual children around you and to say, "Here am I, and these whom you have given me."

Through the Bible in One Year: 1 Chronicles 13–16

Carry Out the Master's Will

❧

"His master replied, 'Well done, good and faithful servant!
You have been faithful with a few things;
I will put you in charge of many things.
Come and share your master's happiness!'"
MATTHEW 25:21

The church's power is twofold. It is a power to testify to the world what Christ has revealed. She is set as a witness, and she must act as such. She has, next, a ministerial power, by which she carries out the will of Christ and does his bidding as Christ's servant and minister. A certain number of servants meet in the servants' hall; they have an order given to do such work, and they have also orders given them how to do it. They then consult with each other as to the minor details, how they can best observe the master's rule and do his bidding. They are perfectly right in so doing. But suppose they began to consult about whether the objects proposed by the master were good, or whether the rules he had laid down might not be altered! They would at once become rebellious and be in danger of discharge. So a church met together to consult how to carry out the Master's will, how to enforce his laws, does rightly; but a church meeting to make new laws, or a church meeting to rule according to its own judgment and opinion, imagining that its decision will have weight, has made a mistake and placed itself in a false position. The one doctrine I have sought to bring forward is this: that he alone who bought the church and saved the church is to rule the church; and surely our hearts, without exception, bow to this.

Through the Bible in One Year: 1 Chronicles 17–19

His Love Is Greater!

Who will bring any charge against those whom God has chosen?
It is God who justifies. Who is he that condemns?
Christ Jesus, who died—more than that, who was raised to life—
is at the right hand of God and is also interceding for us.
Who shall separate us from the love of Christ? Shall trouble or hardship
or persecution or famine or nakedness or danger or sword?

ROMANS 8:33–35

Have we during the past week fallen into a signal state of gross unbelief? Have we been thinking hard thoughts of God? Has some sin suspended our communion with our Savior? Are we now cold at heart and void of spiritual emotion? Do we feel quite unworthy to draw near unto him who loved us with so great a love? Be not desponding. The God of all patience will not desert you. The love that our Lord Jesus Christ bears to his people is so great that he passes by their transgression, iniquity, and sin. No, there is no anger on his part to divide you from your Lord. Since he thus graciously comes to you, will you not gladly come to him? Do not think for a moment that he will frown or repulse you. He will not remind you of your cold prayers, your neglected closet, your unread Bible, nor will he chide you for losing occasions of fellowship; but he will receive you graciously and love you freely and grant you just what at this moment you need.

Through the Bible in One Year: 1 Chronicles 20–23

Slow Learners

❧

If you have any encouragement from being united with Christ,
if any comfort from his love, if any fellowship with the Spirit,
if any tenderness and compassion, then make my joy complete by being
like-minded, having the same love, being one in spirit and purpose.
PHILIPPIANS 2:1–2

You and I are neither the Alpha nor Omega to the law, for we have broken it altogether. We have not even learned its first letter—"Thou shalt love the Lord thy God with all thy heart," and certain I am we know but very little of the next—"Love thy neighbour as thyself." Even though renewed by grace, we are very slow to learn the holiness and spirituality of the law; we are so staggered by the letter that we often miss its spirit altogether. But, beloved, if you would see the law fulfilled, look to the person of our blessed Lord and Master. What love to God is there!

Jesus loved in such a way that all the love that ever gleamed in human bosom, if it could be gathered together, would be but as a spark, while his great love to man would be as a flaming furnace heated seven times hotter than human imagination can conceive. Do not, beloved friends, if you are in Christ Jesus, permit legal fears to distress you at the remembrance of your failures in obedience, as though they would destroy your soul. Seek after holiness, but never make holiness your trust. Seek after virtue, pant for it; but when you see your own imperfections, do not therefore despair. Your saving righteousness is the righteousness of Christ; that in which God accepts you is Christ's perfect obedience; and we say of that again, in the words of the text, Jesus Christ is "Alpha and Omega, the beginning and the end" (Revelation 22:13).

Through the Bible in One Year: 1 Chronicles 24–26

The Godly Man

Know that the LORD has set apart the godly for himself.
PSALM 4:3

All men are not godly. Alas, the ungodly are the great majority of the human race. And all men who are to some extent godly are not equally godly. The man who fears God and desires truly to know him has some little measure of godliness. The man who has begun to trust the Savior whom God has set forth as the great propitiation for sin has a blessed measure of godliness. The man whose communion with God is constant, whose earnest prayers and penitential tears are often observed of the great Father, and who sighs after fuller and deeper acquaintance with the Lord—this man is godly in a still higher sense. And he who by continual fellowship with God has become like him, upon whom the image of Christ has been photographed, for he has looked on him so long and rejoiced in him so intensely—he is *the* godly man. The man who finds his God everywhere, who sees him in all the works of his hands, the man who traces everything to God, whether it be joyful or calamitous; the man who looks to God for everything, takes every suit to the throne of grace and every petition to the mercy seat; the man who could not live without his God, to whom God is his exceeding joy, the help and the health of his countenance; the man who dwells in God—this is the godly man. This is the man who shall dwell forever with God, for he has a godlikeness given to him; and in the Lord's good time he shall be called away to that blessed place where he shall see God and shall rejoice before him forever and ever.

Through the Bible in One Year: 1 Chronicles 27–29

The Prayerful Life

❧

And pray in the Spirit on all occasions
with all kinds of prayers and requests.
With this in mind, be alert and
always keep on praying for all the saints.
EPHESIANS 6:18

Some praying takes the form of action, and an act may be a prayer. To love our fellow men and to desire their good is a kind of consolidated practical prayer. There comes to be a prayer to God in giving alms, or in preaching the gospel, or in trying to win a wanderer, or in taking a child upon your knee and talking to him about the Savior. Such acts are often most acceptable prayers. But when you cannot act thus, it is well to pour out your heart before the Lord in words. And when you cannot do that, it is sweet to sit quite still and look up to him, and even as the lilies pour out their fragrance before him who made them, so do you, even without speaking, worship God in that deep adoration that is too eloquent for language, that holy nearness that, because it is so near, dares not utter a sound lest it should break the spell of the divine silence that engirds it. Frost of the mouth but flow of the soul is often a good combination in prayer. It is blessed prayer to lie on your face before God in silence, or to sigh and cry, or to moan and wail as the Holy Spirit moves you. All this is prayer, whatever shape it assumes, and it is the sign and token of a true believer's life.

Through the Bible in One Year: 2 Thessalonians 1–3

Heaven upon Earth

*I have no greater joy than to hear
that my children are walking in the truth.*
3 JOHN 4

I have had some very happy days in my life, but my happiest times have been such as I had one day last week, when I shook hands with somewhere about a hundred persons who called me their spiritual father. It seemed to them to be quite a grand day to touch my hand, while to me—the tears standing in my eyes as I saw each one of them—it was as the days of heaven upon earth, for I had never seen all those people before. Perhaps some of them had been in this house now and then, but I went from village to village and found them standing at their doors, begging me to stop just to hear how such a sermon was "blessed to me," and "My old father read your sermons and died in peace after reading them"—there, I could have died of joy, for this is the truest happiness we can have on earth. Seek sinners, my brethren; seek their conversion with all your heart and soul. If you would be happy men and women and would sing the sweetest song that could be sung on earth, let it be "praise unto our God"; not yours alone, but the God also of those whom infinite mercy shall permit you to bring to the same dear Savior's feet.

Through the Bible in One Year: 2 Chronicles 1–4

While We Speak

❧

As soon as you began to pray, an answer was given,
which I have come to tell you, for you are highly esteemed.
DANIEL 9:23

Is there any limitation in the Spirit of God? Why should not the feeblest minister become the means of salvation to thousands? Is God's arm shortened? When I bid you pray that God would make the ministry quick and powerful, like a two-edged sword, for the salvation of sinners, I am not setting you a hard, much less an impossible, task. We have but to ask and to get. Before we call, God will answer; and while we are yet speaking, he will hear. God alone can know what may come of this sermon, if he chooses to bless it. From this moment you may pray more; from this moment God may bless the ministry more. From this hour other pulpits may become more full of life and vigor than before. From this moment the Word of God may flow and run and rush and get to itself an amazing and boundless victory. Only wrestle in prayer, meet together in your houses, go to your closets, be instant, be earnest in season and out of season, agonize for souls, and all that you have heard shall be forgotten in what you shall see; and all that others have told you shall be as nothing compared with what you shall hear with your ears and behold with your eyes in your own midst.

Through the Bible in One Year: 2 Chronicles 5–8

A Broken Spirit

The sacrifices of God are a broken spirit;
a broken and contrite heart,
O God, you will not despise.
PSALM 51:17

If you and I have a broken spirit, *all idea of our own importance is gone*. What is the use of a broken heart? Why, much the same as the use of a broken pot, or a broken jug, or a broken bottle! Men throw it on the dunghill. Hence, David says, "A broken and a contrite heart, O God, thou wilt not despise" (Psalm 51:17 KJV), as if he felt that everyone else would despise it. Now, do you feel that you are of no importance? Though you know that you are a child of God, do you feel that you would not give a penny for yourself? You would not wish to claim the first place; the rear rank suits you best, and you wonder that you are in the Lord's army in any rank at all. O brothers, I believe that the more God uses us, the less we shall think of ourselves; and the more he fills us with his Spirit, the more will our own spirit sink within us in utter amazement that he should ever make use of such broken vessels as we are! Well, now, indulge that feeling of nothingness and unimportance; not only indulge it as a feeling, but go and act upon it, and be you in the midst of your brethren less than the least; humble yourselves in wonder that God should permit your name to stand on the roll of his elect at all. Admire the grace of God to you, and marvel at it in deep humiliation of spirit. That is part of the sacrifice that God will not despise.

Through the Bible in One Year: 2 Chronicles 9–12

Make No Pretenses

*The LORD is close to the brokenhearted
and saves those who are crushed in spirit.*

PSALM 34:18

If you and I have a broken and contrite heart, it means that *frivolity and trifling have gone from us*. There are some who are always trifling with spiritual things, but he who gets a broken heart has done with that sort of spirit. A broken heart is serious and solemn and in earnest. A broken heart never tries to play any tricks with God and never shuffles texts as though even Scripture itself were meant only to be an opportunity for testing our wit. A broken spirit is tender, serious, weighed down with solemn considerations. Indulge that spirit now, be solemn before God, grasp eternal things, let slip these shadows; what are they worth? But set you your soul on things divine and everlasting. Pursue that vein of thought, and so bring God a broken and a contrite spirit.

Further, a broken spirit is one out of which *hypocrisy has gone*. That vessel, whole and sealed up, may contain the most precious essence of roses, or it may contain the foulest filth; I know not what is in it. But break it, and you will soon see. There is no hypocrisy about a broken heart. O brethren and sisters, be before men what you are before God! Seem to be what you really are. Make no pretenses. I am afraid that we are all hypocrites in a measure; we both pray and preach above our own actual experience full often, and we perhaps think that we have more faith than we actually have, and more love than we have ever known. The Lord make us to have a broken heart that is revealed by being broken!

Through the Bible in One Year: 2 Chronicles 13–16

The Joy of a Broken Heart

*While he was in Bethany, reclining at the table in the home
of a man known as Simon the Leper, a woman came
with an alabaster jar of very expensive perfume, made of pure nard.
She broke the jar and poured the perfume on his head.*
MARK 14:3

A broken spirit signifies that now *all secrets and essences of the spirit have flowed out.* You remember what happened when that holy woman broke the alabaster box; we read that "the house was filled with the odour of the ointment" (John 12:3 KJV). A broken heart cannot keep secrets. Now is all revealed; now its essence goes forth. Far too much of our praying and of our worship is like closed-up boxes; you cannot tell what is in them. But it is not so with broken hearts; when broken hearts sing, they do sing. When broken hearts groan, they do groan. Broken hearts never play at repenting nor play at believing. There is much of religion nowadays that is very superficial; it is all on the surface; a very small quantity of gospel paint, with just a little varnish of profession, will go a very long way and look very bright. But broken hearts are not like that; with broken hearts, the hymn is a real hymn, the prayer is a real prayer, the hearing of sermons is earnest work, and the preaching of them is the hardest work of all. Oh, what a mercy it would be if some of you were broken all to pieces! Oh, to worship God in spirit and truth! One has well said, "No one ever worshiped God with his whole heart unless he worshiped him with a broken heart; and there never was a heart that was truly broken that did not thereby become a whole heart."

Through the Bible in One Year: 2 Chronicles 17–20

Our Compass

The watchman opens the gate for him, and the sheep listen to his voice.
He calls his own sheep by name and leads them out.
When he has brought out all his own, he goes on ahead of them,
and his sheep follow him because they know his voice.
JOHN 10:3–4

Hundreds of years ago, when men went to sea at all, their boats kept always within sight of shore. Your Greek or Roman mariner might be quite master of his galley, but he could not bear to lose sight of a headland that he knew, for he had no compass and knew little or nothing of astronomical observations. Here and there a lighthouse might be placed, but it would be regarded as a wonder. But at this day a ship may not sight land for a month, and yet its position on the chart will be as certain as your position in the pew. The vessel will be steered entirely by observations of the heavenly bodies and by chart and compass, and yet at the end of thirty days, it will reach a point that was never within sight, and reach it as accurately as if it had been running on a tramline instead of sailing over the pathless ocean. Its way is as certain as if it had traversed a railway from port to port. Such is the life of a Christian—the life of faith. We see not spiritual things, but yet we steer for them with absolute certainty. We are guided by the Word of God, which is our chart, and by the witness of the blessed Spirit within, which is our compass. We see him who is invisible, and we seek a heaven full of "things not seen as yet." Glory be to God, we shall reach the harbor as sure as a bullet goes to the mark.

Through the Bible in One Year: 2 Chronicles 21–24

A Hazardous Road

*People who want to get rich fall into temptation and a trap
and into many foolish and harmful desires that plunge men into ruin
and destruction. For the love of money is a root of all kinds of evil.
Some people, eager for money, have wandered from the faith
and pierced themselves with many griefs.*

1 TIMOTHY 6:9–10

O Christian, if you keep to the King's highway, you will be safe, but there are byways and, alas, crooked lanes down which you must not go; if you do go there, you will go at your own hazard. There are hundreds and I fear thousands of church members who say that they are the people of God, yet they appear to live entirely in the world. Their great aim is moneymaking and personal aggrandizement, just as much as it is the aim of altogether ungodly men. The kingdom of Christ, the needs of his church, the wants of perishing souls, have a very slender place in their hearts; but they live wholly for themselves, only they try to conceal it under the plea of providing for their families. "Seek ye first the kingdom of God, and his righteousness; and all these things shall be added unto you" is a text from which we need to preach to professing Christians throughout London and throughout the whole world.

There is also the way of pride that many tread. To be great, to be famous, to be esteemed, to keep up a high repute—it is for this that they live. I do not believe there is any higher life in this world than the life of God that is given to everyone who believes on the Lord Jesus Christ.

Through the Bible in One Year: 2 Chronicles 25–28

Safe Ways

He who trusts in himself is a fool,
but he who walks in wisdom is kept safe.
PROVERBS 28:26

Do what God tells you, as God tells you, and because God tells you, and no hurt can come to you. The Lord told Moses to take by the tail the serpent from which he fled; he did so, and he was not bitten, but the serpent stiffened into a wonder-working rod. Obey the Lord in all things. Mind the jots and the tittles, for whosoever shall break one of the least of Christ's commandments, "and shall teach men so, he shall be called the least in the kingdom of heaven: but whosoever shall do and teach them, the same shall be called great in the kingdom of heaven" (Matthew 5:19 KJV).

There is, also, the way of childlike trust in providential guidance. Happy is that man who always waits upon God to know what he shall do, who asks the Lord ever to guide him, and who dares not lean upon his own understanding. Watch the Lord's providential leadings; wait for divine guidance. It is far better to stand still than to run in the wrong road. Pause awhile, and pray for direction, and do not move until you hear the voice behind you saying, "This is the way, walk ye in it" (Isaiah 30:21 KJV).

And I am quite sure that the way of consecrated service for God's glory is another of these safe ways. It is well when a man says, "I choose my path by this rule: 'How can I best serve my God?' 'In what course of life can I best glorify God?'" That is your way to heaven, Christian, the way in which your Master can get the most glory out of you; if you walk in that way, you may depend upon it—you will be protected by his sovereign power.

Through the Bible in One Year: 2 Chronicles 29–32

Faithful to Your Convictions

We have a strong city; God makes salvation its walls and ramparts.
Open the gates that the righteous nation may enter,
the nation that keeps faith. You will keep in perfect peace him
whose mind is steadfast, because he trusts in you.
Isaiah 26:1–3

Be you determined that if others do as they please, you are not accountable for their action; but you will do what you believe to be right. If you are a Christian, go through with it; be a follower of Christ in every respect as far as the Word of God and your own conscience lead you. I found that the habit of beginning to think for myself and to follow my convictions was useful to me, and it has been useful to me to this day; and at this moment, before the living God, I am able to stand on my own feet, to lean neither on this man nor on that, but only on that eternal arm which will support any man and every man who, in the sight of God, determines to follow the truth wherever it may lead him.

Now, I earnestly pray every Christian person here, especially in the beginning of life, to look well to this matter, for the joy of your life, the peace of your life, the inward rest of your life, will much depend under God upon your being faithful to your convictions in every point as God shall help you. The great King himself seems to say tonight, "Mine eyes shall be upon the faithful in the land, that they may dwell with me: he that walketh in a perfect way, he shall serve me" (Psalm 101:6 KJV). He is the man whom I will pick out for my servant.

Through the Bible in One Year: 2 Chronicles 33–36

A God of Flesh

His pleasure is not in the strength of the horse,
nor his delight in the legs of a man;
the LORD delights in those who fear him,
who put their hope in his unfailing love.
PSALM 147:10–11

It is a good thing to be learned and wise, and the more you can cultivate your minds, the better; but remember the words of the apostle: "Not many wise men after the flesh, not many mighty, not many noble, are called" (1 Corinthians 1:26 KJV). And oftentimes, the wisdom that is merely that of the mind may even prove like scales upon the spiritual eye, hiding from the soul the blessed sight that alone can save it. It is true mentally as well as physically that the Lord takes no pleasure in any of the faculties that a man possesses if he be destitute of grace.

Another thing in which the Lord takes no pleasure is that *self-reliance* which is much cried up nowadays. This is only another form of "the strength of the horse" and "the legs of a man." Some persons proudly say that they are self-made men, and I generally find that they worship their makers! Having made themselves, they are peculiarly devoted to themselves; but a man who is self-made is badly made. That which comes of man is but a polluted stream from an impure source; out of evil comes evil, and from a depraved nature comes depravity. It is only when God makes us new creatures in Christ Jesus that it is any joy for us to be creatures at all, and all the praise must be given to him. It is foolish to worship a god of wood or of stone; it is equally foolish to worship a god of flesh, and it is most foolish when that god of flesh is yourself.

Through the Bible in One Year: 1 Timothy 1–2

God's Delight in You

The LORD delights in those who fear him,
who put their hope in his unfailing love.
PSALM 147:11

When God takes pleasure in any man, the outcome of his favor may be learned from the pleasure we take in our own child. Now, without enlarging upon this point, I will say that if you fear the Lord and hope in his mercy, God takes as much delight in you as you do in your dear child, and far more, because God's is an infinite mind, and from it there comes infinite delight, so that he views you with infinite complacency.

Can you believe it? You do not view yourself so; I hope that you do not, but God sees you in Christ. He sees in you that which is yet to be in you. He sees in you that which will make you to grow into a heavenly being, and therefore he takes delight in you. It does not matter what others think of you. I want you just to go home and feel, "If my heavenly Father takes delight in me, it really does not concern me if my fellow creatures do not understand or appreciate me." If you and I want to be pleased by other people's good opinion, we shall lay ourselves open to be wounded by other people's bad opinion. Live so as to please God, and if your fellows are not pleased, well, then, they must be displeased. It should be the one aim of your life to be able to say, "I do always those things which please him." Walk with God by faith, as Enoch did, that you may have a like testimony to his: "He pleased God." And if you have pleased God, what matters it who is not pleased?

Through the Bible in One Year: 1 Timothy 3–4

The Beauty of Meekness

Blessed are the meek,
for they will inherit the earth.
MATTHEW 5:5

In the Scriptures, you will find that the most beautiful persons were the meek persons. I remember only three persons whose faces are said to have shone; you recollect those three, do you not? There was, first, the Lord Jesus Christ, whose face shone when he came down from the Mount of Transfiguration so that the people came running together unto him. How meek and lowly of heart was he! Another person whose face shone was Moses, when he came down from the mount of communion with God, and of him we read, "Now the man Moses was very meek" (Numbers 12:3 KJV). The third man whose face shone was Stephen, when he stood before the council and in the meekest manner pleaded for his Lord and Master. If ever your face is to shine, you must get rid of a high and haughty spirit; you must be meek, for the brightness of the divine light will never rest on the forehead that flashes with anger. Be gentle, quiet, yielding, like your Lord, and he will then beautify you. The Lord does give great beauty to his people who are very quiet and submissive. If you can bear and forbear, if you will not be provoked to speak a hasty word, that meekness of yours is itself a beauty.

Beside that, God beautifies meek people with peace. They have not to go and beg pardon and make up quarrels, as others have, for they have had no quarrel. They have not to think at night, "I really said what I ought not to have said," for they have not done so. There is a great beauty about the peace that comes of meekness.

Through the Bible in One Year: 1 Timothy 5–6

Beauty in Meekness

Refrain from anger and turn from wrath;
do not fret—it leads only to evil. For evil men will be cut off,
but those who hope in the LORD will inherit the land.

A little while, and the wicked will be no more;
though you look for them, they will not be found.
But the meek will inherit the land and enjoy great peace.

PSALM 37:8–11

Another beauty God puts on the meek is contentment. They who are of a quiet and gentle spirit through the grace of God are satisfied with their lot. They thank God for little; they are of the mind of the godly woman who ate the crust of bread and drank a little water and said, "What! All this, and Jesus Christ too?" There is a great charm about contentment, while envy and greed are ugly things in the eyes of those who have anything like spiritual perception. So meekness, through bringing contentment, beautifies us.

Out of meekness also comes holiness, and who has not heard of "the beauty of holiness"? When one is made to subdue his temper and curb his will and yield his mind sweetly up to Christ, then obedience to God's will follows, and the whole life becomes lovely. Let us praise the Lord that ever he put any beauty upon any of us, and let us bless God for the holiness of his people whenever we see it. It is a pity that there should be so little of it, but what a comfort it is that the Lord has some among his people who are of a meek and gentle spirit, whom he beautifies with salvation!

Through the Bible in One Year: Ezra 1–3

The Consecrated Man

Command those who are rich in this present world
not to be arrogant nor to put their hope in wealth,
which is so uncertain, but to put their hope in God,
who richly provides us with everything for our enjoyment.
Command them to do good, to be rich in good deeds,
and to be generous and willing to share.
1 TIMOTHY 6:17–18

Every child of God is a consecrated man. His consecration is not typified by any outward symbol; we are not commanded to let our hair grow forever, nor to abstain from meats or drinks. The Christian is a consecrated man, but his consecration is unseen by his fellows, except in the outward deeds that are the result thereof.

"But," says someone, "can we be consecrated to Christ? I thought that was for ministers only." Oh no, my brethren; all God's children must be consecrated men. What are you? Are you engaged in business? If you are what you profess to be, your business must be consecrated to God. Perhaps you have no family whatever and you are engaged in trade and are saving some considerable sum a year; let me tell you the example of a man thoroughly consecrated to God. There lives in Bristol a man whose income is large, and what does he do with it? He labors in business continually that this income may come to him, but of it, every farthing every year is expended in the Lord's cause except that which he requires for the necessaries of life. He makes his necessities as few as possible, that he may have the more to give away. He is God's man in his business. Brethren, you in business may be as much consecrated to Christ as the minister in his pulpit; you may make your ordinary transactions in life a solemn service of God.

Through the Bible in One Year: Ezra 4–7

The Separated Life

Do not be misled: "Bad company corrupts good character."
1 CORINTHIANS 15:33

It may be that some of you professedly Christian people have been living at a distance from God. You have not led the separated life; you have tried to be friendly with the world as well as with Christ, and your children are not growing up as you wish they would. You say that your sons are not turning out well and that your girls are dressy and flighty and worldly. Do you wonder that it is so? "Oh!" you say, "I have gone a good way to try to please them, thinking that perhaps by so doing, I might win them for Christ." Ah! You will never win any soul to the right by a compromise with the wrong. It is decision for Christ and his truth that has the greatest power in the family and the greatest power in the world too.

Nobody doubts that evil company tends to make a man bad, and it is equally sure that good companionship has a tendency to influence men toward that which is good. It is a happy thing to have side by side with you one whose heart is full of love to God. It is a great blessing to have as a mother a true saint or to have as a brother or a sister one who fears the Lord, and it is a special privilege to be linked for life, in the closest bonds, with one whose prayers may rise with ours and whose praises may also mingle with ours. There is something about Christian companionship that must tell in the right direction unless the heart be resolutely bent on mischief.

Through the Bible in One Year: Ezra 8–10

The True God

*I am astonished that you are so quickly deserting
the one who called you by the grace of Christ and are turning
to a different gospel—which is really no gospel at all.*
GALATIANS 1:6–7

At the present day, I am afraid that nine people out of ten do not believe in the God who is revealed to us in the Bible. I can point you to newspapers, to magazines, to periodicals, and also to pulpits by the score in which there is a new god set up to be worshiped—not the God of the Old Testament; he is said to be too strict, too severe, too stern for our modern teachers. They shudder at the very mention of the God of the Puritans. If Jonathan Edwards were to rise from the dead, they would not listen to him for a minute; they would say that they had quite a new god since his day. But, brethren, I believe in the God of Abraham and of Isaac and of Jacob; this God is my God—aye, the God who drowned Pharaoh and his host at the Red Sea and moved his people to sing, "Hallelujah!" as he did it; the God who caused the earth to open and swallow up Korah, Dathan, and Abiram and all their company. A terrible God is the God whom I adore—he is the God and Father of our Lord and Savior Jesus Christ, full of mercy, compassion, and grace, tender and gentle, yet just and dreadful in his holiness and terrible out of his holy places. This is the God whom we worship, and he who comes to him in Christ and trusts in him will take him to be his instructor, and so shall he learn aright all that he needs to know.

Through the Bible in One Year: 2 Timothy 1–2

The Imperfect Church

❧

Be imitators of God, therefore, as dearly loved children
and live a life of love, just as Christ loved us and gave himself up
for us as a fragrant offering and sacrifice to God.
EPHESIANS 5:1–2

I have heard people find fault with the members of our churches and say that they cannot join with them, for they are such inferior sort of people. Well, I know a great many different sorts of people, and after all, I shall be quite content to be numbered with God's people as I see them even in his visible church, rather than to be numbered with any other persons in the whole world. I count the despised people of God the best company I have ever met with.

"Oh," says one, "I will join the church when I can find a perfect one." Then you will never join any. "Ah," you say, "but perhaps I may." Well, but it will not be a perfect church the moment after you have joined it, for it will cease to be perfect as soon as it receives you into its membership. I think that if a church is such as Christ can love, it is such as I can love; and if it is such that Christ counts it as his church, I may well be thankful to be a member of it. Christ "loved the church, and gave himself for it" (Ephesians 5:25 KJV); then may I not think it an honor to be allowed to give myself to it? Shame on those who think to join the church for what they can get! Yet the loaves and fishes are always a bait for some people.

Through the Bible in One Year: 2 Timothy 3–4

Care for the Young Converts

❧

*We who are strong ought to bear with the failings of the weak
and not to please ourselves. Each of us should please his neighbor
for his good, to build him up.*
ROMANS 15:1–2

You who have long been believers in the Lord Jesus, who have grown rich in experience, who know the love and faithfulness of our covenant God, and who are strong in the Lord and in the power of his might, I want you to make a point of looking out for the young converts and speaking to them goodly words and comfortable words, whereby they may be cheered and strengthened. Why are we so reticent when a word would send our weaker brethren on their way rejoicing? Therefore, I do entreat all of you whom God has greatly blessed to look after those who are of low estate in spiritual things and try to cheer and encourage them. As you do this, God will bless you in return, but if you neglect this tender duty, it may be that you yourselves will grow despondent and be yourselves in need of friendly succor.

We should, in all probability, see a much more rapid growth in grace among our young converts if they were better nursed and watched over. Some of us owed much to older, experienced Christians in our younger days. I know I did. Let it be said of us, when we too grow old, that those who were children when we were young were helped by us to become useful in their riper years.

Through the Bible in One Year: Nehemiah 1–3

The Full Reward

For the Lord himself will come down from heaven,
with a loud command, with the voice of the archangel
and with the trumpet call of God, and the dead in Christ will rise first.
After that, we who are still alive and are left will be caught up together
with them in the clouds to meet the Lord in the air.
And so we will be with the Lord forever.
Therefore encourage each other with these words.

1 THESSALONIANS 4:16–18

What is the full reward of those who come to trust under the wings of God? I would answer that a full reward will come to us in that day when we lay down these bodies of flesh and blood, that they may sleep in Jesus, while our unclothed spirits are absent from the body but present with the Lord. In the disembodied state we shall enjoy perfect happiness of spirit; but a fuller reward will be ours when the Lord shall come a second time and our bodies shall rise from the grave to share in the glorious reign of the descended King. Then in our perfect manhood we shall behold the face of him we love and shall be like him. Then shall come the adoption, to wit, the redemption of our body; and we, as body, soul, and spirit, a trinity in unity, shall be forever with Father, Son, and Holy Ghost, our triune God. This unspeakable bliss is the full reward of trusting beneath the wings of Jehovah.

Through the Bible in One Year: Nehemiah 4–7

The Joyful Life

For what is our hope, our joy, or the crown in which
we will glory in the presence of our Lord Jesus when he comes?
Is it not you? Indeed, you are our glory and joy.
1 Thessalonians 2:19–20

They who trust in God and follow him have another full reward, and that is the bliss of doing good. Can any happiness excel this? This joy is a diamond of the first water. Match me, if you can, the joy of helping the widow and the fatherless! Find me the equal of the delight of saving a soul from death and covering a multitude of sins! It would be worth worlds to have faith in God, even if we lived here forever, if our sojourn could be filled up with doing good to the poor and needy and rescuing the erring and fallen. If you desire to taste the purest joy that ever flowed from the founts of paradise, drink of the unselfish bliss of saving a lost soul. When faith in God teaches you to forgo self and live wholly to glorify God and benefit your fellow men, it puts you on the track of the Lord of angels, and by following it you will come to reign with him.

I believe, brethren, that our lot, even when we are poor and sorrowful and cast down, is infinitely to be preferred to that of the loftiest emperor who does not know the Savior. Oh, poor kings, poor princes, poor peers, poor gentry, who do not know Christ! But happy paupers who know him! Happy slaves who love him! Happy dying men and women who rejoice in him! Those have solid joy and lasting pleasure who have God to be their all in all.

Through the Bible in One Year: Nehemiah 8–10

Feeding on the Word of God

Oh, how I love your law! I meditate on it all day long.
Your commands make me wiser than my enemies,
for they are ever with me. I have more insight than all my teachers,
for I meditate on your statutes.
PSALM 119:97–99

Nothing can be more fattening to the soul of the believer than feeding upon the Word and digesting it by frequent meditations. No wonder that some grow so little when they meditate so little. We must take the truth and roll it over and over again in the inward parts of our spirit, and so we shall extract divine nourishment therefrom. Is not meditation the land of Goshen to you? If men once said, "There is corn in Egypt," may they not always say that the finest of the wheat is to be found in secret prayer? Private devotion is a land that flows with milk and honey, a paradise yielding all manner of fruits, a banqueting house of choice wines. Where can we feed and lie down in green pastures in so sweet a sense as we do in our musings on the Word? Meditation distills the quintessence from the Scriptures and gladdens our mouth with a sweetness that exceeds the virgin honey dropping from the honeycomb. Your retired seasons and occasions of prayer should be to you regal entertainments, or at least refreshing seasons, in which, like the reapers at noonday, you sit with Boaz and eat of your Master's generous provisions.

Through the Bible in One Year: Nehemiah 11–13

Saving Faith

❧

Show me your faith without deeds, and I will show you my faith
by what I do. You believe that there is one God. Good!
Even the demons believe that—and shudder.
JAMES 2:18–19

If I say that I believe in God yet continue to live in sin willfully and knowingly, then I have not so good a faith as the devils have, for they "believe, and tremble." There are some men who profess to believe in God yet who do not tremble before him but are impudent and presumptuous. That is not the kind of faith that saves the soul; saving faith is that which produces good works, which leads to repentance or is accompanied by it, and which leads to love of God and to holiness and to a desire to be made like unto the Savior. Good works are not the root of faith, but they are its fruit. A house does not rest upon the slates of its roof, yet it would not be fit to live in if it had not a roof; and in like manner, our faith does not rest upon our good works, yet it would be a poor and useless faith if it had not some of the fruit of the Spirit to prove that it had come from God. Jesus Christ can tell us how a man can aim at being holy as God is holy and yet never talk about his holiness or dream of trusting in it. We would live as if we were to be saved by our own works, yet place no reliance whatever upon them but count them as dross, that we may win Christ and be found in him, not having our own righteousness, which is of the law, but that which is through the faith of Christ, the righteousness that is of God by faith.

Through the Bible in One Year: Titus 1–3

Can God Forget?

*When you were dead in your sins and in the uncircumcision
of your sinful nature, God made you alive with Christ.
He forgave us all our sins, having canceled the written code,
with its regulations, that was against us and that stood opposed to us;
he took it away, nailing it to the cross.*

COLOSSIANS 2:13–14

How can God, who sees all things, no longer see any sin in believers? That is a puzzle that many cannot understand. God is everywhere, and everything is present to his all-seeing eyes, yet he says, through the prophet Jeremiah, "In those days, and in that time, saith the LORD, the iniquity of Israel shall be sought for, and there shall be none" (Jeremiah 50:20 KJV). I venture to say that even God himself cannot see that which no longer exists; even his eye rests not on a thing that is not. And thus is it with the sin of those who have believed in Jesus: it has ceased to be. God himself has declared, "I will remember their sin no more." But can God forget? Of course he can, as he says that he will. The work of the Messiah was described to Daniel in these remarkable words: "to finish the transgression, and to make an end of sins, and to make reconciliation for iniquity, and to bring in everlasting righteousness" (Daniel 9:24 KJV). Well, then, there *is* an end of them, according to that other gracious, divine declaration, "I have blotted out, as a thick cloud, thy transgressions, and, as a cloud, thy sins" (Isaiah 44:22 KJV). Hence, they are gone, they have ceased to be, Christ has obliterated them, and therefore God no longer sees them. Oh, the splendor of the pardon that God has bestowed upon all believers, making a clean sweep of all their sins forever!

Through the Bible in One Year: Esther 1–3

Let God Lead You

*However, when the people of Gibeon heard what Joshua
had done to Jericho and Ai, they resorted to a ruse:
They went as a delegation whose donkeys were loaded
with worn-out sacks and old wineskins, cracked and mended.*

JOSHUA 9:3–4

I believe that our trials usually come out of the things that we do not take to the Lord, and moreover, I am sure that we make greater blunders in what we consider to be simple matters, which we do not take to the Lord, than we do in far more difficult matters, which we do take to him. The men of Israel were deceived by the Gibeonites because they had on old shoes and clouted, and had moldy bread in their wallets, and the Israelites said, "It is perfectly clear that these men must have come from a long distance; look at their old boots and their ragged garments." So they made a covenant with them and inquired not the will of the Lord. If it had not appeared to them to be quite so clear a case, they would have asked the Lord for direction, and then they would have been rightly guided. It is when you think you can see your way that you go wrong; when you cannot see your way but trust to God to lead you by a way that you know not, you will go perfectly right. I am persuaded that it is so—that the simplest and plainest matter, kept away from Christ, will turn out to be a maze, while the most intricate labyrinth, under the guidance of Christ, will prove to have in it a straight road for the feet of all those who trust in the infallible wisdom of their Lord and Savior.

Through the Bible in One Year: Esther 4–7

Ask and Commune

*"You did not choose me, but I chose you and appointed you
to go and bear fruit—fruit that will last.
Then the Father will give you whatever you ask in my name."*
JOHN 15:16

If you do not come to Jesus and commune with him of all that is in your heart, you will lose his counsel and help, and the comfort that comes from them. I do not suppose anybody here knows what he has lost in this way, and I can hardly imagine how you are to calculate what you have lost of spiritual good that you might have had. There is many a child of God, who might be rich in all the intents of bliss, who continues to be as poor as Lazarus the beggar; he has hardly a crumb of comfort to feed upon and is full of doubts and fears when he might have had full assurance long ago. There is many an heir of heaven who is living upon mere husks of gospel food when he might be eating the rich fare of which Moses speaks: "Butter of kine, and milk of sheep, with fat of lambs, and rams of the breed of Bashan, and goats, with the fat of kidneys of wheat" (Deuteronomy 32:14 KJV). Very often, beloved, you have not because you ask not; or because you believe not, or because you do not confide in Jesus and commune with him. How strong the weakling might be if he would go to Jesus more frequently! How rich the poor soul might be if it would draw continually from Christ's inexhaustible treasury! Might we not live in the suburbs of heaven and often, as it were, be close to the pearly gates, if we would but go and tell all to Jesus and commune with him concerning all that is in our heart?

Through the Bible in One Year: Esther 8–10

God's Providence

❧

There is a time for everything,
and a season for every activity under heaven.

ECCLESIASTES 3:1

Now, brethren, whatever mischief may be brewing against the cause of God and truth, and I daresay there is very much going on at this moment, for neither the devil nor the Jesuits nor the atheists are long quiet, this we are sure of: the Lord knows all about it, and he has his Esther and his Mordecai ready at their posts to frustrate their designs.

Every child of God is where God has placed him for some purpose, and the practical use of this first point is to lead you to inquire about the practical purpose for which God has placed each one of you where you now are. You have been wishing for another position where you could do something for Jesus: do not wish anything of the kind, but serve him where you are. If you are sitting at the King's gate, there is something for you to do there, and if you were on the queen's throne, there would be something for you to do there; do not ask either to be gatekeeper or queen, but whichever you are, serve God therein.

Esther did well, because she acted as an Esther should, and Mordecai did well, because he acted as a Mordecai should. I like to think, as I look over you all—God has put each one of them in the right place, even as a good captain well arranges the different parts of his army, and though we do not know his plan of battle, it will be seen during the conflict that he has placed each soldier where he should be. Forget not, then, the fact that God in his providence places his servants in positions where he can make use of them.

Through the Bible in One Year: Philemon

July 28

Destiny and Choice

In love he predestined us to be adopted as his sons through Jesus Christ,
in accordance with his pleasure and will—to the praise
of his glorious grace, which he has freely given us in the One he loves.
EPHESIANS 1:4–6

It is clear that the divine will is accomplished, and yet men are perfectly free agents. "I cannot understand it," says one. My dear friend, I am compelled to say the same—I do not understand it either. I have known many who thought they comprehended all things, but I fancy they had a higher opinion of themselves than truth would endorse. Certain of my brethren deny free agency and so get out of the difficulty; others assert that there is no predestination and so cut the knot. As I do not wish to get out of the difficulty and have no wish to shut my eyes to any part of the truth, I believe both free agency and predestination to be facts. How they can be made to agree, I do not know or care to know; I am satisfied to know anything God chooses to reveal to me, and equally content not to know what he does not reveal. There it is; man is a free agent in what he does, responsible for his actions, and verily guilty when he does wrong. And he will be justly punished too, and if he be lost, the blame will rest with himself alone. But yet there is One who rules over all, who, without complicity in their sin, makes even the actions of wicked men to subserve his holy and righteous purposes. Believe these two truths and you will see them in practical agreement in daily life, though you will not be able to devise a theory for harmonizing them on paper.

Through the Bible in One Year: Job 1–4

Danger

Therefore I do not run like a man running aimlessly;
I do not fight like a man beating the air.
No, I beat my body and make it my slave so that
after I have preached to others,
I myself will not be disqualified for the prize.
1 CORINTHIANS 9:26–27

I feel I have to come, Sabbath after Sabbath, and weekday after weekday, and tell you a great many precious things about Christ, and sometimes I enjoy them myself. And if nobody else gets blessed by them, I do, and I go home and praise the Lord for it. But my daily fear is lest I should be a handler of texts for you and a preacher of good things for others and yet remain unprofited in my own heart. My prayer is that the Lord Jesus will show me where he feeds his people and let me feed with them, that then I may conduct you to the pastures where he is and be with him myself at the same time that I bring you to him. You Sabbath-school teachers and evangelists and others, my dear, earnest comrades, for whom I thank God at every remembrance, I feel that the main point you have to watch about is that you do not lose your own spirituality while trying to make others spiritual. Appeal to the Well Beloved, and entreat him to let you feed your flock where he is feeding his people, that he would let you sit as his feet, like Mary, even while you are working in the house, like Martha. Do not do less, but rather more; but ask to do it in such communion with him that your work shall be melted into his work, and what you are doing shall be really only his working in you and your rejoicing to pour out to others what he pours into your own soul.

Through the Bible in One Year: Job 5–8

Mechanical?

❧

Vindicate me, O LORD, for I have led a blameless life;
I have trusted in the LORD without wavering.
Test me, O LORD, and try me, examine my heart and my mind;
for your love is ever before me, and I walk continually in your truth.

PSALM 26:1–3

I dread very much the tendency to do Christ's work in a cold, mechanical spirit, but above even that I tremble, lest I should be able to have warmth for Christ's work and yet should be cold toward the Lord himself. I fear that such a condition of heart is possible—that we may burn great bonfires in the streets for public display and scarcely keep a live coal upon our hearth for Jesus to warm his hands at. When we meet in the great assembly, the good company helps to warm our hearts, and when we are working for the Lord with others, they stimulate us and cause us to put forth all our energy and strength, and then we think, "Surely my heart is in a healthy condition toward God." But, beloved, such excitement may be a poor index of our real state. I love that quiet, holy fire that will glow in the closet and flame forth in the chamber when I am alone, and that is the point I am more fearful about than anything else, both for myself and for you, lest we should be doing Christ's work without Christ; having much to do but not thinking much of *him*; cumbered about much serving, and forgetting him. Why, that would soon grow into making a Christ out of our own service, an antichrist out of our own labors. Love your work, but love your Master better; love your flock, but love the Great Shepherd better still, and ever keep close to him, for it will be a token of unfaithfulness if you do not.

Through the Bible in One Year: Job 9–12

The Glad Soul

ॐ

*To those who have been called, who are loved by God the Father
and kept by Jesus Christ: Mercy, peace and love be yours in abundance.*
JUDE 1–2

Gracious souls are never perfectly at ease except they are in a state of nearness to Christ; for mark you, when they are not near to Christ, they lose their *peace*. The nearer to Jesus, the nearer to the perfect calm of heaven; and the further from Jesus, the nearer to that troubled sea that images the continual unrest of the wicked. There is no peace to the man who does not dwell constantly under the shadow of the cross; for Jesus is our peace, and if he be absent, our peace is absent too. I know that being justified, we have peace with God, but it is "through our Lord Jesus Christ," so that the justified man himself cannot reap the fruit of justification except by abiding in Christ Jesus, who is the Lord and giver of peace. The Christian without fellowship with Christ loses all his *life* and energy; he is like a dead thing. He is without vivacity; yea, more, he is without animation till Jesus comes. But when the Lord sensibly sheds abroad his love in our hearts, then *his* love kindles ours; then our blood leaps in our veins for joy, like the Baptist in the womb of Elizabeth. The heart when near to Jesus has strong pulsations, for since Jesus is in that heart, it is full of life, of vigor, and of strength.

Beloved, all the joys of life are nothing to us; we have melted them all down in our crucible and found them to be dross. Being in a state of dissatisfaction with all mortal things, we have learned through divine grace that none but Jesus, none but Jesus can make our souls glad.

Through the Bible in One Year: Job 13–16

God's Standard

The Lord was standing by a wall that had been built true to plumb, with a plumb line in his hand.

AMOS 7:7

Everything that God builds is built plumb and straight and square and fair. You see that rule at work in nature; there is nothing out of proportion there. Those who understand these things and look deeply into them will tell you that the very form and size of the earth have a connection with the blooming of a flower or the hanging of a dewdrop upon a blade of grass, and that if the sun were larger or smaller than it is, or if the material of which the earth is formed were denser or different in any degree from what it is, then everything, the most magnificent and the most minute, would be thrown out of gear.

In spiritual matters, it is very manifest that whenever God is dealing with souls, he always uses the plumb line. In beginning with us, he finds that the very foundation of our nature is out of the perpendicular, and therefore he does not attempt to build upon it, but commences his operations by digging it out. The first work of divine grace in the soul is to pull down all that nature has built up. The man has taken a great deal of pains in putting it together, but it must all come out, and there must be a great hole left; the man must feel himself emptied and abused and humbled in the sight of God. For if God is to be everything to the man, then he himself must be nothing; and if Christ is to be his Savior, he must be a complete Savior, from beginning to end. So the foundation of the human merit must be cleared right out and flung away, for God could not build squarely upon it.

Through the Bible in One Year: Job 17–20

Confident Even in Death

*For I am already being poured out like a drink offering,
and the time has come for my departure. I have fought the good fight,
I have finished the race, I have kept the faith.
Now there is in store for me the crown of righteousness.*

2 TIMOTHY 4:6–8

How very confidently Paul contemplates the prospect of death! He betrays no trembling apprehensions. With the calmness and serenity not only of resignation and submission, but of assurance and courage, he appears joyous and gladsome and even charmed with the hope of having his body dissolved and being girt about with the new body that God has prepared for his saints. He who can talk of the grave and of the hereafter with such intelligence, thoughtfulness, faith, and strong desire as Paul did is a man to be envied. Princes might well part with their crowns for such a sure and certain hope of immortality. If able to say with him, "We are confident, I say, and willing rather to be absent from the body, and to be present with the Lord" (2 Corinthians 5:8 KJV), they might well barter earthly rank for such a requital.

This side of heaven, what can be more heavenly than to be thoroughly prepared to pass through the river of death? On the other hand, what a dreary and dreadful state of mind must they be in who, with nothing before them but to die, have no hope and see no outlet—the pall and the shroud their last adorning; the grave and the sod their destination. Without hope of rising again in a better future; with no prospects of seeing God face-to-face with rejoicing, well may men dislike any reference to death.

Through the Bible in One Year: Job 21–24

God's Timing

❧

I eagerly expect and hope that I will in no way be ashamed,
but will have sufficient courage so that now as always Christ
will be exalted in my body, whether by life or by death.
For to me, to live is Christ and to die is gain.

PHILIPPIANS 1:20–21

The time of our departure, though unknown to us, is fixed by God, unalterably fixed; so rightly, wisely, lovingly settled and prepared for that no chance or haphazard can break the spell of destiny. The wisdom of divine love shall be proven by the carefulness of its provision.

Dire calamities befell Job when he was bereaved of his children and his servants, his herds and his flocks. Yet he took little heed of the different ways in which his troubles were brought about, whether by an onslaught of the Sabeans or by a raid of the Chaldeans: whether the fire fell from heaven or the wind came from the wilderness, it mattered little. Whatever strange facts broke on his ear, one thought penetrated his heart, and one expression broke from his lips. "The LORD gave, and the LORD hath taken away; blessed be the name of the LORD" (Job 1:21 KJV). So too, beloved, when the time of your departure arrives—be it by disease or decay, be it by accident or assault, that your soul quits its present tenement—rest assured that "thy times are in his hand"; and know of a surety that "all his saints are in his hand" likewise. There is a time to depart, and God's time to call me is my time to go.

Through the Bible in One Year: Job 25–28

Shut Your Eyes to Sin

*Don't you know that a little yeast works
through the whole batch of dough?*
1 CORINTHIANS 5:6

Oh, if our mother Eve had shut her eyes when the serpent pointed out yon rosy apple on the tree! Oh, that she had shut her eyes to it! Oh, that she had said, "No, I will not even look at it." Looking leads to longing, and longing leads to sin. Do you say, "There can be no harm in looking, just to see for yourself; are we not told to prove all things?" "Just come here, young man," says the tempter; "you do not know what life is; one evening will suffice to show you a little gaiety. Just come for an hour or two and look on." "Oh no," says the man whose eyes are to see the King in his beauty, "the Tree of Knowledge of Good and Evil never brought any man good yet, so please let me alone. I shut my eyes from the sight of it. I do not want to participate, even as a spectator."

Remember you cannot have a half of Christ. You cannot have him as your Redeemer but not as your Ruler. You must take him as he is. He is a Savior, but he saves his people from their sins. Now, if you have ever seen Christ as your Savior, you have seen beauty in him; he is lovely in your eyes, for the loveliest sight in the world to a sinner is his Savior. Be it so, and you will henceforth shut your eyes from seeing, stop your ears from hearing, shake your hands from all iniquity, and turn aside your feet from it, to live the life you live in the flesh by the faith of the Son of God, to his honor and glory.

Through the Bible in One Year: Job 29–32

The Believer's Inheritance

❧

In his great mercy he has given us new birth into a living hope
through the resurrection of Jesus Christ from the dead,
and into an inheritance that can never perish, spoil or fade—
kept in heaven for you.
1 PETER 1:3–4

Now, an inheritance is not a thing that is bought with money, earned by labor, or won by conquest. If any man hath an inheritance, in the proper sense of that term, it came to him by birth. It was not because of any special merit in him, but simply because he was his father's son that he received the property of which he is now possessed. So is it with heaven. The man who shall receive this glorious heritage will not obtain it by the works of the law, nor by the efforts of the flesh; it will be given to him as a matter of most gracious right because he has been "begotten . . . again unto a lively hope by the resurrection of Jesus Christ from the dead" (1 Peter 1:3 KJV) and has thus become an heir of heaven by blood and birth.

They who come unto glory are sons, for is it not written, the captain of our salvation "bringeth many sons unto glory" (Hebrews 2:10 KJV)? They come not there as servants; no servant has any right to the inheritance of his master. Let him be ever so faithful, yet is he not his master's heir. But because you are sons—sons by God's adoption, sons by the Spirit's regeneration—because by supernatural energy you have been born again—you become inheritors of eternal life and you enter into the many mansions of our Father's house above. Let us always understand, then, when we think of heaven, that it is a place that is ours and a state that we are to enjoy as the result of birth—not as the result of work.

Through the Bible in One Year: Job 33–36

The Deliciousness of Work

❧

Therefore, "they are before the throne of God
and serve him day and night in his temple."
REVELATION 7:15

A true idea of heaven is that it is a place of uninterrupted service. It is a land where they serve God day and night in his temple and never know weariness and never require to slumber. Do you know the deliciousness of work? Although I must complain when people expect impossibilities of me, it is the highest enjoyment of my life to be busily engaged for Christ. Tell me the day when I do not preach, and I will tell you the day in which I am not happy; but the day in which it is my privilege to preach the gospel and labor for God is generally the day of my peaceful and quiet enjoyment after all. Service is delight. Praising God is pleasure. Laboring for him is the highest bliss a mortal can know. Oh, how sweet it must be to sing his praises and never feel that the throat is dry! Oh, how blessed to flap the wing forever and never feel it flag! Oh, what sweet enjoyment to fly upon his errands evermore, to circle round the throne of God in heaven while eternity shall last and never once lay the head on the pillow, never once feel the throbbing of fatigue, never once the pangs that admonish us that we need to cease, but to keep on forever like eternity's own self—a broad river rolling on with perpetual floods of labor! Oh, that must be enjoyment! That must be heaven, to serve God day and night in his temple! Many of you have served God on earth and have had foretastes of that bliss.

Through the Bible in One Year: Job 37–39

Stay the Course

❧

Timothy, guard what has been entrusted to your care.
Turn away from godless chatter and the opposing ideas of what
is falsely called knowledge, which some have professed
and in so doing have wandered from the faith.

Grace be with you.
1 TIMOTHY 6:20–21

No mischief that ever befalls our Christian communities is more lamentable than that which occurs from the defections of the members. The devil himself is not such a subtle foe to the church as Judas, when, after the sop, Satan entered into him. Judas was a friend of Jesus. Jesus addressed him as such. And Judas said, "Hail, Master," and kissed him. But Judas it was who betrayed him. That is a picture that may well appall you; that is a peril that may well admonish you. In all our churches, among the many who enlist, there are some who desert. They continue awhile, and then they go back to the world. The radical reason why they retract is an obvious incongruity. "They went out from us, but they were not of us; for if they had been of us, they would no doubt have continued with us" (1 John 2:19 KJV).

Those who go aside—what becomes of them? Well, if they are God's children, I will tell you what becomes of them, for I have seen it scores of times. Though they go aside, they are not happy. They cannot rest, for they are miserable even when they try to be cheerful. After a while they begin to remember their first husband, for then it was better with them than now. They return; but there are scores and scores, to say nothing of the shame that they have to carry with them to the grave, who are never the men they were before.

Through the Bible in One Year: Job 40–42

Apostasy

*Do your best to present yourself to God as one approved,
a workman who does not need to be ashamed
and who correctly handles the word of truth.*

2 TIMOTHY 2:15

Look narrowly at the various causes or excuses for defection. Why do they renounce the religious profession they once espoused? The fundamental reason is want of grace, a lack of true faith, an absence of vital godliness. It is, however, the outward reasons that expose the heart's inward apostasy from Christ of which I am anxious to treat. Some there are in these days, as there were in our Lord's own day, who depart from Christ because they cannot bear his doctrine. There are many points and particulars in which the gospel is offensive to human nature and revolting to the pride of the creature.

Unsound doctrine occasions many to apostatize. They begin cautiously by reading works with a view to answer scientific or intellectual skepticism. They read a little more and dive a little deeper into the turbid stream, because they feel well able to stand against the insidious influence. They go on, till at last they are staggered. They do not repair to those who could help their scruples, but they continue to flounder on till at last they have lost their footing, and he that said he was a believer has ended in stark atheism, doubting even the existence of God. Oh, that those who are well taught would be content with their teaching! Why meddle with heresies? What can they do but pollute your minds? Keep to the study of the Word of God. If it be your duty to expose these evils, encounter them bravely, with prayer to God to help you. But if not, as a humble believer in Jesus, what business have you to taste and test such noxious fare when it is exposed in the market?

Through the Bible in One Year: Hebrews 1–2

The Man Who Is Careful

Blessed is the man who does not walk in the counsel of the wicked
or stand in the way of sinners or sit in the seat of mockers.
PSALM 1:1

It is not for you to be seen standing, much less to be found sitting down with men of loose manners and lewd converse. You may have heard the story—but it is so good it will bear repeating—of the lady who advertised for a coachman and was waited upon by three candidates for the situation. She put to the first one this question: "I want a really good coachman to drive my pair of horses, and therefore I ask you, how near can you drive to danger and yet be safe?" "Well," he said, "I could drive very near indeed; I could go within a foot of a precipice without fear of any accident so long as I had the reins." She dismissed him with the remark that he would not do. To the next one who came, she put the same question. "How near could you drive to danger?" Being determined to get the place, he said, "I could drive within a hair's breadth and yet skillfully avoid any mishap." "You will not do," said she. When the third one came in, his mind was cast in another mold, so when the question was put to him, "How near could you drive to danger?" he said, "Madam, I never tried. It has always been a rule with me to drive as far off from danger as I possibly can." The lady engaged him at once. In like manner, I believe that the man who is careful to run no risks and to refrain from all equivocal conduct, having the fear of God in his heart, is most to be relied upon.

Through the Bible in One Year: Hebrews 3–4

The Blessed Fellowship

They devoted themselves to the apostles' teaching and to the fellowship, to the breaking of bread and to prayer.
ACTS 2:42

You who have never been converted find very noisy fellowship, I am afraid, in this world; you do not get much companionship that helps you, blesses you, gives you rest of mind. But if you had been gathered to the Lord Christ, you would have found that there are many sweetnesses in this life in being beneath the wings of the Most High. He who comes to Christ finds father and mother and sister and brother; he finds many dear and kind friends who are themselves connected with Christ and who therefore love those who are joined to him. Amongst the greatest happiness of my life, certainly, I put down Christian fellowship; and I think that many who have come from the country to London have for a long time missed much of this fellowship, till at last they have fallen in with Christian people and they have found themselves happy again. O lonely sinner, you who come in and out of this place and say, "Nobody seems to care about me," if you will come to Christ and join with the church that is gathered beneath his wings, you will soon find happy fellowship! I remember that in the times of persecution, one of the saints said that he had lost his father and his mother by being driven away from his native country, but he said, "I have found a hundred fathers and a hundred mothers, for into whatsoever Christian house I have gone, I have been looked upon with so much kindness by those who have received me as an exile from my native land that everyone has seemed to be a father and a mother to me."

Through the Bible in One Year: Hebrews 5–6

The Last Great Day

When the perishable has been clothed with the imperishable,
and the mortal with immortality, then the saying that is written
will come true: "Death has been swallowed up in victory."

"Where, O death, is your victory? Where, O death, is your sting?"

1 CORINTHIANS 15:54–55

There shall be a second death, but over us it shall have no power. Do you understand the beauty of the picture? As if we may walk through the flames of hell and they should have no power to devour us any more than when the holy children paced with ease over the hot coals of Nebuchadnezzar's seven-times-heated furnace. Death may bend his bow and fit the arrow to the string. But we laugh at you, O death! And you, O hell, we will despise! For over both of you, you enemies of man, we shall be more than conquerors through him who has loved us. We shall stand invulnerable and invincible, defying and laughing to scorn our every foe. And all this because we are washed from sin and covered with a spotless righteousness.

When we shall rise again, we shall be freed from all corruption: no evil tendencies shall remain in us. "I will cleanse their blood that I have not cleansed: for the LORD dwelleth in Zion" (Joel 3:21 KJV). "Not having spot, or wrinkle, or any such thing" (Ephesians 5:27 KJV), without even the shadow of a spot that the eye of omniscience could discover, we shall be as pure as Adam before his fall, as holy as the immaculate manhood when it first came from the divine hand. We shall be better than Adam, for Adam might sin, but we shall be so established in goodness, in truth, and in righteousness that we shall not even be tempted again, much less shall we have any fear of falling. We shall stand spotless and faultless at the last great day.

Through the Bible in One Year: Hebrews 7–9

Christic and His Perfection

※

You have come to God, the judge of all men,
to the spirits of righteous men made perfect.
HEBREWS 12:23

Perhaps the chief point in which Christ will be glorified will be the absolute perfection of all the saints. They shall then be without "spot, or wrinkle, or any such thing" (Ephesians 5:27 KJV). We have not experienced what perfection is, and therefore we can hardly conceive it; our thoughts themselves are too sinful for us to get a full idea of what absolute perfection must be. But we shall have no sin left in us, for we shall be "without fault before the throne of God" (Revelation 14:5 KJV), and we shall have no remaining propensity to sin. There shall be no bias in the will toward that which is evil, but it shall be fixed forever upon that which is good. The affections will never be wanton again; they will be chaste for Christ. The understanding will never make mistakes. You shall never put bitter for sweet, nor sweet for bitter; you shall be "perfect, even as your Father which is in heaven is perfect" (Matthew 5:48 KJV), and truly, brethren, he who works this in us will be a wonder. Christ will be admired and adored because of this grand result. O mighty Master, with what strange moral alchemy did you work to turn that morose-dispositioned man into a mass of love! How did you work to lift that selfish Mammonite up from his hoarded gains to make him find his gain in you? How did you overcome that proud spirit, that fickle spirit, that lazy spirit, that lustful spirit—how did you contrive to take all these away? How did you extirpate the very roots of sin, and every little rootlet of sin, out of your redeemed, so that not a tiny fiber can be found?

Through the Bible in One Year: Hebrews 10–11

Jewels in His Crown

✧

*For what is our hope, our joy, or the crown in which
we will glory in the presence of our Lord Jesus when he comes?
Is it not you? Indeed, you are our glory and joy.*
1 THESSALONIANS 2:19–20

The Thessalonians were heathens plunged in sin, and this poor tent maker came in among them and told them of Jesus Christ and his gospel. His testimony was believed, that belief changed the lives of his hearers and made them holy, and they being renewed came at length to be perfectly holy, and there they are, and Jesus Christ is glorified in them.

Will it not be a delightful thing throughout eternity to contemplate that you went into your Sunday-school class this afternoon, and you were afraid you could not say much, but you talked about Jesus Christ with a tear in your eye, and you brought a dear girl to believe in his saving name through your testimony? In years to come that girl will be among those who shine out to the glory of Christ forever. Or you will talk in a lodging house to some of those poor vagrants or one of the fallen women of the story of your Lord's love and blood, and the poor broken heart will catch at the gracious word and come to Jesus, and then a heavenly character will be begun, and another jewel secured for the Redeemer's diadem. Methinks you will admire his crown all the more, because as you see certain stones sparkling in it, you will say, "Blessed be his name forever; he helped me to dive into the sea and find that pearl for him," and now it adorns his sacred brow. Now, get at it, all of you!

Through the Bible in One Year: Hebrews 12–13

Not Here

※

*"If the world hates you, keep in mind that it hated me first.
If you belonged to the world, it would love you as its own.
As it is, you do not belong to the world, but I have chosen you out
of the world. That is why the world hates you."*

JOHN 15:18–19

I never try to teach a horse astronomy, and to teach an unconverted man spiritual experience would be a folly of the same sort. I might stand and preach until midnight concerning my Lord, but all that men who are unconverted would gain would be to hear what I have to tell and then to say, "Perhaps it is true." But they could not possibly discern it; the thing is beyond the cognizance of sense. So is our spiritual life. Beloved, you may reign over sin, but the sinner does not comprehend your being a king. You may officiate as a priest before God, but the ungodly man does not perceive your priesthood and your worship. Do not expect him to do so; your labor is lost if you try by any way to introduce him to these mysteries, except by the same door through which you came yourself.

What did the world do with Christ as soon as they saw him? Set him in the chair of state and fall down and worship his absolute perfection? No, not they: "He is despised and rejected of men; a man of sorrows, and acquainted with grief" (Isaiah 53:3 KJV). Outside the camp was his place; cross-bearing was for him the occupation, not of one day, but of every day. Such you must expect to be the lot of the part of your spiritual life that men can see; as soon as they see it to be spiritual life, they will treat it as they treated the Savior. They will despise it.

Through the Bible in One Year: Psalms 1–4

True to Your Master

*"Be on your guard against men; they will hand you over
to the local councils and flog you in their synagogues.
On my account you will be brought before governors and kings
as witnesses to them and to the Gentiles."*
MATTHEW 10:17–18

You dream that men will admire you, that the holier you are and the more Christlike you are, the more peaceable people will be toward you. You do not know what you are driving at. "It is enough for the disciple that he be as his master, and the servant as his lord. If they have called the master of the house Beelzebub, how much more shall they call them of his household?" (Matthew 10:25 KJV). I believe if we were more like Christ, we should be much more loved by his friends and much more hated by his enemies. I do not believe the world would be half so lenient to the church nowadays if it were not that the church has grown complacent to the world. When any of us speak up boldly, mercenary motives are imputed to us, our language is turned upside down, and we are abhorred of men. We get smooth things, brethren, because I am afraid we are too much like the prophets who prophesied peace, peace, where there was no peace. Let us be true to our Master, stand out and come out and be like him, and we must expect the same treatment that he had.

Through the Bible in One Year: Psalms 5–8

The Sustainer of Faith

*When he had gone indoors, the blind men came to him,
and he asked them, "Do you believe that I am able to do this?"*

"Yes, Lord," they replied.

*Then he touched their eyes and said, "According to your faith
will it be done to you"; and their sight was restored.
Jesus warned them sternly, "See that no one knows about this."*

MATTHEW 9:28–30

If you have faith, the Lord has dealt with you; this is the mark of his hand upon you.

Not a grain of faith exists in all the world except that which he has himself created. By faith he has brought you out of your death in sin and the natural darkness of your mind. "Thy faith hath saved thee," for it is the candlestick that holds a candle by which the chamber of your heart is enlightened. Your God and Savior has put this faith in you. Our Lord is also the sustainer of faith, for faith is never independent of him upon whom it relies. The greatest believer would not believe for another moment unless grace were constantly given him to keep the flame of faith burning. If you have had any experience of the inner life at all, you know that he who first made you live must keep you alive, or else you will go back to your natural death. Since faith from day to day feeds at the table of Jesus, then he knows where it is. It is well for us that we have one looking for faith who, on account of his having created and sustained it, will be at no loss to discern it.

Through the Bible in One Year: Psalms 9–12

Launching Faith

*"I tell you the truth, anyone who has faith in me will do what
I have been doing. He will do even greater things than these."*
JOHN 14:12

Oh, to have done with all glory but glorying in the cross! For my
part, I am content to be a fool if the old gospel be folly. What is
more, I am content to be lost if faith in the atoning sacrifice will
not bring salvation. I am so sure about the whole matter that if I
were left alone in the world as the last believer in the doctrines of
grace, I would not think of abandoning them, nor even toning
them down to win a convert.

"When the Son of man cometh, shall he find faith on the
earth" such as he deserves at our hands (Luke 18:8 KJV)? Do we
believe in Jesus practically, in matter-of-fact style? Is our faith fact
and not fiction? If we have the truth of faith, have we the degree
of faith that we might have? Just think of this: "If ye have faith as
a grain of mustard seed, ye shall say unto this mountain, Remove
hence to yonder place; and it shall remove" (Matthew 17:20 KJV).
What does this mean? Brethren, are we not off the rails? Do we
even know what faith means? I begin sometimes to question
whether we believe at all. What signs follow our believing? When
we think what wonders faith could have done, when we consider
what marvels our Lord might have wrought among us if it had not
been for our unbelief, are we not humiliated? Have we ever
launched out into the deep in clear reliance upon the Eternal God?
Have we clung to the naked promise of God and rested upon the
bare arm of omnipotence, which in and of itself is more than sufficient for the fulfillment of every promise?

Through the Bible in One Year: Psalms 13–16

The Full Influence of the Invisible

*Therefore we do not lose heart. Though outwardly we are wasting away,
yet inwardly we are being renewed day by day.
For our light and momentary troubles are achieving
for us an eternal glory that far outweighs them all.
So we fix our eyes not on what is seen, but on what is unseen.
For what is seen is temporary, but what is unseen is eternal.*

2 CORINTHIANS 4:16–18

Paul ranks among the bravest of the brave. We note also with admiration how the hero of so many dangers and conflicts, who could glow and burn with fervor, was yet among the calmest and quietest of spirits. He had learned to live beyond those present circumstances that worry and disturb; he had stolen a march upon the shadows of time and entered into possession of the realities of eternity. He looked not on the things that are seen, but he set his whole regard on the things that are not seen; and by this means he entered into a deep and joyful peace that made him strong, resolute, steadfast, immovable. I would to God that we had all acquired Paul's art of being "always confident"—his habit of having the inward man renewed day by day. Are we not too apt to live in the immediate present that is revealed by the senses? The ox projects no thought upward or beyond: to stand in the cool brook or lie down in the fat pasturage is its all in all. Even thus is it with the mass of men; their souls are tethered to their bodies, imprisoned within the circumstances of the day. If we could be completely delivered from the thralldom of things seen and felt, and could feel the full influence of the invisible and the eternal, how much of heaven we might enjoy before the celestial shores are reached!

Through the Bible in One Year: Psalms 17–20

Like Our Lord

❧

How great is the love the Father has lavished on us,
that we should be called children of God!
1 JOHN 3:1

When you were new born as a Christian, you were born as Jesus Christ was, for you were born of the Holy Ghost. What happened after that? The devil tried to destroy the new life in you, just as Herod tried to kill your Lord: you were with Christ in danger, early and imminent. You grew in stature and in grace, and while yet grace was young, you staggered those who were about you with the things you said and did and felt, for they could not understand you; even thus when he went up to the temple, our Lord amazed the doctors who gathered around him. The Spirit of God rested upon you, not in the same measure, but still as a matter of fact it did descend upon you as it did upon your Lord. You have been with him in Jordan's stream and have received the divine acknowledgment that you are indeed the son of God. Your Lord was led into the wilderness to be tempted, and you too have been tempted of the devil. You have been with the Lord all along, from the first day until now. If you have been by grace enabled to live as you should, you have trodden the separated paths with Jesus; you have been in the world but not of it, holy, harmless, undefiled, and separate from sinners. Therefore, you have been despised; you have had to take your share of being unknown and misrepresented, because you are even as he was in the world.

Through the Bible in One Year: Psalms 21 – 24

We Are His

"No eye has seen, no ear has heard,
no mind has conceived what God has prepared
for those who love him."
1 Corinthians 2:9

Oh, the delight of being joint heirs with Christ and with him in the possession of all that he possesses. What is heaven? It is the place that his love suggested, that his genius invented, that his bounty provided, that his royalty has adorned, that his wisdom has prepared, that he himself glorifies; in that heaven you are to be with him forever. You shall dwell in the King's own palace. Its gates of pearl and streets of gold shall not be too good for you. You who love him are to abide forever with him, not near him in a secondary place, as a servant lives at the lodge gate of his master's mansion, but with him in the selfsame palace in the metropolis of the universe.

In a word, believers are to be identified with Christ forever. Do they ask for the Shepherd? They cannot behold him to perfection except as surrounded by his sheep. Will the King be illustrious? How can that be if his subjects are lost? Do they ask for the Bridegroom? They cannot imagine him in the fullness of joy without his bride. Will the Head be blessed? It could not be if it were separated from the members. Will Christ be forever glorified? How can he be if he shall lose his jewels? He is a foundation, and what would he be if all his people were not built upon him into the similitude of a palace? O brethren, there shall be no Christ without Christians; there shall be no Savior without the saved ones; there shall be no Elder Brother without the younger brethren; there shall be no Redeemer without his redeemed.

Through the Bible in One Year: Psalms 25–28

The All-Conquering Church

❧

Indeed, of Zion it will be said,
"This one and that one were born in her,
and the Most High himself will establish her."
PSALM 87:5

Of old, the church was like Mount Zion, a very little hill. What saw the nations of the earth when they looked upon it?—a humble Man with twelve disciples. But that little hill grew, and some thousand were baptized in the name of Christ; it grew again and became mighty. The stone cut out of the mountain without hands began to break in pieces kingdoms, and now at this day the hill of Zion stands a lofty hill. But still compared with the colossal systems of idolatry, she is but small. The Hindu and the Chinese turn to our religion and say, "It is an infant of yesterday; ours is the religion of ages." The Easterns compare Christianity to some miasma that creeps along the fenny lowlands, but their systems they imagine to be like the Alps, outsoaring the heavens in height. Ah, but we reply to this, "Your mountain crumbles and your hill dissolves, but our hill of Zion has been growing, and strange to say, it has life within its bowels, and grow on it shall, grow on it must, till all the systems of idolatry shall become less than nothing before it, till false gods being cast down, mighty systems of idolatry being overthrown, this mountain shall rise above them all, and on and on and on shall this Christian religion grow until, converting into its mass all the deluded followers of the heresies and idolatries of man, the hill shall reach to heaven, and God in Christ shall be all in all." Such is the destiny of our church; she is to be an all-conquering church, rising above every competitor.

Through the Bible in One Year: Psalms 29–32

For Jesus

❧

Then shall the King say unto them on his right hand,
Come, ye blessed of my Father, inherit the kingdom prepared
for you from the foundation of the world.
MATTHEW 25:34 KJV

Now, notice that Christ, as it were, inferentially tells us that the actions that will be mentioned at the judgment day, as the proof of our being the blessed of the Lord, spring from the grace of God, for he says, "Ye blessed of my Father, inherit the kingdom prepared for you from the foundation of the world." They fed the hungry, but sovereign grace first fed them. They clothed the naked, but infinite love first clothed them. They went to the prison, but free grace first set them free from a worse prison. They visited the sick, but the Good Physician in his infinite mercy first came and visited them. They evidently had no idea that there was anything meritorious in what they did; they had never dreamed of being rewarded for it. When they stand before the judgment seat, the bare idea of there being any excellence in what they have done will be new to the saints, for they have formed a very lowly estimate of their own performances, and what they have done seems to them too faulty to be commended. The saints fed the hungry and clothed the naked because it gave them much pleasure to do so. They did it because they could not help doing it; their new nature impelled them to it. They did it because it was their delight to do good and was as much their element as water for a fish or the air for a bird. They did good for Christ's sake, because it was the sweetest thing in the world to do anything for Jesus.

Through the Bible in One Year: Psalms 33–36

Have You Searched Intently?

*Concerning this salvation, the prophets, who spoke of the grace
that was to come to you, searched intently and with the greatest care,
trying to find out the time and circumstances to which the Spirit of Christ
in them was pointing when he predicted the sufferings of Christ
and the glories that would follow. It was revealed to them
that they were not serving themselves but you, when they spoke
of the things that have now been told you by those who have preached
the gospel to you by the Holy Spirit sent from heaven.
Even angels long to look into these things.*
1 PETER 1:10–12

God is to be worshiped by us devoutly, and we are to take pains to worship him in his own way. How many people have a kind of—what shall I call it?—a happy-go-lucky religion. Whatever their mother or their father was, that are they. A great many of you go to certain places of worship, not because you have ever inquired whether the sect you belong to is right or not, but because you have drifted that way, and there you stick. How few take the Bible and search for themselves; yet no man has obeyed God aright who has not done so. If I could not honestly say, "I am a member of this denomination because I have weighed the truths that are held by my brethren, and I believe them to be according to God's Book," I could not feel that I had done right toward the Most High.

Through the Bible in One Year: Psalms 37–40

Trifling with Conscience

*"Be strong and courageous, because you will lead these people
to inherit the land I swore to their forefathers to give them.
Be strong and very courageous. Be careful to obey all the law my servant
Moses gave you; do not turn from it to the right or to the left,
that you may be successful wherever you go. Do not let this
Book of the Law depart from your mouth; meditate on it day and night,
so that you may be careful to do everything written in it.
Then you will be prosperous and successful."*

JOSHUA 1:6–8

The idea that there are good people in all sects is well enough, but a great many have perverted it into an excuse for never caring what God's truths or ordinances are. Rest assured that he who neglects one of the least of Christ's ordinances and teaches men so, the same shall be least in the kingdom of heaven. Every truth is important. Trifling with conscience is the sin of the present age. Men have even come to occupy pulpits in churches when they do not believe the fundamental doctrines of the church. We have heard them even claim a right to retain their pulpits after they have denied the doctrines of the denomination to which they belong. From any power to believe in such a conscience, may God deliver every one of us. Be right even in little things. Be precise: you serve a precise God. Charity toward others is one thing; laxity for yourselves is quite another thing.

Through the Bible in One Year: Psalms 41–44

Scraps of Time

🌾

What I mean, brothers, is that the time is short.
1 CORINTHIANS 7:29

Could it be possible for me to come to every one of you personally and grasp you by the hand, I would with most affectionate earnestness—yea, even with tears—pray you by him to whom you owe your souls, awake and render personal service to the Lover of your souls; make no excuse, for no excuse can be valid from those who are bought with so great a price. Your business, you will tell me, requires so much of your thoughts—I know it does; then use your business in such a way as to serve God in it. Still there must be some scraps of time that you could devote to holy service; there must be some opportunities for directly aiming at conversions. To some of you the excuse of "business" would not apply, for you have seasons of leisure. Oh, I beseech you, let not that leisure be driveled away in frivolities, in mere talk, in sleep and self-indulgence! Time is hastening and men are perishing. With such awful demands upon us, we cannot afford to trifle. Oh, that I had the power to stir the heart and soul of all my fellow Christians by a description of this huge city wallowing in iniquity. Surely sin, the grave, and hell are themes that might create a tingling even in the dull, cold ear of death. Oh, that I could set before you the Redeemer upon the cross dying to ransom souls! Oh, that I could depict the heaven that sinners lose, and their remorse when they shall find themselves self-excluded!

Through the Bible in One Year: Psalms 45–48

A Valuable Weapon

For though we live in the world, we do not wage war
as the world does. The weapons we fight with are not the weapons
of the world. On the contrary, they have divine power
to demolish strongholds.
2 CORINTHIANS 10:3–4

Intercede for your friends. Plead with Christ on their account; mention their names in your constant prayers; set apart special times in which you plead with God for them. Let your dear sister's case ring in the ears of the Mediator; let your dear child's name be repeated again and again in your intercessions. As Abraham pleaded for Ishmael, so let your cry come up for those who are round about you, that the Lord would be pleased to visit them in his mercy. Intercession is a true bringing of souls to Christ, and this means will avail when you are shut out from employing any other. Here is a valuable weapon for those who cannot preach or teach: they can wield the sword of all-prayer. When hearts are too hard for sermons, and good advice is rejected, it still remains to love to be allowed to plead with God for its wayward one. Tears and weepings are prevalent at the mercy seat, and if we prevail there, the Lord will be sure to manifest his prevailing grace in obdurate spirits.

Through the Bible in One Year: Psalms 49–52

Your Niche

The eye cannot say to the hand, "I don't need you!"
And the head cannot say to the feet, "I don't need you!"
On the contrary, those parts of the body that seem
to be weaker are indispensable, and the parts that we think
are less honorable we treat with special honor.
1 CORINTHIANS 12:21–23

Now, you young men, if you become diligent in tract distribution, diligent in the Sunday school, you are likely men to be made into ministers; but if you stop and do nothing until you can do everything, you will remain useless—an impediment to the church instead of being a help to her. Dear sisters in Jesus Christ, you must none of you dream that you are in a position in which you can do nothing at all. That would be such a mistake in providence as God cannot commit. You must have some talent entrusted to you and something given you to do that no one else can do. Out of this whole structure of the human body, every little muscle, every single cell, has its own secretion and its own work; and though some physicians have said this and that organ might be spared, I believe that there is not a single thread in the whole embroidery of human nature that could well be spared—the whole of the fabric is required. So in the mystical body, the church, the least member is necessary; the most uncomely member of the Christian church is needful for its growth. Ask God to tell you what is your niche, and stand in it, occupying the place till Jesus Christ shall come and give you your reward.

Through the Bible in One Year: Psalms 53–56

God Will Bless

❧

As for those who seemed to be important—whatever they were
makes no difference to me; God does not judge by external appearance—
those men added nothing to my message. On the contrary, they saw
that I had been entrusted with the task of preaching the gospel
to the Gentiles, just as Peter had been to the Jews. For God,
who was at work in the ministry of Peter as an apostle to the Jews,
was also at work in my ministry as an apostle to the Gentiles. James,
Peter and John, those reputed to be pillars, gave me and Barnabas
the right hand of fellowship when they recognized the grace given to me.
They agreed that we should go to the Gentiles, and they to the Jews.

GALATIANS 2:6–9

Oh, what a mercy it is that the imperfections of our ministry do not prevent God's saving souls by us! If it were not so, how little good would be done in the world! Mr. John Wesley preached most earnestly one view of the gospel, and William Huntingdon preached quite another view of it. The two men would have had a holy horror of each other and censured each other most conscientiously, yet no rational man dare say that souls were not saved under John Wesley, or under William Huntingdon either, for God blessed them both. Both ministers were faulty, but both were sincere and both made useful. So is it with all our testimonies. They are all imperfect, full of exaggerations of one truth and misapprehensions of another, but as long as we witness to the true Christ foretold by Moses and the prophets, our mistakes shall be forgiven, and God will bless our ministry, despite every flaw.

Through the Bible in One Year: Psalms 57–60

Meeting Together

❦

Let us hold unswervingly to the hope we profess,
for he who promised is faithful. And let us consider how we may
spur one another on toward love and good deeds. Let us not
give up meeting together, as some are in the habit of doing,
but let us encourage one another—and all the more
as you see the Day approaching.
HEBREWS 10:23–25

When the apostles met on the first Lord's Day after Jesus had risen, Thomas was the only disciple absent out of the eleven; on the second Lord's Day, Thomas was there, and he was the only disciple doubting out of the eleven. How much the fact of his doubting was occasioned and helped by the fact of his former absence I cannot say, but still it looks highly probable that had he been there at the first, he would have enjoyed the same experience as the other ten and would have been able to say as they did, "We have seen the Lord." Let us not forsake the assembling of ourselves together as the manner of some is, for we cannot tell what loss we may sustain thereby. Though our Lord may reveal himself to single individuals in solitude as he did to Mary Magdalene, yet he more usually shows himself to two or three, and he delights most of all to come into the assembly of his servants. The Lord seems most at home when, standing in the midst of his people, he says, "Peace be unto you." Let us not fail to meet with our fellow believers. For my part, the assemblies of God's people shall ever be dear to me. Where Jesus pays his frequent visits, there would I be found.

Through the Bible in One Year: Psalms 61–64

Even Thomas Was Convinced

Now Thomas (called Didymus), one of the Twelve,
was not with the disciples when Jesus came.
So the other disciples told him "We have seen the Lord!"

But he said to them, "Unless I see the nail marks in his hands
and put my finger where the nails were,
and put my hand into his side, I will not believe it."

JOHN 20:24–25

If you tell me that the resurrection of our Lord from the dead was witnessed by men who were prepared to believe it, I reply that the statement is totally false. Not one among that company even knew the meaning of the Lord's prophecy that he would rise again from the dead. It was hard to make any of them catch the idea. In Thomas we have a man who was specially hard to be convinced, a man who was so obstinate as to give the lie to ten of his friends with whom he had been associated for years. Now, if I had a statement to make that I wished to have well attested, I should like to place in the witness box a person who was known to be exceedingly cautious and wary. I should be glad if it were known that at the first he had been suspicious and critical, but had at length been overwhelmed by evidence so as to be compelled to believe. I am sure that such a man would give his evidence with the accent of conviction, as indeed Thomas did when he cried, "My Lord and my God." We cannot have a better witness to the fact that the Lord is risen indeed than that this cool, examining, prudent, critical Thomas arrived at an absolute certainty.

Through the Bible in One Year: Psalms 65–68

Divine Visitations

*"Forget the former things; do not dwell on the past.
See, I am doing a new thing!
Now it springs up; do you not perceive it?"*
ISAIAH 43:18–19

It is very possible that in addition to cultivating a vehement desire for the revival of religion, we may have been forecasting in our minds a conception of the form that the divine visitation shall take. Perhaps you have planned in your mind that God will raise up an extraordinary preacher whose ministry will attract the multitude, and while he is preaching, God the Holy Spirit will attend the word so that hundreds will be converted under every sermon; other evangelists will be raised up of a like spirit, and from end to end this island shall hear the truth and feel its power.

Now it may be that God will so visit us. It may be that such signs and wonders as have frequently attended revivals may be again witnessed. His Holy Spirit may reveal himself like a mighty river swollen with floods and sweeping all before its majestic current, but if so he wills, he may rather unveil his power as the gentle dew, which, without observation, refreshes all the earth. It may happen unto us as unto Elias [Elijah] when the fire and the wind passed before him, but the Lord was not in either of those mighty agencies; he preferred to commune with his servant in a still, small voice. Perhaps that still, small voice is to be the language of grace in this congregation. It will be useless then for us to be mapping out the way of the Eternal God, idle for us to be rejecting all the good that he may be pleased to give us because it does not happen to come in the shape that we have settled in our own minds to be the proper one.

Through the Bible in One Year: Psalms 69–72

God's Dwelling

Do you not know that your body is a temple of the Holy Spirit,
who is in you, whom you have received from God?
1 CORINTHIANS 6:19

Is your house fit for the Lord to enter and abide there? I know some houses where my Lord could not lodge for a single night— the table, the talk, the whole surroundings would be so uncongenial to him. Are you prepared, then, to put away everything that would displease him and to have your house cleansed of all that is evil? You cannot expect the Lord Jesus to come into your house if you invite the devil to come too. Christ would not remain in the same heaven with the devil; as soon as ever Satan sinned, Christ hurled Satan out of the holy place. Christ could not endure to have a sinful spirit, the spirit of evil, there, and he will not come and live in your house if you make provision for the lust of the flesh, the lust of the eyes, and the pride of life and all those evil things that he abhors. Are you prepared, by his grace, to make a clean sweep of these things?

Further, we must admit none who would grieve our Guest. It is hard to lodge with some people because their children are so badly behaved. My Lord loves not to dwell in families where Eli is at the head of the household and where the children and young people live as they like; but if he comes to your house, he will want you to be like Abraham, of whom he said, "I know him, that he will command his children and his household after him, and they shall keep the way of the LORD" (Genesis 18:19 KJV). Do you not wish that it may be so in your house? Do you not ardently desire it? I trust that you do.

Through the Bible in One Year: Psalms 73–76

September 2

Honoring God

※

Six days before the Passover, Jesus arrived at Bethany,
where Lazarus lived, whom Jesus had raised from the dead.
Here a dinner was given in Jesus' honor.
JOHN 12:1–2

I frequently used to go and preach in a country place, where I stayed at a farm, and the dear old man who lived there used to have about a hundred pounds of beef, at the very least, on his table. And when, year after year, I noticed such enormous joints, I said to him one day, "You must have a very curious idea of my appetite; it is not possible that I should ever get through these masses of meat that you put on your table." "Oh," he replied, "we get through it all very easily after you are gone, for there are plenty of poor people and plenty of farm laborers round about, and they soon clear it up." "But," I inquired, "why do you have so much when I come?" "Bless you, sir," he answered, "I would give you a piece as big as a house if I could get it, I would indeed, just to show you how welcome you are in my home." I understood what he meant and appreciated his kindness, and in a far higher sense, let us all do as much as ever we possibly can to show the Lord Jesus how welcome he is to our heart and our home.

How welcome he ought always to be when he comes, as our blessed Savior, to put away our sin, and change our nature, and honor us with his royal company, and keep and preserve us even to the end, that he may take us up, and our children too, to dwell at his right hand forever! Oh, there ought to be grand entertainment for such a Guest as he is!

Through the Bible in One Year: Psalms 77–80

The Human Heart

❧

He approached Jesus to kiss him, but Jesus asked him,
"Judas, are you betraying the Son of Man with a kiss?"
LUKE 22:47–48

One reason for the appointment of the betrayal lay in the fact that
it was ordained that man's sin should reach its culminating point
in Jesus' death. God, the great owner of the vineyard, had sent
many servants, and the husbandmen had stoned one and cast out
another; last of all, he said, "I will send my Son; surely they will
reverence my Son." When they slew the heir to win the inheritance, their rebellion had reached its height. The murder of our
blessed Lord was the extreme of human guilt; it developed the
deadly hatred against God that lurks in the heart of man. When
man became a deicide, sin had reached its fullness; and in the
black deed of the man by whom the Lord was betrayed, that fullness was all displayed. If it had not been for a Judas, we would not
have known how black, how foul, human nature may become. I
scorn the men who try to apologize for the treachery of this son of
perdition, this foul apostate. My brethren, we should feel a deep
detestation of this master of infamy; he has gone to his own place,
and the anathema of David, part of which was quoted by Peter,
has come upon him: "When he shall be judged, let him be condemned: and let his prayer become sin. Let his days be few; and
let another take his office" (Psalm 109:7–8 KJV). Surely, as the
devil was allowed unusually to torment the bodies of men, even so
was he let loose to get possession of Judas as he has seldom gained
possession of any other man, that we might see how foul, how des-
perately evil, is the human heart.

Through the Bible in One Year: Psalms 81–84

Dangerous Ground

❧

*Some people, eager for money, have wandered from the faith
and pierced themselves with many griefs.*
1 TIMOTHY 6:10

I do solemnly believe that of all hypocrites, those are the persons of whom there is the least hope whose God is their money. You may reclaim a drunkard; thank God—we have seen many instances of that; and even a fallen Christian, who has given way to vice, may loathe his lust and return from it; but I fear me that the cases in which a man who is cankered with covetousness has been saved are so few that they might be written on your fingernail. This is a sin that the world does not rebuke; the most faithful minister can scarce smite its forehead. God knows what thunders I have launched out against men who are all for this world and yet pretend to be Christ's followers, but yet they always say, "It is not for me." What I should call stark-naked covetousness, they call prudence, discretion, economy, and so on; and actions that I would scorn to spit upon, they will do, and think their hands quite clean after they have done them, and still sit as God's people sit, and hear as God's people hear, and think that after they have sold Christ for paltry gain, they will go to heaven. O souls, souls, souls, beware, beware, beware, most of all of greed! It is not money, nor the lack of money, but *the love* of money that is the root of all evil. It is not getting it; it is not even keeping it; it is loving it; it is making it your god; it is looking at that as the main chance, and not considering the cause of Christ, nor the truth of Christ, nor the holy life of Christ, but being ready to sacrifice everything for gain's sake.

Through the Bible in One Year: Psalms 85–88

What God Reveals

All Scripture is God-breathed and is useful for teaching, rebuking, correcting and training in righteousness, so that the man of God may be thoroughly equipped for every good work.
2 TIMOTHY 3:16–17

I have heard it said that there are certain truths in God's Word that it is better for us not to preach. It is admitted that they are true, but it is alleged that they are not edifying. I will not agree to any such plan; this is just going back to Rome's method. Whatsoever it has seemed good to God's wisdom to reveal, it is wise for God's servants to proclaim. Who are we that we are to judge between this truth and that, and to say that this we are to preach, and that we are to withhold? This system would make us to be, after all, the judges of what Christ's gospel is to be. It must not be so among us; that would be assuming a responsibility that we are quite unable to bear.

Whatsoever the Lord has taught to you by his Spirit, my brother, tell to others. According as you have opportunity, reveal to them what God has revealed to you; remember how Christ himself charged his disciples, "What I tell you in darkness, that speak ye in light: and what ye hear in the ear, that preach ye upon the housetops" (Matthew 10:27 KJV).

All truths are to be preached in due proportion; there is a time for this and a time for that, and none must be omitted. At the end of our ministry, may we be able to say, "I have kept back nothing; all that Christ taught me, I have taught to others, and so I have made full proof of my ministry."

Through the Bible in One Year: Psalms 89–90

Will You Carry His Cross?

As they led him away, they seized Simon from Cyrene,
who was on his way in from the country, and put the cross on him
and made him carry it behind Jesus.

LUKE 23:26

So far as atonement is concerned, the Lord has trodden the winepress alone, and of the people there was none with him; but as far as the conversion of the world is concerned, and its rescue from the power of error and wickedness, Christ is not alone. We are workers together with God. We are ourselves to be in the hands of God part bearers of the sorrow and travail by which men are to be delivered from the bondage of sin and Satan and brought into the liberty of truth and righteousness. Hence, it became important that in the bearing of the cross, though not in the death upon it, there should be yoked with the Christ one who should follow close behind him. To bear the cross after Jesus is the office of the faithful. Simon the Cyrenian is the representative of the whole church of God and of each believer in particular. Often had Jesus said, "Except a man take up his cross daily, and follow me, he cannot be my disciple"; and now at last he embodies that sermon in an actual person. The disciple must be as his Master: he who would follow the Crucified must himself bear the cross: this we see visibly set forth in Simon of Cyrene with the cross of Jesus laid upon his shoulder.

> Shall Simon bear the cross alone,
> And all the rest go free?
> No; there's a cross for everyone,
> And there's a cross for me.

Through the Bible in One Year: Psalms 91–94

So Blessed a Burden

Let us fix our eyes on Jesus, the author and perfecter of our faith,
who for the joy set before him endured the cross, scorning its shame,
and sat down at the right hand of the throne of God.
HEBREWS 12:2

Of course the easy way is to turn monk and live quietly in a cloister and serve God by doing nothing; or to turn nun and dwell in a convent and expect to win the battle of life by running out of it. Is not this absurd? You men and women who are Christians must stand up and stand out for Jesus where the providence of God has cast you: if your calling is not a sinful one, and if the temptations around you are not too great for you, you must "hold the fort" and never dream of surrender. If your load is hard, look upon it as Christ's cross, and bow your back to the load. Your shoulder may be raw at first, but you will grow stronger before long, for as your day your strength shall be. "It is good for a man that he bear the yoke in his youth" (Lamentations 3:27 KJV), but it is good for a man to bear the cross in his old age as well as in his youth; in fact, we ought never to be quit of so blessed a burden. What wings are to a bird, and sails to a ship, the cross becomes to a man's spirit when he fully consents to accept it as his life's beloved load. Now, Simon, where are you? Shoulder the cross, man, in the name of God!

Through the Bible in One Year: Psalms 95–98

Wholly Consecrated

Now listen, you who say, "Today or tomorrow
we will go to this or that city, spend a year there,
carry on business and make money."
Why, you do not even know what will happen tomorrow.
What is your life? You are a mist that appears
for a little while and then vanishes.
JAMES 4:13–14

What is the life of a man who toils in business, makes money, becomes rich, and dies? It winds up with a paragraph in the *Illustrated London News*, declaring that he died worth so much: the wretch was not worth anything himself; his estate had value; he had none. Had he been worth anything, he would have sent his money about the world doing good, but as a worthless steward he laid his Master's stores in heaps to rot. The life of multitudes of men is self-seeking. But a life spent for Jesus, though it involve cross-bearing, is noble, heroic, sublime. A life wholly consecrated to Christ and his cross is life indeed; it is akin to the life of angels; aye, higher still, it is the life of God within the souls of man. O you who have a spark of true nobility, seek to live lives worth living, worth remembering, worthy to be the commencement of eternal life before the throne of God.

Some of you ought to feel the cross coming upon your shoulders now when you think of the needs of those among whom you live. They are dying, perishing for lack of knowledge, rich and poor alike ignorant of Christ, multitudes of them wrapped up in self-righteousness. They are perishing, but have you no bowels of compassion? Are your hearts turned to steel? I am sure you cannot deny that the times demand of you earnest and forceful lives.

Through the Bible in One Year: Psalms 99–102

The Thief Who Believed

Then he said, "Jesus, remember me
when you come into your kingdom."
LUKE 23:42

Observe that this man believed in Christ when he literally saw him dying the death of a felon, under circumstances of the greatest personal shame. You have never realized what it was to be crucified. It stands beyond us. This man saw it with his own eyes, and for him to call him "Lord" who was hanging on a gibbet was no small triumph of faith. For him to ask Jesus to remember him when he came into his kingdom, though he saw Jesus bleeding his life away and hounded to the death, was a notable act of reliance—a noble achievement of faith.

Recollect too that at that time, when the thief believed in Christ, all the disciples had forsaken him and fled. John might have been lingering at a little distance, and holy women may have stood farther off, but no one was present bravely to champion the dying Christ. Judas had sold him, Peter had denied him, and the rest had forsaken him; and it was then that the dying thief called him "Lord" and said, "Remember me when thou comest into thy kingdom." I call that glorious faith. Why, some of you do not believe, though you are surrounded by Christian friends—though you are urged on by the testimony of those whom you regard with love; but this man, all alone, comes out and calls Jesus his Lord! The centurion bore witness afterwards, when Jesus expired, but this thief was a lone confessor, holding on to the Savior when nobody would say "Amen" to what he said.

Through the Bible in One Year: Psalms 103–6

Why Are We Still Here?

One of the criminals who hung there hurled insults at him:
"Aren't you the Christ? Save yourself and us!"

But the other criminal rebuked him.
LUKE 23:39–40

Why is it that our Lord does not emparadise all of us at once? It is because there is something for us to do on earth. *Are you doing it?* Some good people are still on earth, but why? What is the use of them? I cannot make it out. If they are indeed the Lord's people, what are they here for? They get up in the morning and eat their breakfast, and in due course they eat their dinner and their supper and go to bed and sleep; at a proper hour they get up the next morning and do the same as on the previous day. Is this living for Jesus? Is this life? It does not come to much. Can this be the life of God in man? O Christian people, do justify your Lord in keeping you waiting here! How can you justify him but by serving him to the utmost of your power? The Lord help you to do so! Why, you owe as much to him as the dying thief! What a debt of obligation young Christians owe to the Lord! And if this poor thief crammed a lifetime of testimony into a few minutes, ought not you and I, who have been spared for years after our conversion, to perform good service for our Lord? Come, let us wake up if we have been asleep! Let us begin to live if we have been half-dead. May the Spirit of God make something of us yet so that we may go as industrious servants from the labors of the vineyard to the pleasures of paradise!

Through the Bible in One Year: Psalms 107–10

In the Midst of His Service

While they were stoning him, Stephen prayed,
"Lord Jesus, receive my spirit."
Then he fell on his knees and cried out,
"Lord, do not hold this sin against them."
When he had said this, he fell asleep.
ACTS 7:59–60

Let us look at Stephen's death and notice its general character. It strikes us at once that it happened in the very midst of his service. He had been appointed an officer of the church at Jerusalem to see that the alms were distributed properly amongst the poor, especially amongst the Grecian widows. He discharged his duty to the satisfaction of the whole church, and thereby he did most useful service, for it gave the apostles opportunity to give themselves wholly to their true work, namely, that of preaching and prayer, and it is no small matter to be able to bear a burden for another if he is thereby set free for more eminent service than we could ourselves perform. But not content with being a deacon, Stephen began to minister in holy things as a speaker of the Word, and that with great power, for he was full of faith and of the Holy Ghost. He stands forth on the page of the church's history, for the time being, as quite a leading spirit; so much so, indeed, that the enemies of the gospel recognized his prominent usefulness and made him the object of their fiercest opposition, for they generally rage most against those who are doing most good. Stephen stood in the front rank of the Lord's host, and yet he was taken away! "A mystery," say some. "A great privilege," say I. Who desires to be removed at any other time? Is it not well to die in harness while yet you are useful? Who wants to linger till he becomes a burden rather than a help?

Through the Bible in One Year: Psalms 111–14

Calm as Heaven Above

*When they heard this, they were furious and gnashed their teeth at him.
But Stephen, full of the Holy Spirit, looked up to heaven
and saw the glory of God, and Jesus standing at the right hand of God.*
ACTS 7:54–55

Stephen's departing moments were calm, peaceful, confident, joyous. He never flinched while he was addressing that infuriated audience. He told them the plain truth, with as much quiet deliberation as if he had been gratifying them with a pleasing discourse. When they grew angry he was not afraid; his lip did not quiver; he did not retract or soften down a single expression, but cut them to the heart with even more fidelity. With the courage of a man of God, his face was set as a flint. Knowing that he was now preaching his last sermon, he used the sharp two-edged sword of the Word, piercing into their very souls. Little cared he how they frowned; nothing was he abashed when they gnashed their teeth. He was as calm as the opened heaven above him and continued so though they hurried him out of the city. When they had dragged him outside the gate and stripped off their clothes to carry out his execution, he did not let fall a single timorous word or trembling cry; he stood up and committed his soul to God with calmness, and when the first murderous stones felled him to the earth, he rose to his knees, still not to ask for pity, nor to utter a craven cry, but to plead with his Lord for mercy upon his assailants; then, closing his eyes like a child tired out with the sport of a long summer's day, and dropping asleep upon its mother's lap, "he fell asleep." Believe, then, O Christian, that if you abide in Christ, the like will be the case with you.

Through the Bible in One Year: Psalms 115–18

Love and Service

The grace of our Lord was poured out on me abundantly,
along with the faith and love that are in Christ Jesus.
1 TIMOTHY 1:14

The grace of God that is able to save the chief of sinners can assuredly save those who are of less degree. If the bridge of grace can carry the elephant, it will certainly carry the mouse. If the mercy of God could bear with the hugest of sinners, it can have patience with you. If a gate is wide enough for a giant to pass through, any ordinary-sized mortal will find space enough. No man can now say that he is too great a sinner to be saved, because the chief of sinners was saved eighteen hundred years ago. So why not you?

After Paul was saved, he became a foremost saint. The Lord did not allot him a second-class place in the church. He had been the leading sinner, but his Lord did not therefore say, "I save you, but I shall always remember your wickedness to your disadvantage." Not so: he counted him faithful, putting him into the ministry and into the apostleship so that he was not a whit behind the very chief of the apostles. There is no reason why, if you have gone very far in sin, you should not go equally far in usefulness. On the contrary, there is a reason why you should do so, for it is a rule of grace that to whom much is forgiven, the same loves much, and much love leads to much service.

Through the Bible in One Year: Psalm 119

Pure Grace

*As he neared Damascus on his journey, suddenly a light
from heaven flashed around him. He fell to the ground and heard
a voice say to him, "Saul, Saul, why do you persecute me?"*

"Who are you, Lord?" Saul asked.

"I am Jesus, whom you are persecuting."
ACTS 9:3–5

Paul's conversion would serve for an outline sketch of the conversion of any one of us. How was that conversion wrought? Well, it is clear that there was nothing at all in Paul to contribute to his salvation. You might have sifted him in a sieve without finding anything upon which you could rest a hope that he would be converted to the faith of Jesus. His natural bent, his early training, his whole surroundings, and his life's pursuits all fettered him to Judaism and made it most unlikely that he would ever become a Christian. The first elder of the church that ever talked to him about divine things could hardly believe in his conversion. "Lord," said he, "I have heard by many of this man, how much evil he hath done to thy saints at Jerusalem" (Acts 9:13 KJV). He could hardly think it possible that the ravening wolf should have changed into a lamb. Nothing favorable to faith in Jesus could have been found in Saul; the soil of his heart was very rocky, the plowshare could not touch it, and the good seed found no roothold. Yet the Lord converted Saul, and he can do the like by other sinners, but it must be a work of pure grace and of divine power, for there is not in any man's fallen nature a holy spot of the size of a pin's point on which grace can light. Transforming grace can find no natural lodgment in our hearts; it must create its own soil. And blessed be God, it can do it, for with God all things are possible.

Through the Bible in One Year: Psalms 120–23

The Surest Antidotes

*As I urged you when I went into Macedonia, stay there in Ephesus
so that you may command certain men not to teach false doctrines
any longer nor to devote themselves to myths and endless genealogies.
These promote controversies rather than God's work—which is by faith.*

1 TIMOTHY 1:3–4

How very remarkable the times repeat themselves! When the
same evils come, we must apply to them the same remedies.
When a disease appears that has done deadly mischief in past
times, physicians inquire for medicines that on a former occasion
curbed the enemy. We are bound to do the same in spiritual matters. We must see what Paul did in his day when the malaria of
false doctrine was in the air. It is remarkable how very simple, as
a rule, everything is that is really effective. If a discovery is made
in science or machinery, it is complicated at first, and that for the
very reason that it is imperfect; but all improvements are in the
direction of simplicity. It is just the same with spiritual teachings.
When we get at reality, we cut off superfluity. Let us not talk of
inventing wise measures for the present distress in the spiritual
world, but let us use the great remedy that was so effectual in
Paul's day. Paul taught young Timothy the gospel himself: he
made him not only hear his doctrine, but see his practice. We cannot force truth upon men, but we can make our own teaching clear
and decided and make our lives consistent therewith. Truth and
holiness are the surest antidotes to error and unrighteousness. The
apostle said to Timothy, "Continue thou in the things which thou
hast learned and hast been assured of, knowing of whom thou hast
learned them" (2 Timothy 3:14 KJV).

Through the Bible in One Year: Psalms 124–27

Preserving

Only be careful, and watch yourselves closely so that you do not forget
the things your eyes have seen or let them slip from your heart
as long as you live. Teach them to your children and to their children.

DEUTERONOMY 4:9

To be prepared for the coming conflict, we have only to preach the gospel and to live the gospel and also to take care that we teach the children the Word of the Lord. This last is specially to be attended to, for it is by the mouth of babes and sucklings that God will still the enemy. Keep to the apostolic plans, and rest assured of apostolic success. Preach Christ, preach the Word in season and out of season, and teach the children. One of God's chief methods for preserving his fields from tares is to sow them early with wheat.

The work of God's grace in Timothy commenced with early instruction—"From a child thou hast known the holy scriptures" (2 Timothy 3:15 KJV). Note the time for instruction. The expression "from a child" might be better understood if we read it, "from a very child," or as the Revised Version has it, "from a babe." It does not mean a well-grown child or youth, but a child just rising out of infancy. From a very child Timothy had known the sacred writings. This expression is, no doubt, used to show that we cannot begin too early to imbue the minds of our children with scriptural knowledge. Babes receive impressions long before we are aware of the fact. During the first months of a child's life, it learns more than we imagine. It soon learns the love of its mother and its own dependence, and if the mother be wise, it learns the meaning of obedience and the necessity of yielding its will to a higher will. This may be the keynote of its whole future life.

Through the Bible in One Year: Psalms 128–31

Leading Little Ones

Train a child in the way he should go,
and when he is old he will not turn from it.
PROVERBS 22:6

The Holy Scripture may be learned by children as soon as they are capable of understanding anything. It is a very remarkable fact, which I have heard asserted by many teachers, that children will learn to read out of the Bible better than from any other book. I scarcely know why: it may, perhaps, be on account of the simplicity of the language, but I believe it is so. A biblical fact will often be grasped when an incident of common history is forgotten. There is an adaptation in the Bible for human beings of all ages, and therefore it has a fitness for children. We make a mistake when we think that we must begin with something else and lead up to the Scriptures. The Bible is the book for the peep of day. Parts of it are above a child's mind, for they are above the comprehension of the most advanced among us. There are depths in it wherein leviathan may swim, but there are also brooks in which a lamb may wade. Wise teachers know how to lead their little ones into the green pastures beside the still waters.

Through the Bible in One Year: Psalms 132–35

A Sacred Trust

My son, do not forget my teaching,
but keep my commands in your heart,
for they will prolong your life many years
and bring you prosperity.

Let love and faithfulness never leave you;
bind them around your neck, write them on the tablet of your heart.
Then you will win favor and a good name
in the sight of God and man.
PROVERBS 3:1–4

O dear mothers, you have a very sacred trust reposed in you by God! He hath in effect said to you, "Take this child and nurse it for me, and I will give thee thy wages." You are called to equip the future man of God, that he may be thoroughly furnished unto every good work. Those who think that a woman detained at home by her little family is doing nothing think the reverse of what is true. Scarcely can the godly mother quit her home for a place of worship, but dream not that she is lost to the work of the church; far from it, she is doing the best possible service for her Lord. Mothers, the godly training of your offspring is your first and most pressing duty.

Through the Bible in One Year: Psalms 136–39

September 19

A Holy Service

*"Anyone who breaks one of the least of these commandments
and teaches others to do the same will be called least
in the kingdom of heaven, but whoever practices and teaches these
commands will be called great in the kingdom of heaven."*
MATTHEW 5:19

Nowadays, since the world has in it, alas, so few of Christian mothers and grandmothers, the church has thought it wise to supplement the instruction of home by teaching held under her fostering wing. Those children who have no such parents the church takes under her maternal care. I regard this as a very blessed institution. I am thankful for the many of our brothers and sisters who give their Sabbath days, and many of them a considerable part of their week evenings also, to the teaching of other people's children, who somehow grow to be very much their own. They endeavor to perform the duties of fathers and mothers, for God's sake, to those children who are neglected by their own parents, and therein they do well. Let no Christian parents fall into the delusion that the Sunday school is intended to ease them of their personal duties. The first and most natural condition of things is for Christian parents to train up their own children in the nurture and admonition of the Lord. Yet it is a Christly work when others undertake the duty that the natural doers of it have left undone. The Lord Jesus looks with pleasure upon those who feed his lambs and nurse his babes, for it is not his will that any of these little ones should perish. Come forward, earnest men and women, and sanctify yourselves for this joyful service.

Through the Bible in One Year: Psalms 140–43

September 20

Early Teaching

❦

> *"From infancy you have known the holy Scriptures,*
> *which are able to make you wise for salvation*
> *through faith in Christ Jesus.*
> 2 TIMOTHY 3:15

Observe that Timothy was taught, not only to reverence holy things in general, but especially to *know the Scriptures*. The teaching of his mother and his grandmother was the teaching of Holy Scripture. Suppose we get the children together on Sabbath days and then amuse them and make the hours to pass away pleasantly; or instruct them, as we do in the weekdays, in the elements of a moral education—what have we done? We have done nothing worthy of the day or of the church of God. Suppose that we are particularly careful to teach the children the rules and regulations of our own church and do not take them to the Scriptures; suppose that we bring before them a book that is set up as the standard of our church but do not dwell upon the Bible—what have we done? The aforesaid standard may or may not be correct, and we may therefore have taught our children truth or taught them error; but if we keep to Holy Scripture, we cannot go aside. With such a standard we know that we are right. This Book is the Word of God, and if we teach it, we teach that which the Lord will accept and bless. O dear teachers—and I speak here to myself also—let our teaching be more and more scriptural! Fret not if our classes forget what *we* say, but pray them to remember what the Lord says. May divine truths about sin and righteousness and judgment to come be written on their hearts! May revealed truths concerning the love of God, the grace of our Lord Jesus Christ, and the work of the Holy Ghost never be forgotten by them!

Through the Bible in One Year: Psalms 144–47

God Is in Control

❧

I know, O LORD, that a man's life is not his own;
it is not for man to direct his steps.
JEREMIAH 10:23

Have you a son who has left home? Is he a willful, wayward young man who has gone away because he could not bear the restraints of a Christian family? It is a sad thing it should be so—a very sad thing, but do not despond or even have a thought of despair about him. You do not know where he is, but God does; and you cannot follow him, but the Spirit of God can. Is he going on a voyage to Shanghai? Ah, there may be a Paul at Shanghai who is to be the means of his salvation, and as that Paul is not in England, your son must go there. Is it to Australia that he is going? There may be a word spoken there by the blessing of God to your son, which is the only word that ever will reach him. I cannot speak it; nobody in London can speak it; but the man there will, and God therefore is letting him go away in all his willfulness and folly that he may be brought under the means of grace, which will prove effectual to his salvation. The worst thing that can happen to a young man is sometimes the best thing that can happen to him.

Through the Bible in One Year: Psalms 148–50

Precious Faith

"When the Son of Man comes,
will he find faith on the earth?"
LUKE 18:8

Our returning Lord will care nothing for the treasures of the rich or the honors of the great. He will not look for the abilities we have manifested, nor the influence we have acquired; but he will look for our faith. It is his glory that he is "believed on in the world," and to that he will have respect. This heavenly merchantman counts faith to be the pearl of great price—faith is precious to Jesus as well as to us. The last day will be occupied with a great scrutiny, and that scrutiny will be made upon the essential point—where is there faith, and where is there no faith? He who believes is saved; he who believes not is condemned. A search warrant will be issued for our houses and our hearts, and the inquiry will be: Where is your faith? Did you honor Christ by trusting his Word and his blood, or did you not? Did you glorify God by believing his revelation and depending upon his prom- ise, or did you not? The fact that our Lord, at his coming, will seek for faith should cause us to think very highly of faith. It is no mere act of the intellect; it is a grace of the Holy Spirit that brings glory to God and produces obedience in the heart. Jesus looks for it because he is the proper object of it, and it is by means of it that his great end in his first advent is carried out. Our Savior is search- ing for faith now. "His eyes behold, his eyelids try, the children of men" (Psalm 11:4 KJV). This is the gold he seeks after amid the quartz of our humanity. This is the object of his royal quest— do you believe in the Lord Jesus Christ?

Through the Bible in One Year: James 1–2

Faith

❧

*So those who have faith are blessed along
with Abraham, the man of faith.*
GALATIANS 3:9

Where is the preaching or the teaching that is done in full faith in what is preached and taught? It is no use flogging other people; let us come home to ourselves. My brothers and sisters, where is our own faith? It seemed almost a novelty in the church when it was stated long ago that Mr. George Mueller walked by faith in regard to temporal things. To feed children by faith in God was looked upon as the belief of a pious freak. We have come to a pretty pass, have we not, when God is not to be trusted about common things. Abraham walked with God about daily life, but nowadays if you meet with a man who walks with God as to his business, trusts God as to every item and detail of his domestic affairs, persons look at him with a degree of suspicious wonder. They think he has grace in his heart, but they also suspect that he has a bee in his bonnet, or he would not act in that sort of way. Oh yes, we have a fancied faith, but when it comes to the stern realities of life, where is our faith?

My brethren, why are you so full of worldly care? Why are you so anxious, if you have faith in God? Why do you display in worldly things almost as much distrust as worldly men? Whence this fear? This murmuring? This worry? O my Savior, if you were to come, we could not defend ourselves for our wretched mistrust, our foolish apprehension, our want of loving reliance upon you. We do not trust you as you ought to be trusted, and if this be the case among those who are such great debtors to your loving faithfulness, where will you find faith on earth?

Through the Bible in One Year: James 3–5

September 24

Why Should I Fear?

On this mountain he will destroy the shroud that enfolds all peoples,
the sheet that covers all nations; he will swallow up death forever.
The Sovereign LORD will wipe away the tears from all faces;
he will remove the disgrace of his people from all the earth.

The LORD has spoken.
ISAIAH 25:7–8

Well, brethren, as surely as Christ rose, so did he guarantee as an absolute certainty the resurrection of all saints into a glorious life for their bodies, the life of their souls never having paused even for a moment. In this he conquered death; and since that memorable victory, every day Christ is overcoming death, for he gives his Spirit to his saints, and having that Spirit within them, they meet the last enemy without alarm; often they confront him with songs; perhaps more frequently they face him with calm countenance and fall asleep with peace. I will not fear you, death; why should I? You look like a dragon, but your sting is gone. Your teeth are broken, old lion; wherefore should I fear you? I know you are no more able to destroy me, but you are sent as a messenger to conduct me to the golden gate wherein I shall enter and see my Savior's unveiled face forever. Expiring saints have often said that their last beds have been the best they have ever slept upon. Many of them have inquired, "Tell me, my soul, can this be death?" To die has been so different a thing from what they expected it to be, so lightsome and so joyous; they have been so unloaded of all care, have felt so relieved instead of burdened, that they have wondered whether this could be the monster they had been so afraid of all their days. Beloved, our exalted Lord has overcome death in all these ways!

Through the Bible in One Year: Proverbs 1–3

Overcomers

※

The last enemy to be destroyed is death.
1 CORINTHIANS 15:26

Notice that death is the last enemy to each individual Christian and the last to be destroyed. Well, now, if the Word of God says it is the last, I want to remind you of a little piece of practical wisdom—leave him to be the last. Brother, do not dispute the appointed order, but let the last be last. I have known a brother wanting to vanquish death long before he died. But, brother, you do not want dying grace till dying moments. What would be the good of dying grace while you are yet alive? A boat will only be needful when you reach a river. Ask for living grace, and glorify Christ thereby, and then you shall have dying grace when dying time comes. Your enemy is going to be destroyed, but not today. There is a great host of enemies to be fought today, and you be content to let this one alone for a while. This enemy will be destroyed, but of the times and the seasons we are in ignorance; our wisdom is to be good soldiers of Jesus Christ as the duty of every day requires. Take your trials as they come, brother! God will in due time help you to overcome your last enemy, but meanwhile see to it that you overcome the world, the flesh, and the devil. If you live well, you will die well.

Through the Bible in One Year: Proverbs 4–6

Our Limited Risk

*Now we know that if the earthly tent we live in is destroyed,
we have a building from God, an eternal house in heaven,
not built by human hands.*
2 CORINTHIANS 5:1

Paul's confident belief that if his body should be dissolved, he would be no loser, kept him from fainting. He knew what the worst would be, and he was prepared for it. Great storms were out, but the apostle knew the limit of his possible loss and so was ready. All we can lose is the frail tent of this poor body. By no possibility can we lose more. When a man knows the limit of his risk, it greatly tends to calm his mind. The undiscoverable and the unmeasured are the worst ingredients of dread and terror: when you can gauge your fears, you have removed them. The apostle felt that he had been sent into the world with the great design of glorifying God, winning souls, and building up saints, and he was fully resolved to keep to the ministry that he had received. He argues with himself that his most dangerous course would be to faint in his life service, for perseverance in his calling could bring with it no greater risk than death, and that he summed up as losing a tent and gaining a mansion. The Roman emperor might strike off his head, or a mob might stone him to death, or he might be crucified like his Master, but he made light of such a fate! It was to him only the coming down of the old tent; it did not affect his undying spirit; he smiled and sang, "For our light affliction, which is but for a moment, worketh for us a far more exceeding and eternal weight of glory" (2 Corinthians 4:17 KJV).

Through the Bible in One Year: Proverbs 7–9

Our Sickle

For the word of God is living and active.
Sharper than any double-edged sword,
it penetrates even to dividing soul and spirit, joints and marrow;
it judges the thoughts and attitudes of the heart.
HEBREWS 4:12

To promulgate a dry creed, and go over certain doctrines, and expound and enforce them logically, but never to deal with men's consciences, never to upbraid them for their sins, never to tell them of their danger, never to invite them to a Savior with tears and entreaties—what a powerless work is this! We want laborers, not loiterers.

Now, see what the laborer brings with him. It is a sickle. His communications with the corn are sharp and cutting. He cuts right through, cuts the corn down, and casts it on the ground. The man whom God means to be a laborer in his harvest must not come with soft and delicate words and flattering doctrines concerning the dignity of human nature and the excellence of self-help and of earnest endeavors to rectify our lapsed condition and the like. Such mealymouthedness may God curse, for it is the curse of this age. The honest preacher calls a sin a sin and a spade a spade and says to men, "You are ruining yourselves; while you reject Christ you are living on the borders of hell, and ere long you will be lost to all eternity. There shall be no mincing the matter; you must escape from the wrath to come by faith in Jesus or be driven forever from God's presence and from all hope of joy." The preacher must make his sermons cut. Our sickle is made on purpose to cut. The gospel is intended to wound the conscience and to go right through the heart, with the design of separating the soul from sin and self, as the corn is divided from the soil.

Through the Bible in One Year: Proverbs 10–12

Godly Skill Is Needed

As Jesus walked beside the Sea of Galilee,
he saw Simon and his brother Andrew casting a net into the lake,
for they were fishermen. "Come, follow me," Jesus said,
"and I will make you fishers of men."
At once they left their nets and followed him.

MARK 1:16–18

In fishing for the souls of men, you need as much judgment as you do in angling, for men are curious fish, and they will often be frightened at a shadow; and in the very way of throwing the line and managing the fly, there is an art not very readily learned. Some never learn the way and are never able to attract souls, while others are endowed with sacred instincts by which they know how to handle men's hearts and win power over them. We must be wise to win souls; souls are not won by fools. We must have a sympathy with men, even reaching to their infirmities, and we must woo them as men, dealing with them not as they ought to be, but as they are, and putting truth in the shape in which it is likely to be acceptable to them. If you bear witness for Christ, ask the Spirit of wisdom to guide you. Pray to be directed lest your earnestness should lead you into an injudicious mode of speech. Let prudence be mingled with your zeal.

Through the Bible in One Year: Proverbs 13–15

By the Spirit

❧

"Not by might nor by power, but by my Spirit,"
says the LORD Almighty.
ZECHARIAH 4:6

There is a secret, subtle power, *spiritual power*, wherein, in the spiritual world, a man is made a prince with God and has power with God; and learning how to prevail with God for men, he catches the art of prevailing with men for God. He is first a wrestler alone by Jabbok; then he becomes a wrestler in the midst of the host of sinners, conquering them for Christ, taking them captive in the name of the Most High. Power in prayer is the highest form of power; and communion with God is power; and holiness, above all things, is a great power among the sons of men.

This spiritual power makes a man influential in a sense very different from that in which the world uses the word *influential*—a disgraceful use of the word. We want men who have influence in the most divine sense, men who, somehow or other, cast a spell over their fellow men. In their presence men cannot do what they are accustomed to do elsewhere; when these men are in any company, they check sin without a word; they incite to righteousness almost without a sentence. They carry everything before them, not by might, nor by power, but by the Spirit of the Lord who dwells in them.

Through the Bible in One Year: Proverbs 16–18

Transformed Lives

Do you not know that the wicked will not inherit the kingdom of God?
Do not be deceived: Neither the sexually immoral nor idolaters nor
adulterers nor male prostitutes nor homosexual offenders nor thieves
nor the greedy nor drunkards nor slanderers nor swindlers will inherit
the kingdom of God. And that is what some of you were.
But you were washed, you were sanctified, you were justified
in the name of the Lord Jesus Christ and by the Spirit of our God.
1 CORINTHIANS 6:9–11

Our Lord is a great transformer of character. I do not like to speak of myself, but I will speak of many a man whom I know. He came into this tabernacle a drunkard, a swearer, a lover of unholy pleasures, and while the Word was preached, the Lord broke him down and melted his heart. Now he hates what once he loved, and as to those pursuits that were once distasteful to him, so that he cursed and swore at the very mention of them, or at least poured ridicule upon others who loved them, he now loves them himself, and it is a wonder to himself to find himself where he now is. Ask his wife whether there is a change in him; ask his little children whether there is a change in him; ask his workmates, ask his employer, ask anybody, and they will all say, "He is not the same man." Oh, if there are any who would learn the way of righteousness and quit the paths of sin, let them believe my testimony, which comes not out of feigned lips! "I speak the truth in Christ, and lie not" (1 Timothy 2:7 KJV). The Lord is able to transform character in a very wonderful way; he has done it for many of us, and if you believe in him, he will do it for you also.

Through the Bible in One Year: Proverbs 19–21

New Evidence

*News of this reached the ears of the church at Jerusalem,
and they sent Barnabas to Antioch. When he arrived
and saw the evidence of the grace of God, he was glad and encouraged
them all to remain true to the Lord with all their hearts.*
Acts 11:22–23

The Spirit of God coming from Christ moves men to high and noble thoughts. Selfishness no longer rules the man who believes in Christ; he loves his fellow men, he desires their good, he can forgive them if they persecute him, he can lay down his life for them. Have we not had many who have gone forth among the heathen and laid down their lives for Christ? I was speaking with a brother from the Congo, and I spoke of the many deaths there, and he said, "Yes, it looks a sad thing that so many missionaries should die; but, sir," he added, "that is the first thing that we have done in Africa that is really hopeful. I have often heard the natives say to me, 'These men must believe a true religion, or else they would not come here to die for us poor black men.' Men begin to believe this new kind of evidence. The blood of the missionary becomes the seed of the church." I do not doubt that it is so; and, beloved, if you and I can live wholly and alone for Christ, if we can live nobly, if we can get out of ourselves, if we can rise superior to worldly advantages and prove that we believe all we say, we shall convince our fellow men of the truth of our religion.

Through the Bible in One Year: Proverbs 22–24

Repentance

*And repentance and forgiveness of sins will be preached
in his name to all nations, beginning at Jerusalem.*
LUKE 24:47

I am glad to find in this verse that old-fashioned virtue called
repentance. It used to be preached, but it has gone out of fashion
now. Indeed, we are told that we always misunderstood the meaning of the word *repentance* and that it simply means a "change of
mind" and nothing more. I wish that those who are so wise in their
Greek knew a little more of that language, for they would not be
so ready with their infallible statements. Gospel repentance is a
change of mind of the most radical sort—such a change as never
was wrought in any man except by the Spirit of God.

We are also to preach the motives of repentance—that men
may not repent from mere fear of hell, but they must repent of sin
itself. Every thief is sorry when he has to go to prison; every murderer is sorry when the noose is about his neck; the sinner must
repent, not because of the punishment of sin, but because his sin
is sin against a pardoning God, sin against a bleeding Savior, sin
against a holy law, sin against a tender gospel. The true penitent
repents of sin against God, and he would do so even if there were
no punishment.

We are to tell of the source of repentance, namely, that the
Lord Jesus Christ is exalted on high to give repentance and remis-
sion of sins. Repentance is a plant that never grows on nature's
dunghill: the nature must be changed, and repentance must be
implanted by the Holy Spirit, or it will never flourish in our
hearts. We preach repentance as a fruit of the Spirit, or else we
greatly err.

Through the Bible in One Year: Proverbs 25–27

October 3

Try It

The word of the LORD came to me, saying, "Before I formed you
in the womb I knew you, before you were born I set you apart;
I appointed you as a prophet to the nations."

"Ah, Sovereign LORD," I said, "I do not know how to speak;
I am only a child."

But the LORD said to me, "Do not say, 'I am only a child.'
You must go to everyone I send you to and say whatever I command you."
JEREMIAH 1:4–7

If we have a very strong aversion to a certain form of Christian work, instead of taking that aversion as a token that we are not called to it, we may regard it as a sign that we ought at least to try it. The devil knows you better than you know yourself. You see, he has been longer in the world than you have, and he knows a great deal more about human nature than you do; and so he comes to you, and he reckons you up pretty accurately and says, "This brother would be very useful in a certain sphere of labor, and I must keep him from it." So he tells the brother that he is not called to it, that it is not the sort of thing for him, and so on; and then he says to himself, "I have turned aside one foe from harming my cause."

Yonder is a good sister. Oh, how much she might do for Christ, but Satan guides her into a work in which she will never shine, while the holy work she could do right well is dreaded by her. We lose hosts of opportunities; I am sure we do. Many ways of doing good have never occurred to our minds, but they ought to occur to us; and when they do occur we should use them.

Through the Bible in One Year: Proverbs 28–29

Glorious Opposition

Finally, brothers, pray for us that the message of the Lord
may spread rapidly and be honored, just as it was with you.
And pray that we may be delivered from wicked and evil men,
for not everyone has faith. But the Lord is faithful,
and he will strengthen and protect you from the evil one.

2 THESSALONIANS 3:1–3

Nothing is much better for the gospel than opposition. A man comes into the tabernacle tonight, and as he goes away, he says, "Yes, I was pleased and satisfied." In that man's case I have failed. But another man keeps biting his tongue, for he cannot endure the preaching. He is very angry: something in the doctrine does not suit him, and he cries, "As long as I live, I will never come here again." That man is hopeful. He begins to think. The hook has taken hold of him. Give us time, and we will have that fish. It is no ill omen when a man gets angry with the gospel. It is bad enough, but it is infinitely better than that horrible lethargy into which men fall when they do not think. Be hopeful of the man who will not let you speak to him; he is one you must approach again. And if, when he does let you speak to him, he seems as if he would spit on you, be grateful for it. He feels your words. You are touching him on a sore place. You will have him yet. When he swears that he does not believe a word of what you say, do not believe a word of what *he* says, for often the man who openly objects secretly believes. Just as boys whistle when they go through a churchyard in order to keep their courage up, so many a blasphemer is profane in order to silence his conscience.

Through the Bible in One Year: Proverbs 30–31

At Work for Christ

*So, because Jesus was doing these things on the Sabbath,
the Jews persecuted him. Jesus said to them,
"My Father is always at his work to this very day,
and I, too, am working."*
JOHN 5:16–17

I think a strong church is a very valuable institution, but I have always deprecated the idea that all of you should sit here Sunday after Sunday and listen to me, and I have spoken to some of you to such purpose that I do not often see you now. Nor do I want to see you, because I know you are serving the Master elsewhere. There are some of our brethren who only come here to the Communion; why? Because they are always at work for Christ in some way or other. They are the best members we have, and we shall not cross their names off the roll because they are not in attendance here. They are at work in some mission station, or trying to open a new room for preaching, or doing something or other for the Master; the Lord bless them! Scatter as widely as ever you can the blessing that you get for yourself; the moment you find the light and realize that the world is in the dark, run away with your match, and lend somebody else a light. If you go to others and say, "I shall have none the less light because I give some to you," by this means God the Holy Spirit will pour upon you fresh beams of light, and you shall shine brighter and brighter even to the perfect day.

Through the Bible in One Year: 1 Peter 1–2

The Lion of Judah

*How beautiful on the mountains are the feet of those
who bring good news, who proclaim peace, who bring good tidings,
who proclaim salvation, who say to Zion, "Your God reigns!"*
ISAIAH 52:7

I believe the best way of defending the gospel is to spread the gospel. A great many learned men are defending the gospel; no doubt it is a very proper and right thing to do, yet I always notice that when there are most books of that kind, it is because the gospel itself is not being preached. Suppose a number of persons were to take it into their heads that they had to defend a lion, a full-grown king of beasts! There he is in the cage, and here come all the soldiers of the army to fight for him. Well, I should suggest to them, if they would not object and feel that it was humbling to them, that they should kindly stand back and open the door and let the lion out! I believe that would be the best way of defending him, for he would take care of himself; and the best "apology" for the gospel is to let the gospel out. Never mind about defending Deuteronomy or the whole of the Pentateuch; preach Jesus Christ and him crucified. Let the Lion out, and see who will dare to approach him. The Lion of the tribe of Judah will soon drive away all his adversaries.

Through the Bible in One Year: 1 Peter 3–5

The God of Variety

Have you comprehended the vast expanses of the earth?
Tell me, if you know all this.
JOB 38:18

If it be true that "order is heaven's first law," I think it must be equally true that variety is the second law of heaven. The line of beauty is not a straight line, but always the curve. The way of God's procedure is not uniform, but diversified. You see this with a glance when you look at the creation around us. God has not made all creatures of one species, but he has created beasts, birds, fishes, insects, reptiles. In any one of the kingdoms of nature, whether it be the animal, vegetable, or mineral, you shall find so many subdivisions that it would need a long schooling to classify them, and a lifetime would not suffice to understand them all.

Certainly this observation holds good in providence. What strange diversity there has been in the dealings of God with his church! Every sinner must be quickened by the same life, made obedient to the same gospel, washed in the same blood, clothed in the same righteousness, filled with the same divine energy, and eventually taken up to the same heaven, and yet in the conversion of no two sinners will you find matters precisely the same; but from the first dawn of the divine life to the day when it is consummated in the noontide of perfect sanctification in heaven, you shall find that God works this way in that one, and that way in the other, and by another method in the third; for God still will be the God of variety.

Through the Bible in One Year: Ecclesiastes 1–4

Look for the Cause

※

After Jesus had gone indoors, his disciples asked him privately,
"Why couldn't we drive it out?"

MARK 9:28

When we are baffled, there must be a cause, and it is well for us to try to find it out. We must go to the Master and ask, "Why could not we cast him out?"

This inquiry, if it leads up to a correct answer, is evidently a very wise one, for every man ought to try to know all he can about himself. If I am successful, why is it that I succeed? Let me know the secret, that I may put the crown on the right head. If I do not succeed, let me know the reason why, that I may at any rate try to remove any impediment, if it be an impediment of my own making. If I am a vessel that is not fit for the Master's use, let me know why I am not fit, that I may, as much as lies in me, prepare myself for the great Master's service. I know that if I am fit to be used, he is sure to use me; and if he does not use me, it will most probably be because there is some unfitness in me.

For whatever may be the reason of your failure, it may be cured. In all probability, it is not a great matter, certainly not an insuperable difficulty to the Lord. By the grace of God, this hindrance may be taken away from you and no longer be allowed to rob you of your power. Search it out, then; look with both your eyes, and search with the brightest light that you can borrow, that you may find out everything that restrains the Spirit of God and injures your own usefulness.

Through the Bible in One Year: Ecclesiastes 5–8

Preparation

David said, "My son Solomon is young and inexperienced,
and the house to be built for the LORD should be of great magnificence
and fame and splendor in the sight of all the nations.
Therefore I will make preparations for it."
So David made extensive preparations before his death.
1 CHRONICLES 22:5

In the early dawn of Christian history, there was a preparation of the church before it received an increase. Look at the obedient disciples sitting in the upper room, waiting with anxious hope: every heart there had been plowed with anguish by the death of the Lord; each one was intent to receive the promised boon of the Spirit. There, with one heart and one mind, they tarried, but not without wrestling in prayer, and so the Comforter was given, and three thousand souls were given also.

A man with no sensibility or compassion for other men's souls may accidentally be the means of a conversion; the good word that he utters will not cease to be good because the speaker had no right to declare God's statutes. But as a rule, those who bring souls to Christ are those who first of all have felt an agony of desire that souls should be saved.

This is imaged to us in our Master's character. He is the great Savior of men, but before he could save others, he learned in their flesh to sympathize with them. He wept over Jerusalem; he sweat great drops of blood in Gethsemane; he was, and is, a High Priest who is touched with the feeling of our infirmities. As the Captain of our salvation, in bringing many sons unto glory, he was made perfect by sufferings. Even Christ went not forth to preach until he had spent nights in intercessory prayer and uttered strong cryings and tears for the salvation of his hearers.

Through the Bible in One Year: Ecclesiastes 9–12

Even a Few

Jonathan said to his young armor-bearer,
"Come, let's go over to the outpost of those uncircumcised fellows.
Perhaps the LORD will act in our behalf. Nothing can hinder
the LORD from saving, whether by many or by few."
1 SAMUEL 14:6

Usually when God intends greatly to bless a church, it will begin
in this way: Two or three persons in it are distressed at the low
state of affairs and become troubled even to anguish. Perhaps they
do not speak to one another or know of their common grief, but
they begin to pray with flaming desire and untiring importunity.
The passion to see the church revived rules them. They think of
it when they go to rest, they dream of it on their bed, they muse on
it in the streets. This one thing eats them up. They suffer great
heaviness and continual sorrow in heart for perishing sinners; they
travail in birth for souls. When the sun rises, the mountaintops
first catch the light, and those who constantly live near to God
will be the first to feel the influence of the coming refreshing. The
Lord give me a dozen importunate pleaders and lovers of souls,
and by his grace we will shake all London from end to end yet.
The work would go on without the mass of you Christians—
many of you only hinder the march of the army. But give us a
dozen lionlike, lamblike men, burning with intense love to Christ
and souls, and nothing will be impossible to their faith.

Through the Bible in One Year: 2 Peter 1–3

Through the Church

And he directed the people to sit down on the grass.
Taking the five loaves and the two fish and looking up to heaven,
he gave thanks and broke the loaves. Then he gave them to the disciples,
and the disciples gave them to the people. They all ate and were satisfied,
and the disciples picked up twelve basketfuls of broken pieces
that were left over. The number of those who ate
was about five thousand men, besides women and children.
MATTHEW 14:19–21

The world is perishing for lack of knowledge. Did anyone among us ever lay China on his heart? Your imagination cannot grapple with the population of that mighty empire, without God, without Christ, strangers to the commonwealth of Israel. But it is not China alone; there are other vast nations lying in darkness; the great serpent has coiled himself around the globe, and who shall set the world free from him? Reflect upon this one city with its millions. What sin the moon sees! What sin the Sabbath sees! Alas, for the transgressions of this wicked city. Babylon of old could not have been worse than London is, nor so guilty, for she had not the light that London has received. Brethren, there is no hope for China, no hope for the world, no hope for our own city, while the church is sluggish and lethargic. It is through the church the blessing is bestowed. Christ multiplies the bread and gives it to the disciples; the multitudes can only get it through the disciples. Oh, it is time, it is high time that the churches were awakened to seek the good of dying myriads.

Through the Bible in One Year: Song of Songs 1–4

More Important Than Breath

If my people, who are called by my name, will humble themselves
and pray and seek my face and turn from their wicked ways,
then will I hear from heaven and will forgive their sin
and will heal their land. Now my eyes will be open
and my ears attentive to the prayers offered in this place.

2 CHRONICLES 7:14–15

Never rest from prayer because you are weary of it. Whenever prayer becomes distasteful, it should be a loud call to pray all the more. No man has such need to pray as the man who does not care to pray. When you can pray and long to pray, why, then you will pray; but when you cannot pray and do not wish to pray, why, then you must pray, or evil will come of it. He is on the brink of ruin who forgets the mercy seat. When the heart is apathetic toward prayer, the whole man is sickening from a grievous disease. How can we be weary of prayer? It is essential to life. When a man grows weary of breathing, surely he is near to dying: when a man grows weary of praying, surely we ought to pray anxiously for him, for he is in an evil case.

Through the Bible in One Year: Song of Songs 5–8

Our Highest Calling

Praise be to the God and Father of our Lord Jesus Christ!
In his great mercy he has given us new birth into a living hope
through the resurrection of Jesus Christ from the dead,
and into an inheritance that can never perish, spoil or fade—
kept in heaven for you, who through faith are shielded
by God's power until the coming of the salvation
that is ready to be revealed in the last time.

1 PETER 1:3–5

It seems to be the opinion of a large party in the present day that the object of the Christian effort should be to *educate* men. I grant you that education is in itself an exceedingly valuable thing, so valuable that I am sure the whole Christian church rejoices greatly that we have a national system of education, which only needs to be carefully carried out and every child in this land will have the keys of knowledge in his hand. But if the church of God thinks that it is sent into the world merely to train the mental faculties, it has made a very serious mistake, for the object of Christianity is not to educate men for their secular callings, or even to train them in the politer arts or the more elegant professions, or to enable them to enjoy the beauties of nature or the charms of poetry. Jesus Christ came not into the world for any of these things, but he came to seek and to save that which was lost, and on the same errand has he sent his church, and she is a traitor to the Master who sent her if she is beguiled by the beauties of taste and art to forget that to preach Christ and him crucified is the only object for which she exists among the sons of men. The business of the church is salvation.

Through the Bible in One Year: 1 John 1–5

All Things to All Men

Though I am free and belong to no man,
I make myself a slave to everyone, to win as many as possible.
1 CORINTHIANS 9:19

Paul went to his work always with an intense sympathy for those he dealt with—a sympathy that made him adapt himself to each case. If he talked to a Jew, he did not begin at once blurting out that he was the apostle of the Gentiles, but he said he was a Jew, as Jew he was. He raised no questions about nationalities or ceremonies. He wanted to tell the Jew of him of whom Isaiah said, "He is despised and rejected of men; a man of sorrows, and acquainted with grief" (Isaiah 53:3 KJV), in order that he might believe in Jesus and so be saved. If he met a Gentile, the apostle of the Gentiles never showed any of the squeamishness that might have been expected to cling to him on account of his Jewish education. He ate as the Gentile ate, and drank as he did, sat with him, and talked with him; he was, as it were, a Gentile with him, never raising any question about circumcision or uncircumcision, but solely wishing to tell him of Christ, who came into the world to save both Jew and Gentile and to make them one. If he met a Greek, he spoke to him as he did at the Areopagus, with language that was fitted for the polished Athenian. He was all things to all men, that he might by all means save some.

So with you, Christian people: your one business in life is to lead men to believe in Jesus Christ by the power of the Holy Spirit, and every other thing should be made subservient to this one object. If you can but get them saved, everything else will come right in due time.

Through the Bible in One Year: Isaiah 1–4

Godlike

*I have become all things to all men so that by all possible means
I might save some. I do all this for the sake of the gospel,
that I may share in its blessings.*

1 CORINTHIANS 9:22–23

To long for the conversion of others makes us godlike. Do we desire man's welfare? God does so. Would we fain snatch them from the burning? God is daily performing this deed of grace. Can we say that we have no pleasure in the death of him who dies? Jehovah has declared the like with an oath. Do we weep over sinners? Did not Jehovah's Son weep over them? Do we lay out ourselves for their conversion? Did he not die that they might live? You are made godlike when this passion glows within your spirit.

This is a vent for your love to God as well as your love to men. Loving the Creator, we pity his fallen creatures and feel a benevolent love toward the work of his hands. If we love God, we feel as he does, that judgment is his strange work, and we cannot bear that those whom he has created should be cast away forever. Loving God makes us sorrow that all men do not love him too. It frets us that the world lies in the wicked one, at enmity to its own Creator, at war with him who alone can bless it.

If we love others, we shall, like Paul, become wise to attract them, wise to persuade them, wise to convince them, wise to encourage them; we shall learn to use means that had lain rusted by, and discover in ourselves talents that else had been hidden in the ground if the strong desire to save men had not cleared away the soil.

Through the Bible in One Year: Isaiah 5 – 8

Tear Down the Idols

*"Do not turn to idols or make gods of cast metal for yourselves.
I am the LORD your God."*
LEVITICUS 19:4

In all ages since the fall, there has been a tendency in the human heart to forget God and get away from him. Idolatry has been the sin of all nations, including God's favored people, the Jews, and including certain persons who call themselves Christians and yet make idols out of crosses and images. This vicious principle of ignoring God and setting up something between our minds and our Creator, crops up everywhere, in every department of thought.

When men study the works of God in nature, they often hang up a veil to hide the great Worker. Because God acts in a certain way, they call his method of action a law, and straightway they speak of these laws as if they were forces and powers in and of themselves, and thus God is banished out of his own universe, and his place is taken up in the scientific world by idols called "natural laws."

Take the region of providence, and here you find persons, instead of seeing the hand of God everywhere, looking to second causes; seeking causes of prosperity and becoming very despondent if they do not appear to exist; or viewing the agents of affliction and becoming angry against them, instead of bowing before the God who has used them for correction. It is easy to make idols out of second causes and to forget the God who is everywhere present, causing all things to work together for good. That this evil principle should intrude into the church is very sad, and yet it is with difficulty excluded. You may bar all your doors as fast as you please, but the idol makers will come in with their shrines.

Elbow Room

❧

Who are you to judge someone else's servant?
To his own master he stands or falls.
And he will stand, for the Lord is able to make him stand.
ROMANS 14:4

If we are all under one Master, do not let us quarrel. It is a great pity when ministers harshly criticize one another and when Sunday-school teachers do the same. It is a miserable business when we cannot bear to see good being done by those of a different denomination who work in ways of their own. If a new laborer comes on the farm, and he wears a coat of a new cut and uses a hoe of a new shape, shall I become his enemy? If he does his work better than I do mine, shall I be jealous?

Brother, if the great Lord has employed you, it is no business of mine to question his right. I do not like the look of you and cannot think how he can have such a fellow upon the farm; but as *he* has employed you, I have no right to judge you, for I daresay I look as strange in your eyes as you do in mine. If new methods of getting a hearing for the gospel are invented by the ingenuity of earnestness, let the brethren use them; and if we cannot imitate them, let us at least feel that we are still one, because "one is our Master, even Christ."

Through the Bible in One Year: Isaiah 13–16

Have Faith in God

Now faith is being sure of what we hope for and certain
of what we do not see. This is what the ancients were commended for.
HEBREWS 11:1–2

Whenever God has done a mighty work, it has been by some very insignificant instrument. When he slew Goliath it was by little David, who was but a ruddy youth. When God would slay Sisera, it was by a woman who must do it with a hammer and a nail. God has done his mightiest works by the meanest instruments: that is a fact most true of all God's works. Peter the fisherman at Pentecost, Luther the humble monk at the Reformation, Whitefield the potboy of the Old Bell Inn at Gloucester in the time of the last century's revival; and so it must be to the end. God works not by Pharaoh's horses or chariot, but he works by Moses' rod; he does not his wonders with the whirlwind and the storm, but he does them by the still, small voice that the glory may be his and the honor all his own.

Does not this open a field of encouragement to you and to me? Why may not we be employed in doing mighty work for God here? Moreover, we have noticed in all these stories of God's mighty works in the olden time that wherever he has done any great thing, it has been by someone who has had very great faith. Men of great faith do great things. It was Elijah's faith that slew the priests of Baal. It was the same with Whitefield; he believed and he expected that God would do great things. When he went into his pulpit, he believed that God would bless the people, and God did do so. Little faith may do little things, but great faith shall be greatly honored.

Through the Bible in One Year: Isaiah 17–20

Past, Present, and Future

※

"The days are coming," declares the LORD,
"when the reaper will be overtaken by the plowman
and the planter by the one treading grapes."

AMOS 9:13

When people hear about what God used to do, one of the things they say is, "Oh, that was a very long while ago." They imagine that times have altered since then. Others among you say, "Oh, well, I look upon these things as great prodigies—miracles. We are not to expect them every day." That is the very reason why we do not get them. If we had learned to expect them, we should no doubt obtain them, but we put them up on a shelf, as being out of the common order of our moderate religion, as being mere curiosities of Scripture history. We imagine such things, however true, to be prodigies of Providence; we cannot imagine them to be according to the ordinary working of his mighty power. I beseech you, my friends, abjure that idea, put it out of your mind. Whatever God has done in the way of converting sinners is to be looked upon as a precedent, for "the LORD's hand is not shortened, that it cannot save; neither his ear heavy, that it cannot hear" (Isaiah 59:1 KJV). Has God changed? Is he not an immutable God, the same yesterday, today, and forever? Does not that furnish an argument to prove that what God has done at one time he can do at another? Nay, I think I may push it a little further and say what he has done once is a prophecy of what he intends to do again—that the mighty works that have been accomplished in the olden time shall all be repeated, and the Lord's song shall be sung again in Zion, and he shall again be greatly glorified.

Through the Bible in One Year: Isaiah 21–24

Hating Our Sin

And now, dear children, continue in him, so that when he appears
we may be confident and unashamed before him at his coming.
1 JOHN 2:28

The law of God, when it says to us, "Thou shalt not," only sets up a danger signal to tell us where it is injurious to go. And when the law says, "Thou shalt," it does but lift up a kindly hand to point out to us the best and safest path. There is nothing in the law of God that will rob you of happiness; it only denies you that which would cost you sorrow. We know that it is so, and therefore we stand here and bow our head and mourn that we should have been so foolish as to transgress, so willfully and suicidally wicked as to do that evil thing that God hates and that so grievously injures us.

You remember that I am talking to those of you who are saved, to those of you whose sins are forgiven. In my heart, I think that I can hear some others say, "Will you not let us join with you in repenting, though we are not pardoned?" Bless your hearts, yes, yes! God help you to join with us; and if you do, you will find pardon too, for pardon comes in this way!

Beloved, the more you love your Lord, the more you will hate sin. If you often sit at the table with him and dip your hand into his dish, if you lean your head upon his bosom with the blessed John, if you are favored and indulged with the choicest brotherliness toward the Well Beloved, I know that you will often find occasion to seek a quiet place where you may shed tears of bitter regret that you should ever have sinned against such a Savior as Jesus is.

Through the Bible in One Year: Isaiah 25–28

We Were There

❧

So then, just as you received Christ Jesus as Lord,
continue to live in him, rooted and built up in him,
strengthened in the faith as you were taught,
and overflowing with thankfulness.
COLOSSIANS 2:6–7

The greatest crime that was ever committed against high heaven was that crime of deicide, when men nailed the Son of God to the tree and put him to death as a criminal. Where are the wretches that did this awful deed? They are *here*; I will not say that they are before us, for each of us harbors one of them within his bosom. How can I speak to you thus? Well, perhaps, all the better, because from my very heart I ask that we may stand together at the foot of the cross and count the purple drops and say, "These have washed away my sins, yet I helped to spill them. Those hands, those feet, have saved me, yet I nailed them there. That opened side is the refuge of my guilty spirit, yet I made that fearful gash by my sin. It was my sin that slew my Savior." O sin, you thrice-accursed thing, away with you! Away with you! Come, let us be filled with mournful joy, with pleasurable sorrow, while we sit beneath the bloody tree and see what sin has done, and yet see how sin itself has been undone by him who died upon the cross of Calvary.

Through the Bible in One Year: Isaiah 29–32

Our Dearest Friend

But when the kindness and love of God our Savior appeared,
he saved us, not because of righteous things we had done,
but because of his mercy. He saved us through the washing of rebirth
and renewal by the Holy Spirit, whom he poured out on us generously
through Jesus Christ our Savior, so that, having been justified
by his grace, we might become heirs having the hope of eternal life.
TITUS 3:4–7

Oh, what do we not owe to the Holy Spirit? I speak to you who know him. It is the Holy Ghost who quickened you, the Holy Ghost who convinced you of sin, the Holy Ghost who comforted you; and oh, how sweetly does that Divine Comforter still comfort! Yet we resisted him and grieved him. Do you not remember, in your youthful days, how you strangled your convictions, how you held down conscience and would not let it reprove you? That blessed Spirit, whom we vexed and spurned, might have left us and gone his way, never to strive with us again; but he loved us so that he came and took up his abode with us, and now he dwells in us. Within the narrow cell of our poor heart, he had condescended to find a temple for his perpetual indwelling. O my soul, how could you ever grieve him? How could you ever have resisted that best and most tender Friend?

Through the Bible in One Year: Isaiah 33–36

Heavenly Protection

*Are not all angels ministering spirits sent
to serve those who will inherit salvation?*
HEBREWS 1:14

How safe and happy we ought to feel when we know that God has charged the angels to take care of us! Do not be so nervous, my dear sister, the next time there is a little storm, or even a great storm. Do not be afraid, my dear friend, when sickness comes into your house.

How holy we ought to be with such holy beings watching over us! If the angels are always hovering round you, mind what you are at. Would you have spoken as you did when you were coming in at that door yonder if you had seen an angel standing by your side, listening to what you were saying? Oh no; you are wonderfully decorous when there is somebody near whom you respect! How often your glib tongue is checked when there is some Christian man or woman, whom you highly esteem, within hearing! How many a thing is done that would not be done under the eye of one whom you love! Whether we are alone or in company, let us not sin, because angels are ever watching us, and the angels' Lord is also watching us. May he graciously keep us in his holy way, and if we are so kept, we shall be preserved from all evil while we are here, and at last we shall see his face with joy and abide with him forever.

Through the Bible in One Year: Isaiah 37–40

Not as It Seems

When I tried to understand all this,
it was oppressive to me till I entered the sanctuary of God;
then I understood their final destiny.
PSALM 73:16–17

There are times when the wicked seem to have things all their own way. This earth is not the realm of final justice; we are not yet standing before the Lord's great judgment seat. God permits many things to be for a while in confusion. They who are highest with him are often lowest with them; and those for whom he has no regard seem to heap up the treasures of the world till their eyes stand out with fatness, and they have more than heart can wish. Let no child of God be astonished at this arrangement.

It is still true that the wicked triumph and the servants of iniquity delight themselves in the high places of the earth. The righteous need not wonder that they suffer now, for that has been the lot of God's people all along, and there have been certain times in human history when God has seemed to be altogether deaf to the cries of his suffering people.

At such times too, we have proved the power of the Word of God. When your vessel is sailing along very smoothly, the Word of God may grow to be a dead letter with you; but when the waves are rolling mountains high and dashing over you, and you are soaked through and through and fear that the deep will swallow you up, then you begin to test the promises and to prove the power of the Word of God. When its inexpressible sweetness reaches your heart, then you can indeed feel that you have been taught out of God's Word. You see that "blessed is the man whom thou chastenest, O LORD, and teachest him out of thy law" (Psalm 94:12 KJV).

Love and Discipline

*In your struggle against sin, you have not yet resisted
to the point of shedding your blood. And you have forgotten
that word of encouragement that addresses you as sons:
"My son, do not make light of the Lord's discipline,
and do not lose heart when he rebukes you, because the Lord disciplines
those he loves, and he punishes everyone he accepts as a son."*

*Endure hardship as discipline; God is treating you as sons.
For what son is not disciplined by his father?*
HEBREWS 12:4–7

Our God is constant in his affection and merciful toward his children; when they go astray, he pities all their guilt and sin. It is true he takes the rod into his hand and sometimes causes them to weep bitterly by reason of the soreness of his chastisement. He applies the rod to their very soul and brings the iron into their inmost spirit; he makes them smart and cry and groan and sigh; but all he does is in pity, because he is determined to save them. He will not let them go unpunished, because he pities them for their folly and their sin. Just as the physician will not let the man go without his medicine, because he pities him in his disease, so God will not let his children go without his chastisement, because he pities them in their sin. And mark too that even this chastisement is one of pity; there is not one twig too many in the rod, nor one stroke over the right number, not one drop of gall too much, and that drop is none too bitter; the affliction is all measured out and weighed in balances and scales, all given as it should be—no more than there is a needs-be for.

Through the Bible in One Year: Isaiah 45 – 48

A Holy Fragance

But thanks be to God, who always leads us in triumphal procession
in Christ and through us spreads everywhere the fragrance
of the knowledge of him. For we are to God the aroma of Christ
among those who are being saved and those who are perishing.
To the one we are the smell of death; to the other, the fragrance of life.
2 CORINTHIANS 2:14–16

The Lord Jesus Christ communicates much to men with whom he comes in contact and has a mighty influence upon them. He is blessed, and he is made a blessing. To those who love him, Jesus Christ becomes a savor of life unto life. To those who are rebellious and continue to despise him, he becomes a savor of death unto death. Our Savior, then, has an influence upon all those with whom he comes in contact and association. If I compare his human nature with clay, I must compare it with the scented clay, which yields a perfume on all sides. You cannot hear of Jesus Christ without either getting a blessing or rejecting a blessing. I repeat it—he becomes a blessing to all those who are round about him, or else, if that blessing be not received, it brings guilt upon the souls of those who reject him. He is either the stone on which we build our hope and our trust, or else he becomes a stone of stumbling and a rock of offense to those who stumble at his Word, being disobedient.

Through the Bible in One Year: Isaiah 49–52

Loyal Subject or Enemy?

Then I looked and heard the voice of many angels,
numbering thousands upon thousands, and ten thousand
times ten thousand. They encircled the throne and the living creatures
and the elders. In a loud voice they sang: "Worthy is the Lamb,
who was slain, to receive power and wealth and wisdom
and strength and honor and glory and praise!"
REVELATION 5:11–12

It is no use for a man to say concerning a monarch, "I have a great respect for the monarch in his private character. I would not do anything to injure him; I would even hold him up to respect in his private character. But as a king I will never yield him loyal homage; I will never obey him. Indeed, I will do all I can to pluck the crown from off his head." Could the king do otherwise than reckon such a person to be his enemy? It would be in vain for the man to say, "I am privately your friend." The king would say, "Oh, but I esteem my crown to be as precious as my life." So the Lord Jesus Christ cannot have the crown rights of his true deity touched. He "thought it not robbery to be equal with God" (Philippians 2:6 KJV), and he is called "God over all, blessed forevermore" (Romans 9:5). He who trod the waves of Galilee's lake, whose voice death heard and gave up its prey, he who opened the gates of paradise to the dying robber, claims to be none other than equal with the Eternal Father, and like him "God over all," and it is in vain for you to say you respect his character as a man if you do not accept him in his deity. Unless you accept him in his official character as the Savior of sinners, you cannot be otherwise than numbered amongst his enemies.

Through the Bible in One Year: Isaiah 53–56

Such a Kinsman

"He has not stopped showing his kindness to the living and the dead."
She added, "That man is our close relative;
he is one of our kinsman-redeemers."
RUTH 2:20

Our temptation is to regard the Lord's humanity as something quite different from our own; we are apt to spiritualize it away and not to think of him as really bone of our bone and flesh of our flesh. All this is akin to grievous error; we may fancy that we are honoring Christ by such conception, but Christ is never honored by that which is not true. He was a man, a real man, a man of our race, the Son of Man; indeed, a representative man, the second Adam: "As the children are partakers of flesh and blood, he also himself likewise took part of the same" (Hebrews 2:14 KJV).

Now this condescending participation in our nature brings the Lord Jesus very near to us in relationship. Inasmuch as he was man, though also God, he was, according to Hebrew law, our *goel*—our kinsman, next of kin. Now it was according to the law that if an inheritance had been lost, it was the right of the next of kin to redeem it. Our Lord Jesus exercised his legal right, and seeing us sold into bondage and our inheritance taken from us, he came forward to redeem both us and all our lost estate. A blessed thing it was for us that we had such a kinsman. When Ruth went to glean in the fields of Boaz, it was the most gracious circumstance in her life that Boaz turned out to be her next of kin; and we who have gleaned in the fields of mercy praise the Lord that his only begotten Son is the next of kin to us, our brother, born for adversity.

Through the Bible in One Year: Isaiah 57–60

Redemptive Election

Paul, a servant of God and an apostle of Jesus Christ for the faith
of God's elect and the knowledge of the truth that leads to godliness.
TITUS 1:1

Now there is one doctrine in Scripture that is peculiar to the Father. It is the doctrine of election. The Father has chosen us to be his people. Everywhere in Scripture it is put down as the work of the first person of the blessed Trinity—to choose a people to himself that shall show forth his praise. Now there are many persons who want to get at that doctrine. I have known many unconverted people who wanted to understand it. I get letters frequently from persons troubled about it. They say that they should feel peace if they could understand that doctrine. But if any such are here tonight, I will speak to them. You cannot get to election; you cannot get to the Father by a direct road from where you are. Just read that signpost: "No man cometh unto the Father, but by [Christ]" (John 14:6 KJV). If, then, you want to understand election, begin with redemption. You will never understand the eternal choice till you begin at the cross. Begin with this: "God was in Christ reconciling the world unto himself, not imputing their trespasses unto them" (2 Corinthians 5:19 KJV).

It would be a strange thing if our children would insist upon going to the university before they went to the grammar school. It would be an odd thing indeed if every man who took down his Bible should always begin it backwards and read first the Revelation, and if every man read the Lord's Prayer beginning at "Amen" and went backwards to "Our Father"; yet some minds will persist in this. There is a charm to them about the mystery of sovereignty and election, and they must begin with that. There is no way to election except through redemption.

Through the Bible in One Year: Isaiah 61–63

Begin and End with Christ

❧

The law was added so that the trespass might increase.
But where sin increased, grace increased all the more,
so that, just as sin reigned in death, so also grace might reign through
righteousness to bring eternal life through Jesus Christ our Lord.
ROMANS 5:20–21

Every day I find it most healthy to my own soul to try to walk as a saint, but in order to do so, I must continually come to Christ as a sinner. I would seek to be perfect, I would strain after every virtue and forsake every false way, but still, as to my standing before God, I find it happiest to sit where I sat when I first looked to Jesus, on the rock of his works, having nothing to do with my own righteousness, but only with his. Depend on it: the happiest way of living is to live as a poor sinner and as nothing at all, having Jesus Christ as all in all. You may have all your growths in sanctification, all your progress in graces, all the development of your virtues that you will; but still I do earnestly pray you never to put any of these where Christ should be. If you have begun in Christ, then finish in Christ. If you have begun in the flesh and then go on in the flesh, we know what the sure result will be. But if you have begun with Jesus Christ as your Alpha, let him be your Omega. I pray you never think you are rising when you get above this, for it is not rising, but slipping downwards to your ruin.

Through the Bible in One Year: Isaiah 64–66

Practical Godliness

*As I urged you when I went into Macedonia, stay there in Ephesus
so that you may command certain men not to teach false doctrines
any longer nor to devote themselves to myths and endless genealogies.
These promote controversies rather than God's work—which is by faith.
The goal of this command is love, which comes from a pure heart
and a good conscience and a sincere faith. Some have wandered away
from these and turned to meaningless talk.*

1 TIMOTHY 1:3–6

Some Christians are very curious, but not obedient. Plain precepts
are neglected, but difficult problems they seek to solve. I remember one who used always to be dwelling upon the vials and seals
and trumpets. He was great at apocalyptic symbols, but he had
seven children, and he had no family prayer. If he had left the vials
and trumpets and minded his boys and girls, it would have been
a deal better. I have known men marvelously great upon Daniel,
and specially instructed in Ezekiel, but singularly forgetful of the
twentieth of Exodus, and not very clear upon Romans the eighth.
I do not speak with any blame of such folks for studying Daniel
and Ezekiel, but quite the reverse; yet I wish they had been more
zealous for the conversion of the sinners in their neighborhoods
and more careful to assist the poor saints. I admit the value of the
study of the feet of the image in Nebuchadnezzar's vision and the
importance of knowing the kingdoms that make up the ten toes,
but I do not see the propriety of allowing such studies to overlay
the commonplaces of practical godliness. If the time spent over
obscure theological propositions were given to a mission in the
dim alley near the good man's house, more benefit would come
to men and more glory to God.

Through the Bible in One Year: 2 John, 3 John, Jude

Depend upon Prayer

❧

Is any one of you in trouble?
He should pray.
JAMES 5:13

Trouble drives away the carnal man from his pretended religion, but it gathers the true sheep together, and being aroused and alarmed, they seek the Good Shepherd. The more of grief we feel, the more of grace we need, and the nearer to our Comforter we come. "Closer to God!" is the cry of the troubled saint. The comfort of a child of God in the darkness is prayer. Adversity, blessed of the Holy Spirit, calls our attention to the promise; the promise quickens our faith; faith betakes itself to prayer; God hears and answers our cry. This is the chain of a tried soul's experience. As we suffer the tribulation, as we know the promise, let us immediately exercise faith and turn in prayer to God; for surely never did a man turn to God but the Lord also turned to him. If we are set a-praying, we may depend upon it—the Lord is set on blessing. Blessings are on the way from heaven; their shadow falls upon us even now. "Make us glad according to the days wherein thou hast afflicted us, and the years wherein we have seen evil" (Psalm 90:15 KJV).

Through the Bible in One Year: Jeremiah 1–4

Spiritual Prisoners

But the Scripture declares that the whole world is a prisoner of sin,
so that what was promised, being given through faith in Jesus Christ,
might be given to those who believe.

Before this faith came, we were held prisoners by the law,
locked up until faith should be revealed.
GALATIANS 3:22–23

Did you ever visit a condemned cell? To peep through the gate and to see a man sitting there condemned to die is enough to make one faint. Suppose it were your boy! Suppose it were your husband! Suppose it were your brother! But listen: "He that believeth not is condemned already" (John 3:18 KJV). Pardon us, dear unconverted relatives, if we say that yours is a terrible plight, to be even now sitting in the condemned cell, doomed to be taken out to execution before long unless infinite mercy shall grant a free pardon. What dreadful sights must meet the eye upon a battle-field. If I see a man bleeding by a common cut, my heart is in my mouth, and I cannot bear the sight; but what must it be to see men dismembered, disemboweled, writhing to and fro in the last agonies of death! What horror to walk among mounds of dead bodies and stumble at each step over a human corpse! Yet what is natural death compared with spiritual death? What terror to dwell in the same house with relatives who are dead while they live—dead unto God. The thought is full of anguish. If God will quicken our spiritually dead, if he will give life to those who are "free among the slain, as they that go down into the pit" (Psalm 88:5), what a consolation we shall find therein!

Through the Bible in One Year: Jeremiah 5–8

Balm of Service

Praise be to the God and Father of our Lord Jesus Christ,
the Father of compassion and the God of all comfort,
who comforts us in all our troubles, so that we can comfort those
in any trouble with the comfort we ourselves have received from God.
2 CORINTHIANS 1:3–4

Our work is often a very effectual means of comfort to us. On the battlefield of Gettysburg, there had been a terrible fight, and among the wounded lay a certain chaplain of the name of Eastman who had been seriously injured in the back by his horse falling upon him. The dark and dreary night came on, and as he lay there in intense pain, unable to rise, he heard a voice at a little distance cry, "O God!" His interest was excited, and he rolled himself over and over through pools of blood and among the slain till he reached the side of the dying man, and there he lay talking of Jesus and his free salvation. The man expired in hope, and just then two soldiers came and told Eastman that a captain was dying a little farther down the field, and they must carry him there: so he was borne in anguish upon the work of mercy, and while the night wore on, he spoke of Jesus to many dying men. Could he have had a surer relief from his pain? I think not. Why, it seems to me that to lie there on his back with nothing to do but moan and groan would have been horrible, but in all his pain and anguish, to be carried about to proclaim mercy to dying men made the anguish of an injured back endurable! So is it when you miss a friend, or have lost property, or are heavy in spirit, you shall find your surest comfort in serving God with all your might.

Through the Bible in One Year: Jeremiah 9–12

Earnest Toil

Then I said to them, "You see the trouble we are in:
Jerusalem lies in ruins, and its gates have been burned with fire.
Come, let us rebuild the wall of Jerusalem, and we will no longer be
in disgrace." I also told them about the gracious hand
of my God upon me and what the king had said to me.

They replied, "Let us start rebuilding." So they began this good work.
NEHEMIAH 2:17–18

I believe the very best working for God is often done in a very irregular manner. I get more and more to feel like the old soldier of Waterloo when he was examined about the best garment that could be worn by a soldier. The Duke of Wellington said to him, "If you had to fight Waterloo over again, how would you like to be dressed?" The answer was, "Please, sir, I should like to be in my shirtsleeves." I think that is about the best. Get rid of everything superfluous, and get at it and hack away. There they are, going down to hell, and we are stickling about this mode and that, and considering the best way not to do it, and appointing committees to consider and debate, to adjourn and to postpone, and to leave the work in abeyance. The best way is to arise and do it and let the committee sit afterwards. God grant we may. My son, go *work* today. Let it be something practical, something real, something actually done.

And by good work is meant something that will involve effort, toil, earnestness, self-denial, perhaps something that will want perseverance. In right earnest you will need to stick to it. You will have heartily to yield yourself up to it and give up a good deal else that might hinder you in doing it.

Through the Bible in One Year: Jeremiah 13–16

Worth Doing Well

Surely you remember, brothers, our toil and hardship;
we worked night and day in order not to be a burden
to anyone while we preached the gospel of God to you.
1 THESSALONIANS 2:9

O Christian men and women, you will not glorify God much unless you really put your strength into the ways of the Lord and throw your body, soul, and spirit—your entire manhood and womanhood—into the work of the Lord Jesus Christ. To do this you need not leave your families or your shops or your secular engagements. You can serve God in these things. They will often be vantage grounds of opportunity for you, but you must throw yourself into it. A man does not win souls to Christ while he is himself half-asleep. The battle that is to be fought for the Lord Jesus must be fought by men who are wide awake and quickened by the Spirit of God. My son, go work today. Do not go and play at teaching in Sunday schools. Do not go and play the preacher. Do not go and play at exhorting people at the corners of streets or even play at giving away tracts. My son, go work. Throw your soul into it. If it is worth doing, it is worth doing well; and if it is worth doing well, it is worth doing better than you have ever done it yet; and even then it will be worth doing better still. For when you have done your best, you have still to reach forward to a some-thing far beyond, for the best of the best is all too little for such a God and for such a service. My son, go work.

Through the Bible in One Year: Jeremiah 17–20

Choose

❦

"No servant can serve two masters."
LUKE 16:13

O unclean man, how can you dream of salvation while you are defiled with filthiness? What, you and your harlot, members of Christ! Oh, you know not my pure and holy Master. He receives sinners, but he rejects those who delight in their iniquities. You must have done with the indulgence of sin if you would be cleansed from the guilt of it. There is no going on in transgression and yet obtaining salvation: it is a licentious supposition. Christ comes to save us from our sins, not to make it safe to do evil. That blood that washes out the stain brings with it also a hatred of the thing that made the stain. Sin must be relinquished, or salvation cannot be received.

I spoke very plainly just now, but some here of pure heart little know how plainly we must speak if we are to reach some men's consciences, for it shames me when I think of some who year after year indulge in secret sin, and yet they are regular frequenters of the house of God. You would think they surely were already converted or soon would be when you saw them here, but if you followed them home, you would quite despair of them. O lovers of sin, do not deceive yourselves; you will surely reap that which you sow. How can grace reign in you while you are the slaves of your own passions? How can it be while you are anchored to a secret sin that you should be borne along by the current of grace toward the desired haven of safety? Either you must leave your sin, or you must leave all hope of heaven; if you hold your sin, hell will ere long hold you. May God deliver us all from the love of sin, for such a deliverance is salvation.

Through the Bible in One Year: Jeremiah 21–24

Really Saved

❦

This is what the Sovereign LORD, the Holy One of Israel, says:
"In repentance and rest is your salvation, in quietness
and trust is your strength, but you would have none of it."
ISAIAH 30:15

Many make a great mistake about salvation; they mistake the meaning of the term, and to them salvation means being delivered from going down into the pit of hell. Now, the right meaning of salvation is purification from evil. There is not much in a man's desiring to be saved if he means by that an escape from the punishment of his offenses. Was there ever a murderer yet who did not wish to be saved from the gallows? When a man is tied up to be flogged for a deed of brutal violence, and his back is bared for the lash, depend upon it—he repents of what he did; that is to say, he repents that he has to suffer for it, but that is all, and a sorry all too. He has no sorrow for the agony he inflicted on his innocent victim, no regret for maiming him for life. What is the value of such a repentance?

Do you wish to have new hearts? Do you wish to be as God would have you to be: just, loving, kind, chaste, after the example of the great Redeemer? If so, then truly the desire you have comes of God; but if all you want is to be able to die without dread, that you may wake up in the next world and not be driven down to the bottomless pit, if that is all, there is nothing gracious in it, and it is no wonder you do not know what being saved means. Seek salvation as the kingdom of God within you; seek it first and seek it now, and you shall not be denied.

Through the Bible in One Year: Jeremiah 25–29

We Are All Answerable

It is written: "'As surely as I live,' says the Lord,
'every knee will bow before me; every tongue will confess to God.'"
So then, each of us will give an account of himself to God.
ROMANS 14:11–12

"Give an account of thy stewardship" is a command that may be addressed to the ungodly (Luke 16:2 KJV). They are accountable to God for all that they have, or ever have had, or ever shall have. The law of the Lord is not relaxed because they have sinned; they still remain responsible to God, even though they attempt to cast off the yoke of the Almighty. As creatures formed by the divine hand and sustained by divine power, they are bound to serve God, and if they do not and will not, his claims upon them do not cease, and to each of them he says, "Give an account of thy stewardship."

This text may also be applied to the children of God, to the godly, in a different sense, however, and after another fashion. For first of all, the godly are God's children; they are accounted as standing in Christ. They are no longer merely God's subjects, for what they owed to God as sinners has all been discharged by Jesus Christ, their Substitute and Savior. They have therefore been placed on a different footing from other men, but having been saved by grace and adopted into God's family, they have had entrusted to them talents that they are to use to his honor and glory. Being the Lord's children and being saved, they become his servants, and as his servants they are under responsibility to God, and they will all have to give to him an account of their stewardship.

Through the Bible in One Year: Jeremiah 30–32

Infinite Value

*"What do you think? If a man owns a hundred sheep,
and one of them wanders away, will he not leave the ninety-nine
on the hills and go to look for the one that wandered off?"*
MATTHEW 18:12

There is a tendency, apparent at this present time, to think little of the conversion of individuals and to look upon the work of the Holy Spirit upon each separate person as much too slow a business for this progressive age. I am bold to assert that if ever we despise the method of individual conversion, we shall get into an unsound order of business altogether and find ourselves wrecked upon the rocks of hypocrisy. Even in those right glorious times when the gospel shall have the freest course, and run the most quickly, and be the most extensively glorified, its progress will still be after the former manner of the conviction, conversion, and sanctification of individuals, who shall each one believe and be baptized, according to the Word of the Lord.

I fear lest in any of you there should be even the least measure of despising the one lost sheep because of the large and philosophical methods that are now so loudly cried up. If the wanderers are to be brought in in vast numbers, as I pray they may be, yet must it be accomplished by the bringing of them one by one. To attempt national regeneration without personal regeneration is to dream of erecting a house without separate bricks. Let us settle in our minds that we cannot do better than obey the example of our Lord Jesus and go after the one sheep that has gone astray.

Through the Bible in One Year: Jeremiah 33–36

The Wandering One

❧

*"And if he find it, I tell you the truth, he is happier about
that one sheep than about the ninety-nine that did not wander off.
In the same way your Father in heaven is not willing that any
of these little ones should be lost."*
MATTHEW 18:13–14

There is always a great deal to do with sheep: they have many diseases, many weaknesses, many needs; but when you have an attached, affectionate flock about you, you feel at home with them. So the Great Shepherd describes himself as leaving the ninety and nine, his choice flock, the sheep that had fellowship with him, and he with them. Yes, he leaves those in whom he could take pleasure to seek one that gave him pain. I will not dwell upon how he left the paradise above and all the joy of his Father's house and came to this bleak world, but I pray you remember that he did so. It was a wonderful descent when he came from beyond the stars to dwell on this beclouded globe and redeem the sons of men. But remember, he still continually comes by his Spirit. His errands of mercy are perpetual. The Spirit of God moves his ministers, who are Christ's representatives, to forgo the feeding of the gathered flock and to seek, in their discourses, the salvation of the wandering ones, in whose character and behavior there is nothing to cheer us. He would not have his church expend all her care on the flock that he has led into her green pastures, but he would have her go afield after those who are not yet in her blessed society.

Through the Bible in One Year: Jeremiah 37–40

Consumed in Service

❧

Though I am free and belong to no man, I make myself
a slave to everyone, to win as many as possible.
1 CORINTHIANS 9:19

If this is our time for doing good, let us do good while we can. I hear people sometimes say, "Mr. So-and-So does too much; he works too hard." Oh, we none of us do half enough. Do not talk about working too hard for Jesus Christ. The thing is impossible. Are souls perishing, and shall I sleep? My idle, lazy flesh, shall you keep me still while men are dying and hell is filling? Let us be lukewarm no longer. If God makes us lights in the world, let us spend ourselves as a candle does, which consumes itself by shining. As the poor work girl, who has but one light, works with desperate pace because that will soon be burned out, so let us be instant in season and out of season, watching, praying, laboring for the souls of men. If we could but see lost souls and understand their unutterable woe, we should shake ourselves from the dust and go forth to work while it is called today.

Through the Bible in One Year: Jeremiah 41–44

His Example

❧

Very early in the morning, while it was still dark, Jesus got up,
left the house and went off to a solitary place, where he prayed.
MARK 1:35

Remember that our Lord did not only inculcate prayer with great earnestness, but he was himself a brilliant example of it. It always gives force to a teacher's words when his hearers well know that he carries out his own instructions. Jesus was a prophet mighty both in deed and in word, and we read of him, "Jesus began both to do and teach" (Acts 1:1 KJV). In the exercise of prayer, "cold mountains and the midnight air" witnessed that he was as great a doer as a teacher. When he exhorted his disciples to continue in prayer and to "pray without ceasing," he only bade them follow in his steps. If any one of all the members of the mystical body might have been supposed to need no prayer, it would certainly have been our Covenant Head, but if our Head abounded in supplication, much more ought we, the inferior members. He was never defiled with the sins that have debased and weakened us spiritually; he had no inbred lusts to struggle with. But if the perfectly pure drew near so often unto God, how much more incessant in supplication ought we to be! So mighty, so great, and yet so prayerful!

Through the Bible in One Year: Jeremiah 45–48

Devoted Praise

Praise the LORD, you his angels,
you mighty ones who do his bidding, who obey his word.
Praise the LORD, all his heavenly hosts,
you his servants who do his will. Praise the LORD,
all his works everywhere in his dominion.

Praise the LORD, O my soul.
PSALM 103:20–22

The whole life of the Christian should be a life of devotion to God. To praise God both with our voices and with our actions for mercies received, and then to pray to God for the mercies that we need, devoutly acknowledging that they come from him—these two exercises in one form or other should make up the sum total of human life. Our life psalm should be composed of alternating verses of praying and of praising until we get into the next world, where the prayer may cease and praise may swallow up the whole of our immortality. "But," says one, "we have our daily business to attend to." I know you have, but there is a way of making business a part of praise and prayer. You say, "Give us this day our daily bread," and that is a prayer as you utter it; you go off to your work, and as you toil, if you do so in a devout spirit, you are actively praying the same prayer by your lawful labor. You praise God for the mercies received in your morning hymn, and when you go into the duties of life and there exhibit those graces that reflect honor upon God's name, you are continuing your praises in the best manner. Remember that with Christians to labor is to pray and that there is much truth in the verse of Coleridge: "He prayeth best who loveth best."

Through the Bible in One Year: Jeremiah 49–52

Persist in Prayer

Each one had a harp and they were holding golden bowls
full of incense, which are the prayers of the saints.
REVELATION 5:8

"Men ought always to pray" (Luke 18:1 KJV). Week by week, month by month, year by year, the conversion of that dear child is to be the father's main plea. The bringing of that unconverted husband is to lie upon the wife's heart night and day till she gets it; she is not to take even ten or twenty years of unsuccessful prayer as a reason why she should cease; she is to set God no times nor seasons, but so long as there is life in her and life in the dear object of her solicitude, she is to continue still to plead with the mighty God of Jacob.

The pastor is not to seek a blessing on his people occasionally, and then in receiving a measure of it to desist from further inter-cession, but he is to continue vehemently without pause, without restraining his energies, to cry aloud and spare not till the windows of heaven be opened and a blessing be given too large for him to house. But how many times we ask of God and have not because we do not wait long enough at the door! Oh, for grace to stand foot to foot with the angel of God and never, never, never relax our hold, feeling that the cause we plead is one in which we must be successful, for souls depend on it, the glory of God is connected with it, the state of our fellow men is in jeopardy. If we could have given up in prayer our own lives and the lives of those dearest to us, yet the souls of men we cannot give up; we must urge and plead again and again until we obtain the answer.

Through the Bible in One Year: Revelation 1–2

Divine Atonement

❧

*He was delivered over to death for our sins
and was raised to life for our justification.*
ROMANS 4:25

The very name of Jesus tells us that he shall save his people from their sins. Let me further say that inasmuch as that salvation of God is a great one, it must have been intended to meet great sins. Would Christ have shed the blood of his heart for some trifling, venial sins that our tears could wash away? Think you God would have given his dear Son to die as a mere superfluity? If sin had been a small matter, a little sacrifice would have sufficed. Think you that the divine atonement was made only for small offenses? Did Jesus die for little sins and leave the great ones unatoned? No, the Lord God measured the greatness of our sin and found it high as heaven, deep as hell, and broad as the infinite, and therefore he gave so great a Savior. He gave his only begotten Son, an infinite sacrifice, an unmeasurable atonement. With such throes and pains of death as never can be fully described, the Lord Jesus poured out his soul in unknown sufferings, that he might provide a great salvation for the greatest of sinners. See Jesus on the cross, and learn that all manner of sin and blasphemy shall be forgiven unto men. Salvation, that is for me, for I am lost. A great salvation, that is for me, for I am the greatest of sinners. Oh, hear my word this day! It is God's word of love, and it rings out like a silver bell. I weep over you, and yet I feel like singing all the time, for I am sent to proclaim salvation from the Lord for the very worst of you.

Through the Bible in One Year: Revelation 3–5

Our Future Reward

*"The LORD rewards every man
for his righteousness and faithfulness."*
1 SAMUEL 26:23

Like the hireling we must fulfill our day, and then at evening we shall have our penny. Too many Christians look for a present reward for their labors, and if they meet with success, they begin doting upon it as though they had received their recompense. Like the disciples who returned saying, "Lord, even the devils are subject unto us" (Luke 10:17 KJV), they rejoice too exclusively in present prosperity; whereas the Master bade them not to look upon miraculous success as being their reward, since that might not always be the case. "Notwithstanding," said he, "in this rejoice not, that the spirits are subject unto you; but rather rejoice, because your names are written in heaven" (Luke 10:20 KJV). Success in the ministry is not the Christian minister's true reward: it is an earnest, but the wages still wait. The approbation of your fellow men you must not look upon as being the reward of excellence, for often you will meet with the reverse; you will find your best actions misconstrued and your motives ill interpreted.

To be despised and rejected of men is the Christian's lot. Among his fellow Christians he will not always stand in good repute. It is not unmitigated kindness nor unmingled love that we receive even from the saints. I tell you if you look for your reward to Christ's bride herself, you will miss it. "When the King shall come in his glory," then is your time of recompense; but not today, nor tomorrow, nor at any time in this world.

Through the Bible in One Year: Revelation 6–8

Our Divine Carpenter

"In my Father's house are many rooms;
if it were not so, I would have told you.
I am going there to prepare a place for you."
JOHN 14:2

The great God has prepared a kingdom for his people; he has thought, "That will please them, and that will bless them, and this other will make them superlatively happy." He prepared the kingdom to perfection, and then, as if that were not enough, the glorious Man, Christ Jesus, went up from earth to heaven; and you know what he said when he departed—"I go to prepare a place for you." We know that the infinite God can prepare a place fitting for a finite creature, but the words smile so sweetly at us as we read that Jesus himself, who is a Man and therefore knows our hearts' desires, has had a finger in it; *he* has prepared it too. It is a kingdom prepared for you, upon which the thoughts of God have been set to make it excellent from before the foundation of the world.

He has prepared a place for *you*. Here is personal election. He has made a distinct ordinance for every one of his people that where he is there shall they be. "Prepared from the foundation of the world." Here is eternal election appearing before men were created, preparing crowns before heads were made to wear them. Our portion, then, is one prepared from all eternity for us according to the election of God's grace, one suitable to the loftiest character to which we can ever attain, which will consist in nearness to Christ, communion with God, and an eternal standing in a place of dignity and happiness.

Through the Bible in One Year: Revelation 9–10

I Am

Immediately he spoke to them and said,
"Take courage! It is I. Don't be afraid."
MARK 6:50

Jesus spoke this message to believers tossed with tempest, and we need it when we are depressed by the surroundings of these evil times. In seasons of depressed trade, great sickness, terrible wars, and public disasters, it is balm to the spirit to know that Jesus is still the same. Sin may abound yet more, the light of the gospel may burn low, and the prince of darkness may widely sway his destroying scepter, but nevertheless, this truth stands sure, that Jesus is the "I Am." At certain periods, diabolical influence seems paramount, the reins of nations appear to be taken out of the hand of the Great Governor, and yet it is not so. Look through the darkness, and you shall see your Lord amid the hurricane, walking the waters of politics, ruling national convulsions, governing, over-ruling, arranging all, making even the wrath of man to praise him, and restraining it according to his wisdom. Above the howling of the blast, I hear his voice announcing, "It is I." When men's hearts sink for fear and the rowers feel their oars ready to snap by the strain of useless toil, I hear that word which is the soul of music: "It is I; be not afraid. I am ruling all things. I am coming to the rescue of the bark, my church; she shall yet float on smooth waters and reach her desired haven."

Through the Bible in One Year: Revelation 11–13

He Still Works Miracles

*Those who belong to Christ Jesus have crucified
the sinful nature with its passions and desires.*
GALATIANS 5:24

The power of sin is shaken in that man who looks to Jesus for deliverance from it. Some sins that have hardened down into habits yet disappear in a moment when Jesus Christ looks upon a man in love. I have known many instances of persons who, for many years, had never spoken without an oath or a filthy expression, who, being converted, have never been known to use such language again and have scarcely ever been tempted in that direction. Others I have known were so altered at once that the very propensity that was strongest in them has been the last to annoy them afterwards: they have had such a reversion of the mind's action that while other sins have worried them for years and they have had to set a strict watch against them, yet their favorite and dominant sin has never again had the slightest influence over them, except to excite an outburst of horror and deep repentance. Oh, that you had faith in Jesus that he could thus cast down and cast out your reigning sins! Believe in the conquering arm of the Lord Jesus, and he will do it. Conversion is the standing miracle of the church. Where it is genuine, it is as clear a proof of divine power going with the gospel as was the casting out of devils or even the raising of the dead in our Lord's day.

Through the Bible in One Year: Revelation 14–16

Obedient Children

꿎

His mother said to the servants,
"Do whatever he tells you."
JOHN 2:5

If you have been saved by the grace of God, your salvation has put you under obligation henceforth to do what Jesus bids you. Are you redeemed? Then you are not your own; you are bought with a price. Have you been adopted into the divine family? Then it clearly follows that because you are sons, you should be obedient to the law of the household; for is not this a first element of sonship, that you should reverence the great Father of the family? The Lord has been pleased to put away your sin; you are forgiven. But does not pardon demand amendment? Shall we go back to the old sins from which we have been cleansed? Shall we live in the iniquities from which we have been washed by the blood of our Lord Jesus?

As Mary said to the waiters at the wedding at Cana, so say I to you—"Whatsoever he saith unto you, do it." Does he bid you pray? Then pray without ceasing. Does he bid you watch as well as pray? Then guard every act and thought and word. Does he bid you love your brethren? Then love them with a pure heart fervently. Does he bid you serve them and humble yourself for his sake? Then do so, and become the servant of all. Has he said, "Be ye holy, for I am holy"? Then aim at this by his Holy Spirit. Has he said, "Be ye perfect, even as your Father which is in heaven is perfect"? Then strive after perfection, for he who made you whole has a right to direct your way, and it will be both your safety and your happiness to submit yourselves to his commands.

Through the Bible in One Year: Revelation 17–19

Holy Fruit

All over the world this gospel is bearing fruit and growing,
just as it has been doing among you since the day you heard it
and understood God's grace in all its truth.

COLOSSIANS 1:6

The church of God on earth at this present time anxiously desires to spread her influence over the world. For Christ's sake we wish to have the truths we preach acknowledged and the precepts we deliver obeyed. But mark, no church will ever have power over the masses of this or any other land, except in proportion as she does them good. Now, if any church under heaven can show that it is making men honest, temperate, pure, moral, holy; that it is seeking out the ignorant and instructing them; that it is turning moral wastes into gardens and taking the weeds and briars of the wilderness and transforming them into precious fruit-bearing trees, then the world will be ready to hear its claims and consider them.

If you have a church that is devout, that is holy, that is living unto God, that does good in its neighborhood, that by the lives of its members spreads holiness and righteousness; in a word, if you have a church that is really making the world whole in the name of Jesus, you shall in the long run find that even the most carnal and thoughtless will say, "The church that is doing this good is worthy of respect; therefore, let us hear what it has to say." A holy church goes with authority to the world in the name of Jesus Christ its Lord, and this force the Holy Spirit uses to bring human hearts into subjection to the truth.

Through the Bible in One Year: Revelation 20–22

God-Ordained Circumstances

❧

A strong wind was blowing
and the waters grew rough.
JOHN 6:18

Do not consider that adverse circumstances are a proof that you have missed your road, for they may even be an evidence that you are in the good old way, since the path of believers is seldom without trial. You did well to embark and to leave the shore; but remember, though our Lord has insured the vessel and guaranteed that you shall reach your haven, he has not promised that you shall sail over a sea of glass; on the contrary, he has told you that "in the world ye shall have tribulation" (John 16:33 KJV), and you may all the more confidently believe in him because you find his warning to be true.

Their Lord had bidden his disciples make for the other side, and therefore they did their best and continued rowing all night, but making no progress whatever because the wind was dead against them. Probably you have heard it said that if a Christian man does not go forward, he goes backward; that is not altogether true, for there are times of spiritual trial when, if a man does not go backward, he is really going forward. The Christian man may make little or no headway, and yet it may be no fault of his, for the wind is contrary. Our good Lord will take the will for the deed and reckon our progress, not by our apparent advance, but by the hearty intent with which we tug at the oars.

Through the Bible in One Year: Lamentations 1–2

God's Cleansing Influence

*"One thing I do know.
I was blind but now I see!"*
JOHN 9:25

Man is blind. Father Adam put out our eyes. We cannot see spiritual things. We have not the spiritual optic; that has gone, gone forever. Christ comes into this world, and his gospel is despicable in men's esteem even as spittle; the thought of it disgusts most men. He puts the gospel on the blind eye—a gospel that, like clay, seems as if it should make men more blind than before, but it is through "the foolishness of preaching" that Christ saves those who believe. The Holy Spirit is like Siloam's pool. We go to him, or rather he comes to us; the convictions of sin produced by the gospel are washed away by the cleansing influences of the Divine Comforter; and behold, we who were once so blind that we could see no beauty in divine things, and no excellence in the crown jewels of God, begin to see things in a clear and heavenly light and rejoice exceedingly before the Lord.

Through the Bible in One Year: Lamentations 3–5

Personal Testimony

"One thing I do know. . . ."
JOHN 9:25

The skeptic will sometimes overwhelm you with his knowledge. Meet them, but be sure you meet them with a knowledge that is better than theirs. Don't attempt to meet them on their own ground; meet them with this knowledge. "Well," you can say, "I know that you understand more than I do; I am only a poor unlettered Christian, but I have a something in here that answers all your arguments, whatever they may be. I do not know what geology says; I may not understand all about history; I may not comprehend all the strange things that are daily coming to light; but one thing I know—it is a matter of absolute consciousness to me—that I, who was once blind, have been made to see." Then just state the difference that the gospel made in you; say that once when you looked at the Bible, it was a dull, dry book; that when you thought of prayer, it was a dreary piece of work. Say that now the Bible seems to you a honeycomb full of honey and that prayer is your vital breath. Say that you once tried to get away from God and could see no excellence in the divine character, but now you are striving and struggling to get nearer to God. Say that you once despised the cross of Christ and thought it a vain thing for you to fly to, but now you love it and would sacrifice your all for it. And this undoubted change in your own consciousness, this supernatural work in your own innermost spirit, shall stand you in the stead of all the arguments that can be drawn from all the sciences; your one thing shall overthrow their thousand things, if you can say, "Whereas I was blind, now I see."

Through the Bible in One Year: Ezekiel 1–4

Praise and Gratitude

Jesus asked, "Were not all ten cleansed? Where are the other nine?
Was no one found to return and give praise to God except this foreigner?"
Then he said to him, "Rise and go; your faith has made you well."
LUKE 17:17–19

If you search the world around, among all choice spices you shall
scarcely meet with the frankincense of gratitude. We do not
praise the Lord fitly, proportionately, intensely. We receive a con-
tinent of mercies and only return an island of praise. He gives us
blessings new every morning and fresh every evening; great is his
faithfulness. And yet we let the years roll round and seldom
observe a day of praise. Sad is it to see God all goodness and man
all ingratitude!

  I put it in another shape to you who are God's people—most
of us pray more than we praise. You pray little enough, I fear; but
praise, where is that? At our family altars we always pray but seldom praise. In our closets we constantly pray, but do we *frequently*
praise? Prayer is not so heavenly an exercise as praise; prayer is
for time, but praise is for eternity. Praise therefore deserves the
first and highest place, does it not? Let us commence the employ-
ment that occupies the celestials. Prayer is for a beggar, but
methinks he is a poor beggar who does not also give praise when
he receives alms. Praise ought to follow naturally upon the heels
of prayer, even when it does not, by divine grace, go before it.

Through the Bible in One Year: Ezekiel 5–8

Our Real Power

"Have faith in God," Jesus answered. "I tell you the truth,
if anyone says to this mountain, 'Go, throw yourself into the sea,'
and does not doubt in his heart but believes that what he says
will happen, it will be done for him. Therefore I tell you, whatever you
ask for in prayer, believe that you have received it, and it will be yours."
MARK 11:22–24

Whether we live or whether we die, let us have faith in God. Whenever we preach or teach the gospel, let us have faith, for without faith we shall labor in vain. Whenever you distribute religious books or visit the sick, do so in faith, for faith is the lifeblood of all our service. If only by faith can a dying Jacob bless his descendants, so only by faith can we bless the sons of men. Have faith in God, and the instruction you give shall really edify, the prayers you offer shall bring down showers of mercy, and your endeavors for your sons and daughters shall be prospered. God will bless what is done in faith, but if we believe not, our work will not be established. Faith is the backbone and marrow of the Christian's power to do good: we are weak as water till we enter into union with God by faith, and then we are omnipotent. We can do nothing for our fellow men by way of promoting their spiritual and eternal interests if we walk according to the sight of our eyes, but when we get into the power of God and grasp his promise by a daring confidence, then it is that we obtain the power to bless.

Through the Bible in One Year: Ezekiel 9–12

Precious Communications

Be joyful in hope,
patient in affliction,
faithful in prayer.
ROMANS 12:12

It is the duty and privilege of every Christian to have set times of prayer. I cannot understand a man's keeping up the vitality of godliness unless he regularly retires for prayer, morning and evening at the very least. Daniel prayed three times a day, and David says, "Seven times a day do I praise thee" (Psalm 119:164 KJV). It is good for your hearts, good for your memory, good for your moral consistency that you should hedge about certain portions of time and say, "These belong to God. I shall do business with God at such and such a time and try to be as punctual to my hours with him as I should be if I made an engagement to meet a friend."

When Sir Thomas Abney was Lord Mayor of London, the banquet somewhat troubled him, for Sir Thomas always had prayer with his family at a certain time. The difficulty was how to quit the banquet to keep up family devotion; but so important did he consider it that he vacated the chair, saying to a person near that he had a special engagement with a dear friend that he must keep. And he did keep it, and he returned again to his place, none of the company being the wiser, but he himself being all the better for observing his wonted habit of worship.

Through the Bible in One Year: Ezekiel 13–16

A Life of Prayer

*Therefore let everyone who is godly pray to you while you may be found;
surely when the mighty waters rise, they will not reach him.
You are my hiding place; you will protect me from trouble
and surround me with songs of deliverance.*

PSALM 32:6–7

I always find I can preach the better if I can pray while I am preaching. And the mind is very remarkable in its activities. It can be praying while it is studying, it can be looking up to God while it is talking to man, and there can be one hand held up to receive supplies from God while the other hand is dealing out the same supplies that he is pleased to give. Pray as long as you live. Pray when you are in great pain; the sharper the pang, then the more urgent and importunate should your cry to God be. And when the shadow of death gathers round you and strange feelings flush or chill you and plainly tell that you near the journey's end, then pray. Short and pithy prayers like this, "Hide not your face from me, O Lord," or this, "Be not far from me, O God," will doubtless suit you. "Lord Jesus, receive my spirit," were the thrilling words of Stephen in his extremity; and "Father, into thy hands I commend my spirit," were the words that your Master himself uttered just before he bowed his head and gave up the ghost. You may well take up the same strain and imitate him.

Through the Bible in One Year: Ezekiel 17–20

The Invisible Majority

※

By faith Noah, when warned about things not yet seen,
in holy fear built an ark to save his family.
By his faith he condemned the world and became heir
of the righteousness that comes by faith.
HEBREWS 11:7

Noah was a very different man from the rest of those who lived in his time. *They* forgot God, and *he* feared him; they lived for things seen and temporal, and he lived in sight of the invisible. When he was building his ark, he was in a miserable minority, and even after one hundred and twenty years' ministry, when his ark was built and his family entered it, they were eight against many millions, an insignificant few, as men would say; a pitiful sect among mankind. Who could imagine that the eight would be right and all the millions wrong? Where God is, there is the majority. But very clearly there was a very marked distinction between Noah and his household, and all the rest of mankind.

Brethren, the church of God stands at the present moment in the world very much in the same conditions as Noah and his family. These make up with us the chosen family of God who shall be safe when the world is deluged with the last devouring fire. But the time comes—it comes to each man in death, and it will come to the whole company of the ungodly in the day when the Lord Jesus shall descend from heaven with a shout—when the door shall be shut, and it shall be said, "Between us and you there is a great gulf fixed: so that they which would pass from hence to you cannot; neither can they pass to us, that would come from thence" (Luke 16:26 KJV). Character will become unchangeable; he who is unjust will be unjust still, and he who is filthy will be filthy still.

Through the Bible in One Year: Ezekiel 21–24

Yielding to the Divine Call

By faith Abraham, when called to go to a place
he would later receive as his inheritance, obeyed and went,
even though he did not know where he was going.
HEBREWS 11:8

Abraham was called, and he obeyed. There is no hint of hesitation, parleying, or delay; when he was called to go out, he went out. The Lord's complaint is, "I have called, and ye refused" (Proverbs 1:24 KJV). Such calls come again and again to many, but they turn a deaf ear to them; they are hearers only and not doers of the Word. Even among the most attentive hearers, how many there are to whom the Word comes with small practical result in actual obedience. How foolish to go on adding sin to sin, increasing the hardness of the heart, increasing the distance between the soul and Christ, and all the while fondly dreaming of some enchanted hour in which it will be easier to yield to the divine call and part with sin.

Abraham had an opportunity, and he had grace to grasp it, and at this day there is not of our race a nobler name than that of "the father of the faithful." He was an imperial man, head and shoulders above his fellows. His heart was in heaven, the light of God bathed his forehead, and his soul was filled with divine influences so that he saw the day of the Lord Jesus and was glad. He was blessed of the Lord who made heaven and earth and was made a blessing to all nations. Some of you will never gain such honor; you will live and die ignoble because you trifle with supreme calls. And yet, did you believe in God, did you but live by faith, there would be before you also a course of immortal honor that would lead you to eternal glory.

Through the Bible in One Year: Ezekiel 25–28

Wear the Image

The LORD was with Joseph and he prospered.
GENESIS 39:2

Man looks at the outward appearance, but the Lord looks upon the heart; and so the scriptural descriptions of men are not of their visible life alone, but of their spiritual life. Here we have Joseph as God saw him, the real Joseph. Externally it did not always appear that God was with him, for he did not always seem to be a prosperous man; but when you come to look into the inmost soul of this servant of God, you see his true likeness—he lived in communion with the Most High, and God blessed him: "The LORD was with Joseph, and he was a prosperous man" (Genesis 39:2 KJV).

This striking likeness of Joseph strongly reminds us of our Master and Lord, that greater Joseph, who is Lord over all the world for the sake of Israel. Peter, in his sermon to the household of Cornelius, said of our Lord that he "went about doing good, and healing all that were oppressed of the devil; for *God was with him*" (Acts 10:38 KJV, emphasis added)—exactly what had been said of Joseph. It is wonderful that the same words should describe both Jesus and Joseph, the perfect Savior and the imperfect patriarch. When you and I are perfected in grace, we shall wear the image of Christ, and that which will describe Christ will also describe us. Those who live with Jesus will be transformed by his fellowship till they become like him.

Through the Bible in One Year: Ezekiel 29–32

God-Consciousness

❧

"No one is greater in this house than I am.
My master has withheld nothing from me except you,
because you are his wife. How then could I do such
a wicked thing and sin against God?"
GENESIS 39:9

Oh, if you and I always felt that God was near, looking steadily upon us, we should not dare to sin. The presence of a superior often checks a man from doing what else he might have ventured on, and the presence of God, if it were realized, would be a perpetual barrier against temptation and would keep us steadfast in holiness. When Joseph afterwards at any time spoke of God, when God helped him not only to stand against temptation, but to do any service, you will notice how he always ascribed it to God. He would not interpret Pharaoh's dream without first telling him, "It is not in me: God hath showed Pharaoh what he is about to do." He was as conscious of the presence of God when he stood before the great monarch as when he refused that sinful woman.

I am afraid that we do not habitually talk in this fashion, but Joseph did. Without the slightest affectation he spoke out of his heart, under a sense of the divine presence and working. How like he is in this to our divine Lord! The presence of God was everything to Christ as it was to Joseph. Now, if you and I set the Lord always before us, if our soul dwells in God, depend upon it—God is with us. There is no mistake about it.

Through the Bible in One Year: Ezekiel 33–36

Instruments in God's Hand

*You yourselves have seen everything the LORD your God has done
to all these nations for your sake; it was the LORD your God
who fought for you. Remember how I have allotted as an inheritance
for your tribes all the land of the nations that remain—the nations
I conquered—between the Jordan and the Great Sea in the west.*

JOSHUA 23:3–4

A great many mistakes are made about the promises of God.
Some think that if God is to be with them, they will have nothing
to do. Joshua did not find it so. He and his troops had to slay every
Amorite and Hittite and Hivite who fell in battle. He had to fight
and use his sword-arm just as much as if there had been no God
at all.

The best and the wisest thing in the world is to work as if it
all depended upon you, and then trust in God, knowing that it all
depends upon him. He will not fail us, but we are not therefore to
fold our arms and sit still. He will not forsake us; we are not therefore to go upstairs to bed and expect that our daily bread will drop
into our mouths. God does not pander to our laziness, and any
man who expects to get on in this world with anything that is good
without work is a fool. Throw your whole soul into the service of
God, and then you will get God's blessing if you are resting upon
him. Oliver Cromwell had a commonsense view of this truth too.
"Trust in God," said he as they went to battle, "but keep your
powder dry." And so must we.

Through the Bible in One Year: Ezekiel 37–40

On Behalf of Another

*I urge, then, first of all, that requests, prayers,
intercession and thanksgiving be made for everyone.*
1 TIMOTHY 2:1

It is a very great privilege to be permitted to pray for our fellow
men. Prayer in each man's case must necessarily begin with personal petitions, for until the man is himself accepted with God,
he cannot act as an intercessor for others; and herein lies part of
the excellence of intercessory prayer, for it is to the man who exercises it aright a mark of inward grace and a token for good from
the Lord. You may be sure that your King loves you when he will
permit you to speak a word to him on behalf of your friend. He
who in answer to his intercession has seen others blessed and
saved may take it as a pledge of divine love and rejoice in the condescending grace of God. Such prayer rises higher than any petition for ourselves, for only he who is in favor with the Lord can
venture upon pleading for others.

Intercessory prayer is an act of communion with Christ, for
Jesus pleads for the sons of men. It is a part of his priestly office
to make intercession for his people. He has ascended up on high
to this end and exercises this office continually within the veil.
When we pray for our fellow sinners, we are in sympathy with our
divine Savior, who made intercession for the transgressors.

Through the Bible in One Year: Ezekiel 41–44

Taught of God

❧

The fruit of the righteous is a tree of life,
and he who wins souls is wise.
PROVERBS 11:30

If I desire salvation of anyone, I ought to tell him as best as I can what his condition is, and what the way of salvation is, and how he may find rest. All men are approachable at some time or in some way. It is very imprudent to rush at everybody as soon as you see them, without thought or ordinary prudence, for you may disgust those whom you wish to win. But those who earnestly plead for others and bestir themselves to seek them are generally taught of God, and so they are made wise as to time, manner, and subject. A man who wishes to shoot birds will, after a while, become expert in the sport, because he will give his mind to it. So he who longs to win souls and puts his heart into it finds out the knack of it by some means, and the Lord gives him success. I could not teach it to you; you must practice in order to find it out. But this I will say: no man is clear of his fellow's blood simply because he has prayed to be so.

I have heard of one who prayed in New York for a certain number of very poor families that he had visited. His little son said, "Father, if I were God, I should tell you to answer your own prayer, for you have plenty of money." Thus the Lord might well say to us when we have been interceding, "Go and answer your own prayer by telling your friends of my Son." There is a power in your gifts; there is a power in your speech; use these powers. Go and teach the good and right way, and then shall your prayers be heard.

Through the Bible in One Year: Ezekiel 45 – 48

Count on It

❧

In addition to all this, take up the shield of faith,
with which you can extinguish all the flaming arrows of the evil one.
EPHESIANS 6:16

Faith is a shield that you may use for warding off every kind of arrow, yea, even the fiery darts of the great enemy, for this shield cannot be penetrated even by javelins of fire. You cannot be cast into a condition in which faith shall not help you. There is a promise of God suitable for every state, and God has wisdom and skill and love and faithfulness to deliver you out of every possible jeopardy; and therefore you have only to confide in God, and deliverance is sure to come.

Even when your trouble has been brought upon you by your own fault, faith is still available. When your affliction is evidently a chastisement for grievous transgression, still trust in the Lord. The Lord Jesus prayed for erring Peter that his faith might not fail him: his hope of recovery lay there. When you have stepped aside and when at last the heavenly Father makes you smart under his rod—to cast yourself upon him then is faith indeed. If any of you at this time are in great distress and are conscious that you richly deserve all your troubles because of your folly, still trust in the mercy of the Lord. Do not doubt the Lord your Savior, for he invites his backsliding children to return unto him.

Through the Bible in One Year: Daniel 1–3

Everyday Faith

❧

*Was not our ancestor Abraham considered righteous
for what he did when he offered his son Isaac on the altar?
You see that his faith and his actions were working together,
and his faith was made complete by what he did.*
JAMES 2:21–22

Trust in the Lord your God. Believe also in his Son, Jesus. Get rid of sham faith, and really believe. Get rid of a professional faith, and trust in the Lord at all times about everything. "What, trust him about pounds, shillings, and pence?" Assuredly. I dread the faith that cannot trust God about bread and garments—it is a lying faith. Depend upon it—that is not the solid, practical faith of Abraham, who trusted God about his tent and his cattle, and about a wife for his son. The faith that made David trust God about the sons and daughters and the spoil, that is the sort of faith for you and for me. If God cannot be trusted about loaves and fishes, how shall he be trusted about the things of eternity and the glories that are yet to be revealed? Stay yourself on God with an everyday faith. Faith in God is the exercise of sanctified common sense. The purest reason approves reliance upon God. The end shall declare the wisdom of believing God. At the last, when we with all believers shall lift up the great hallelujah unto the Lord God of Israel who reigns over all things for his people, it shall be known by all that faith is honorable and unbelief contemptible.

Through the Bible in One Year: Daniel 4–6

Steadfast Servants

❧

*Then they said to the king, "Daniel, who is one of the exiles
from Judah, pays no attention to you, O king, or to the decree
you put in writing. He still prays three times a day."*
DANIEL 6:13

Daniel had been exalted to very great worldly prosperity, but his soul had prospered too. Oftentimes outward advancement means inward decline. Tens of thousands have been intoxicated by success. Though they bade fair in starting in the race of life to win the prize, they were tempted to turn aside to gather the golden apples, and so they missed the crown. It was not so with Daniel—he was as perfect before God in his high estate as in his lowlier days, and this is to be accounted for by the fact that he sustained the energy of his outward profession by constant secret communion with God. He was, we are told, a man of excellent spirit and a man abundant in prayer; hence, his head was not turned by his elevation, but the Lord fulfilled in him his promise to "make his servant's feet like hinds' feet, that they may stand upon their high places." Yet although Daniel preserved his integrity, he did not find a position of greatness to be one of rest.

The example of Daniel I present for your observation today, believing that these are times when we need to be as firm and resolute as he, and that at any rate, occasions will come to every one of us, before we win our crown, when we shall need to put our foot down firmly and be steadfast and unflinching for the Lord and his truth.

Through the Bible in One Year: Daniel 7–9

In God's Strength

Finally these men said, "We will never find
any basis for charges against this man Daniel unless
it has something to do with the law of his God."
DANIEL 6:5

Remember that Daniel is a type of our Lord Jesus Christ. Jesus had enemies who sought to destroy him; they could find nothing against him except "touching his God." They accused him of blasphemy, and then afterwards, as they did against Daniel, they brought a charge of sedition. He was cast into the den, into the grave: his soul was among the lions. They sealed his tomb with their signet, lest any should steal him by night, but he arose as Daniel did, alive and unhurt, and his enemies were destroyed. Now, if Daniel is a type of Christ, and the Lord Jesus is the great representative Man for all who are in him, you, believer, must expect that there will be those who will attack you, who will assail you especially in your religion. You must expect too that they will prevail against you for a time so that you may be cast into the den, that they will seek to fasten you in as though you were destroyed forever; but there will be a resurrection not only of bodies, but of reputations, and you shall arise.

Oh, to be a follower of Jesus, the great Daniel! To tread in his footsteps wherever he goes! To be much with him, whether in private or public! This is a thing to be desired, and though I exhort you to it, I do not expect you to attain to it in your own strength, but I point you to the Holy Ghost, who can work this in you and make you to be greatly beloved as was this prophet of old.

Through the Bible in One Year: Daniel 10–12

Celestial Shade

❧

Tychicus will tell you all the news about me.
He is a dear brother, a faithful minister
and fellow servant in the Lord.
COLOSSIANS 4:7

I know some of God's saints who live very near to him, and they are evidently a tree of life, for their very shadow is comforting, cooling, and refreshing to many weary souls. I have known the young, the tried, and the downcast go to them, sit beneath their shade, and pour out the tale of their troubles, and they have felt it a rich blessing to receive their sympathy, to be told of the faithfulness of the Lord, and to be guided in the way of wisdom. There are a few good men in this world whom to know is to be rich. Their character is a true and living tree; it is not a mere post of the dead wood of doctrine, bearing an inscription and rotting while it does so, but it is a vital, organized, fruit-producing thing, a plant of the Lord's right-hand planting.

Not only do some saints give comfort to others, but they also yield them spiritual nourishment. Well-trained Christians become nursing fathers and nursing mothers, strengthening the weak and binding up the wounds of the brokenhearted. So too the strong, bold, generous deeds of largehearted Christians are of great service to their fellow Christians and tend to raise them to a higher level. You feel refreshed by observing how they act; their patience in suffering, their courage in danger, their holy faith in God, their happy faces under trial—all these nerve you for your own conflicts. In a thousand ways the sanctified believer's example acts in a healing and comforting way to his brethren and assists in raising them above anxiety and unbelief.

Through the Bible in One Year: Hosea 1–4

From Youth

*Train a child in the way he should go,
and when he is old he will not turn from it.*
PROVERBS 22:6

To reclaim the prodigal is well, but to save him from ever being a prodigal is better. To bring back the thief and the drunkard is a praiseworthy action, but so to act that the boy shall never become a thief or a drunkard is far better; hence, Sabbath-school instruction stands very high in the list of philanthropic enterprises, and Christians ought to be most earnest in it. He who converts a child from the error of his way prevents as well as covers a multitude of sins.

And moreover, it gives the church the hope of being furnished with the best of men and women. The church's Samuels and Solomons are made wise in their youth; Davids and Josiahs were tender of heart when they were tender in years. Read the lives of the most eminent ministers and you shall usually find that their Christian history began early. Though it is not absolutely needful, yet it is highly propitious to the growth of a well-developed Christian character that its foundation should be laid on the basis of youthful piety. I do not expect to see the churches of Jesus Christ ordinarily built up by those who have through life lived in sin, but by the bringing up in their midst, in the fear and admonition of the Lord, young men and women who become pillars in the house of our God. If we want strong Christians, we must look to those who were Christians in their youth.

Through the Bible in One Year: Hosea 5–8

Our Highest Joy

I lift up my eyes to you,
to you whose throne is in heaven.
PSALM 123:1

It is a great pity that people should go into any man's house and see there everything except the man himself. They admire his carpets, they rejoice at the regularity with which the meals are put upon the table, they see that there are certain laws that make provision for the breakfast and the dinner of all the household; they approve of the "laws" that have kept the house clean and the "laws" that have decorated it and the "laws" that govern everything. But where is the master who made those laws? Alas, they do not want to see him! They like to look at what he has provided, they like to sit with their legs under his mahogany, but they do not want to see the master of the house. Surely, this must arise from a lack of understanding. When I am staying with a friend, I am pleased with his entertainment, but I want to spend as much time as possible with *him*. It is the host, and not his dinner, who makes the true enjoyment of a visit; and in the world it is God himself, and not his laws, nor all the products of them, who affords us the highest joy. As he would be unwise who paid a visit and forgot to commune with his friend, but only noticed his house and grounds, so is he most unwise who, in this matchless world, sees everything save him who is everywhere and who made it all. This is folly indeed.

Through the Bible in One Year: Hosea 9–11

The Enmity of God

But as for me, my feet had almost slipped;
I had nearly lost my foothold.
For I envied the arrogant
when I saw the prosperity of the wicked.
PSALM 73:2–3

When God is turned to be a man's enemy and fights against him, he is in a desperate plight. With other enemies we may contend with some hope of success, but not with the Omnipotent. The enmity of others is an affliction, but the enmity of God is destruction. If he turns to be our enemy, then everything is turned against us. "If God be for us, who can be against us?" (Romans 8:31 KJV). But if God be against us, who can be for us?

Men may try to persuade themselves that God does not care, that it is nothing to him how men act, whether they break or keep his laws. Men may plead that he is "kind unto the unthankful and to the evil" (Luke 6:35 KJV), and the same event happens unto all, both to the righteous and to the wicked; and so indeed it seems for the present. Our shortsightedness may even assure us that the ungodly prosper and have the best of it, but this is only our blindness.

God hates sin now and always. He would not be God if he did not. God is stirred with righteous indignation against every kind of evil; it moves his Spirit to anger. Some believe in an impassive God, but certainly the God of the Bible is never so described. He is represented in Holy Scripture after the manner of men. If he were represented after the manner of God, you and I could understand nothing at all of the description; but as he is represented to us in Scripture, the Lord notes sin, feels sin, grows angry with sin, is provoked, and his Holy Spirit is vexed by the rebellion of men.

Through the Bible in One Year: Hosea 12–14

The Weight of Sin

Let the wicked forsake his way and the evil man his thoughts.
Let him turn to the LORD, and he will have mercy on him,
and to our God, for he will freely pardon.

"For my thoughts are not your thoughts, neither are your ways my ways,"
declares the LORD.
ISAIAH 55:7–8

At first, men have very low ideas of sin. It is a trifle, a mere mistake, a failure of judgment, a little going aside; but when the Holy Spirit begins to deal with them, sin grows to be an intolerable burden, a fearsome thing, full of horror and dismay. The more men know of the evil of sin, the more astounded they are that they ever should have found any pleasure in it or could have made any excuse for it. Now, it is well when men begin to see the truth about themselves, for even if that truth breaks them into pieces, it is well that they are delivered from the dominion of falsehood.

Sin is great, and for that reason the sinner thinks it cannot be pardoned, as if he measured the Lord by his sin and fancied that his sin was greater than the mercy of God. Hence, our difficulty with men who are really awakened is to raise their thoughts of God's mercy in proportion to their raised idea of the greatness of sin. While they do not feel their sin, they say that God is merciful and talk very flippantly about it, as if pardon were a trifle. But when they feel the weight of sin, then they think it impossible that sin should be forgiven. In our text God in condescension helps the sinner to believe in pardon by elevating his idea of God. Because God is infinitely superior to man, he can abundantly pardon.

Through the Bible in One Year: Joel 1–3

Beyond Comprehension

How great are your works, O LORD,
how profound your thoughts!
PSALM 92:5

It is quite certain that the best thoughts—the most logical thoughts, the most original thoughts, the most correct thoughts you have ever had—are not worthy to be compared with God's thoughts. Now, look at nature. The things you see in nature were, at first, thoughts in God's mind, and he embodied them. Did you ever think such thoughts as God has thought in creation? You look up at the stars, and your thoughts are that they are mere points of light. His thoughts are not your thoughts, for when you look through the telescope, you discover that these are majestic orbs, and you can hardly get God's great thought of the heavens into your head.

It has even been so in your own mind as to the future. Read the prophecies, and see what is yet to be. God's thoughts about a new heaven and a new earth—how far above ours! The book of Revelation, which gives us parts of God's thought about the future, is not to be understood by us as yet. We have to wait till facts explain it, for God's thoughts are above our thoughts. Why, take a simple matter like the resurrection of the dead. We bury the departed, and their bodies are dissolved. God's thought is that they shall rise again. The seed shall become the flower. God's thoughts are far above any thoughts that can arise in your soul.

Through the Bible in One Year: Amos 1–3

The Grave of Legal Hope

❧

*Now we know that whatever the law says, it says to those who
are under the law, so that every mouth may be silenced
and the whole world held accountable to God. Therefore no one
will be declared righteous in his sight by observing the law;
rather, through the law we become conscious of sin.*
ROMANS 3:19–20

If a man does nothing wrong, yet he fails to do that which is right,
he is guilty. Omission is as truly a defect as commission. If you
have omitted, at any time, to love the Lord your God with the
whole force and intensity of your nature, if you have omitted in
any degree to love your neighbor as thyself, you have committed
a breach of the law. Not to obey is to disobey. Who can plead inno-
cence, if this be so? How cutting is the sentence "Cursed is every
one that continueth not in all things which are written in the book
of the law *to do them*" (Galatians 3:10 KJV, emphasis added)! It is
an awful passage. It seems to me to shut up the gate of hope by
works, yea, to nail it up. I bless God it does fasten this door effectually, for if there seemed to be half a chance of getting through
it, we should find men still struggling for entrance. Salvation by
self is man's darling hope: salvation by doings, feelings, or something or other of their own is the favorite delusion of sinners. We
may bless God that he has rolled a great stone at the mouth of the
grave of legal hope. He has dashed as with a rod of iron the earthen
vessel that held the treasures of our conceit. "By the deeds of the
law there shall no flesh be justified" (Romans 3:20 KJV).

Through the Bible in One Year: Amos 4–6

Perfect Reconciliation

For this reason Christ is the mediator of a new covenant,
that those who are called may receive the promised eternal inheritance—
now that he has died as a ransom to set them free
from the sins committed under the first covenant.
HEBREWS 9:15

Reconciliation, wrought out by Christ, is absolutely perfect. It means eternal life. If Jesus reconciles you to God now, you will never quarrel with God again, nor God with you. If the Mediator takes away the ground of feud—your sin and sinfulness—he will take it away forever. He will cast your iniquities into the depths of the sea, blotting out your sins like a cloud, and like a thick cloud your transgressions. He will make such peace between you and God that he will love you forever, and you will love him forever, and nothing shall separate you from the love of God that is in Christ Jesus our Lord. I have heard of some mend-all that so puts the pieces of broken plates together that the articles are said to be stronger than they were before they were broken. I know not how that may be. This I know: the union between God and the sinner, reconciled by the blood of Jesus, is closer and stronger than the union between God and unfallen Adam. That was broken by a single stroke, but if Christ joins you to the Father by his own precious blood, he will keep you there by the inflowing of his grace into your soul; for who shall separate us from the love of God that is in Christ Jesus our Lord? Lay hold on Christ as mediator, and trust ourselves with him, that he may make peace between us and God. And to his name shall be glory forever and ever!

Through the Bible in One Year: Amos 7–9

Our Rescuer

God is our refuge and strength,
an ever-present help in trouble.
PSALM 46:1

Now, beloved friends, if any of you are in great difficulty and trouble, tempted to do wrong, nay, pressed to do it, and if you do what is right, it looks as if you will be great losers and great sufferers, believe this: God can deliver you. He can prevent you having to suffer what you suppose you may, and if he does not prevent that, he can help you to bear it, and in a short time, he can turn all your losses into gains, all your sufferings into happiness. He can make the worst thing that can happen to you to be the very best thing that ever did happen to you. If you are serving God, you are serving an omnipotent Being; and that omnipotent Being will not leave you in the time of difficulty, but he will come to your rescue. Many of us can say with Paul, "We should not trust in ourselves, but in God which raiseth the dead: Who delivered us from so great a death, and doth deliver: in whom we trust that he will yet deliver us" (2 Corinthians 1:9–10 KJV). The Lord has helped us in the past, he is helping us in the present, and we believe that he will help us all the way through. He will help you too if you just follow his Word and by a simple faith do the right thing. I believe that we have reason to expect interpositions of providence to help us when we are called to suffer for Christ's sake.

Through the Bible in One Year: Obadiah

Beauty from Ashes

❧

Consider it pure joy, my brothers, whenever you face trials
of many kinds, because you know that the testing of your faith
develops perseverance. Perseverance must finish its work so
that you may be mature and complete, not lacking anything.
JAMES 1:2–4

Do you know that God has beauties for every part of the world, and he has beauties for every place of experience? There are views to be seen from the tops of the Alps that you can never see elsewhere. Aye, but there are beauties to be seen in the depths of the dell that you could never see on the tops of the mountains; there are glories to be seen on Pisgah, wondrous sights to be beheld when by faith we stand on Tabor, but there are also beauties to be seen in our Gethsemanes, and some marvelously sweet flowers are to be culled by the edge of the dens of the leopards. Men will never become great in divinity until they become great in suffering. "Ah," said Luther, "affliction is the best book in my library." And let me add that the best leaf in the book of affliction is the blackest of all the leaves, the leaf called heaviness, when the spirit sinks within us, and we cannot endure as we could wish.

Those who have been in the chamber of affliction know how to comfort those who are there. Do not believe that any man will become a physician unless he walks the hospitals, and I am sure that no one will become a divine or become a comforter unless he lies in the hospital as well as walks through it and has to suffer himself.

Through the Bible in One Year: Jonah 1–4

Blessed Advent

"Today in the town of David a Savior has been born to you;
he is Christ the Lord. This will be a sign to you:
You will find a baby wrapped in cloths and lying in a manger."
LUKE 2:11–12

See the glory of our Lord Jesus Christ, even in his state of humiliation! He is born of lowly parents, laid in a manger, and wrapped in swaddling bands, but lo, the principalities and powers in the heavenly places are in commotion. First, one angel descends to proclaim the advent of the newborn King, and suddenly there is with him a multitude of the heavenly host singing glory unto God. Nor is the commotion confined to the spirits above, for in the heavens that overhang this earth, there is a stir. A star is deputed on behalf of all the stars. This star is put in commission to wait upon the Lord, to be his herald to men afar off, his usher to conduct them to his presence, and his bodyguard to sentinel his cradle.

Earth too is stirred. Shepherds have come to pay homage of simpleminded ones: with all love and joy, they bow before the mysterious child, and after them from afar come the choice and flower of their generation, the most studious minds of the age. Making a long and difficult journey, they too at last arrive, the representatives of the Gentiles. Lo, the kings of Seba and Sheba offer gifts—gold, frankincense, and myrrh. Wise men, the leaders of their peoples, bow down before him and pay homage to the Son of God.

Through the Bible in One Year: Micah 1–3

Bow before Him

After Jesus was born in Bethlehem in Judea, during the time
of King Herod, Magi from the east came to Jerusalem and asked,
"Where is the one who has been born king of the Jews?
We saw his star in the east and have come to worship him."
MATTHEW 2:1–2

My intense desire is that we all may pay homage to him of whom we sing, "Unto us a child is born; unto us a son is given." Let those of us who have long worshiped worship anew with yet lowlier reverence and more intense love. And God grant—oh, that he would grant it!—that some who are far off from him spiritually, as the Magi were far off locally, may come today and ask, "Where is he that is born king of the Jews? For we have come to worship him." May feet that have been accustomed to broad roads, but unaccustomed to the narrow path, this day pursue that way till they see Jesus and bow before him with all their hearts, finding salvation in him. These wise men came naturally, traversing the desert; let us come spiritually, leaving our sins. These were guided by the sight of a star; let us be guided by faith in the divine Spirit, by the teaching of his Word and all those blessed lights that the Lord uses to conduct men to himself. Only let us come to Jesus. It was well to come unto the babe Jesus, led by the feeble beams of a star; you shall find it still more blessed to come to him now that he is exalted in the highest heavens and by his own light reveals his own perfect glory. Delay not, for this day he cries, "Come unto me, all ye that labour and are heavy laden, and I will give you rest" (Matthew 11:28 KJV).

Through the Bible in One Year: Micah 4–7

A Holy Mission

֍

For the Son of Man came to seek and to save what was lost.
LUKE 19:10

Jesus was not originally known as "the Son of Man," but as "the Son of God." Before all worlds, he dwelt in the bosom of the Father and "thought it not robbery to be equal with God" (Philippians 2:6 KJV). But in order to redeem men, the Son of the Highest became "the Son of Man." He was born of the Virgin and by birth inherited the innocent infirmities of our nature and bore the sufferings incident to those infirmities. Then did he also take upon himself our sin and its penalty and therefore died upon the cross. He was in all points made like unto his brethren. He could not be the Shepherd of men without becoming like to them, and therefore the Word condescended to be made flesh. Behold the stupendous miracle of incarnation! Nothing can excel this marvel— Immanuel, God with us! "Being found in fashion as a man, he humbled himself and became obedient unto death, even the death of the cross" (Philippians 2:8 KJV). O lost one, conscious of your loss, take heart today when the name of Jesus is named in your hearing: he is God, but he is man, and as God-and-man he saves his people from their sins.

Through the Bible in One Year: Nahum 1–3

He Came

❧

"The Son of Man did not come to be served,
but to serve, and to give his life as a ransom for many."
MATTHEW 20:28

The Son of Man came. Strange the errand, and unique as the blessed Person who undertook it. Thus to come he stooped from the highest throne in glory down to the manger of Bethlehem, and on his part it was voluntary. We are, as it were, thrust upon the stage of action; it is not of our will that we have come to live on this earth. But Jesus had no need to have been born of the Virgin. It was his own consent, his choice, his strong desire, that made him take upon himself our nature, of the seed of Abraham. He came voluntarily on an errand of mercy to the sons of men. Dwell upon this thought for a moment; let it sink into your mind; he who was King of Kings and Lord of Lords, the Mighty God, the Everlasting Father, the Prince of Peace, voluntarily, cheerfully descended that he might dwell among the sons of men, share their sorrows, bear their sins, and yield himself up a sacrifice for them, the innocent victim of their intolerable guilt.

Through the Bible in One Year: Habakkuk 1–3

God with Us

*"Therefore the Lord himself will give you a sign:
The virgin will be with child and will give birth to a son,
and will call him Immanuel."*

ISAIAH 7:14

"God with us": he has not lost that name. Jesus had that name on earth, and he has it now in heaven. He is now "God with us." Believer, he is God with you, to protect you; you are not alone, because the Savior is with you. Put me in the desert, where vegetation grows not; I can still say, "God with us." Put me on the wild ocean, and let my ship dance madly on the waves; I would still say, "Immanuel, God with us." Mount me on the sunbeam, and let me fly beyond the western sea; still I would say, "God with us." Let my body dive down into the depths of the ocean, and let me hide in its coverns; still I could, as a child of God, say, "God with us." Aye, and in the grave, sleeping there in corruption, still I can see the footmarks of Jesus; he trod the path of all his people, and still his name is "God with us."

But would you know this name most sweetly, you must know it by the teaching of the Holy Spirit. Has God been with us this morning? What is the use of coming to chapel if God is not there? We might as well be at home if we have no visits of Jesus Christ, and certainly we may come, and come, and come, as regularly as that door turns on its hinges. It is useless unless it is "God with us" by the influence of the Holy Ghost. Unless the Holy Spirit takes the things of Christ and applies them to our heart, it is not "God with us."

Through the Bible in One Year: Zephaniah 1–3

December 25

Lay Hold and Grow

❧

But grow in the grace and knowledge
of our Lord and Savior Jesus Christ.
To him be glory both now and forever! Amen.
2 PETER 3:18

How is eternal life grasped? Well, it is laid hold of by faith in Jesus Christ. It is a very simple thing to trust the Lord Jesus Christ, and yet it is the only way of obtaining the eternal life. Jesus saith, "He that believeth in me, though he were dead, yet shall he live: And whosoever liveth and believeth in me shall never die. Believest thou this?" (John 11:25–26 KJV). By faith we have done with self and all the confidences that can ever grow out of self, and we rely upon the full atonement made by the Lord Jesus, whom God has set forth to be a propitiation: it is thus that we come to live. Faith and new life go together and can never be divided.

This life, once laid upon, is exercised in holy acts. From day to day we lay hold on eternal life by exercising ourselves unto godliness in deeds of holiness and loving-kindness. Let your life be one of prayer and praise, for these are the breath of the new life. We still live the animal and mental life, but these must be the mere outer courts of our being: our innermost life must be spiritual and be wholly consecrated to God. Henceforth be devotion your breathing, faith your heartbeat, meditation your feeding, self-examination your washing, and holiness your walking.

In laying hold upon it, remember that it is increased by growth. Zealously grasp more and more of it. Do not be afraid of having too much spiritual life. Lay hold on it, for Christ has come not only that we may have life, but that we may have it more abundantly.

Through the Bible in One Year: Haggai 1–2

His Handiwork

And in him you too are being built together
to become a dwelling in which God lives by his Spirit.
EPHESIANS 2:22

A child may forget the mother; it receives much from her, and gratitude does not always come to her in return. But the mother never forgets the child to whom she has given much; what she has given is a firmer bond between her and the child than ever gratitude is from the child to the mother. Now, God has done so much for us already that this is why he continues to love us. Jesus remembers that he died for us, the Holy Ghost remembers that he strove with us, the Great Father remembers how he has preserved us, and because of all this goodness in the past, he takes pleasure in us.

Moreover, I think that the Lord takes pleasure in us not only because of all that he has done, but because he sees something in us that pleases him, something that is his own work. A sculptor, when he commences on the marble, has only a rough block, but after days and weeks of hard working, he begins to see something like the image he is aiming at producing. So I believe that God is pleased when he sees in any of us some grace, some repentance, some faith, some beginnings of that sanctification that will one day be perfect. You know how pleased you are with your children when they begin to talk; yet it is poor talk, is it not? So does God take pleasure in the tears of penitence, in the broken confession, in the first evidences of faith, in the tremblings of hope, because he has wrought all this, and he is pleased with what he has done, pleased to see that so far his handiwork has been successful.

Through the Bible in One Year: Zechariah 1–4

Faith's Twin

❧

*Godly sorrow brings repentance that leads to salvation
and leaves no regret, but worldly sorrow brings death.*
2 CORINTHIANS 7:10

Perhaps you have the notion that repentance is a thing that happens at the commencement of the spiritual life and has to be gone through as one undergoes a certain operation, and there is an end of it. If so, you are greatly mistaken; repentance lives as long as faith. Toward faith I might almost call it a Siamese twin. We shall need to believe and to repent as long as ever we live. Perhaps you have the idea that repentance is a bitter thing. It is sometimes bitter: they "shall be in bitterness for him, as one that is in bitterness for his firstborn" (Zechariah 12:10 KJV). But that is not the kind of repentance that I am talking of now. Surely that bitterness is past; it was all over long ago. But this is a sweet bitterness that attends faith so long as ever we live, and becomes a source of tender joy.

The most intense happiness I have ever felt has not been when I have been exhilarated and full of spirits, but when I have leaned very low on the bosom of God and felt it so sweet to be so low that one could scarcely be lower, and yet did not wish to be any higher. I want you to indulge yourselves in this rarest delight of sorrow at the feet of Jesus—not sorrow for unpardoned sin, but sorrow for pardoned sin, sorrow for that which is done with, sorrow for that which is forgiven, sorrow for that which will never condemn you, for it was laid on Christ long ago and is put away forever.

Through the Bible in One Year: Zechariah 5–8

İt Shall Be Done

I obey your precepts and your statutes,
for all my ways are known to you.
PSALM 119:168

O that every Christian were altogether and evermore obedient to heavenly rule. As the planet revolves undeviatingly in its orbit, because with the law imposed upon it there has come forth a constraining and impelling force, so may we also pursue our course of duty, because we not only have heard the divine precept, but feel the sacred energy of the Holy Spirit leading us in the prescribed path. Brethren, how safe we feel, and how happy in our consciences, if we are certain that we have the authority of the Great King for all our actions! The business of a Christian upon earth is not an independent one; he is not acting on his own account, but he is a steward for Christ.

Now, if we serve ourselves or the world, we must take the consequences of our unfaithfulness, but if we honestly serve the Lord, all is clear. When a Christian can say concerning any course of conduct, "I am bidden to do this by Christ Jesus my Lord; I can find chapter and verse to authorize my acts," when he can feel that he is working for Christ and not for himself, with a single eye to the glory of God and not with sinister aims and selfish motives, then he treads as on a rock and defies the censures of his enemies. When positive duty is concerned, your language will be, "This action I find that I must do, for I see an express command for it, and therefore it shall be done; be it difficult, it shall be achieved; be it impossible, I will wait on him who enables faith to remove mountains."

Through the Bible in One Year: Zechariah 9–11

A Heart like His

My command is this: Love each other as I have loved you.
JOHN 15:12

Among all of those who know that we are Christ's disciples, there is one very important person, and that is yourself. If you have love toward Christ's disciples, you will know that you are one of his disciples, for how does the beloved apostle John put it? "We know that we have passed from death unto life, because we love the brethren" (1 John 3:14 KJV). It will be one of the clearest evidences to your own heart that you are really a disciple of Jesus when you realize that for Christ's sake, you love the redeemed family of God. By this test shall all men know that you are his disciples.

By this test shall your fellow Christians also know that you are Christ's disciples. I do not know of anything that more commends a Christian to his fellow Christian than a true spirit of love. No sermon can be so eloquent to the world as a true manifestation of the love of Christ, and when God restores to his church genuine, hearty, and sincere Christian love—I trust we have not wholly lost it—but when he gives us much more of it, then shall the world be more impressed by the gospel than it is at present.

If ours is not a loving church, I have labored in vain and spent my strength for nought. If you love not one another, surely you do not love the Savior; but if you are knit together in love, then is our joy fulfilled in you, and Christ also rejoices over you.

Through the Bible in One Year: Zechariah 12–14

Sunday Work

*So, because Jesus was doing these things on the Sabbath,
the Jews persecuted him. Jesus said to them, "My Father is always
at his work to this very day, and I, too, am working."*
JOHN 5:16–17

Let me stir up God's people here to do this. Go and tell out the gospel, tell out the gospel. I think I have to a large extent attained my wish in this congregation. I miss such a large number of our friends on Sunday nights, and I am delighted to miss them, for they have no business to be here then. They are out preaching, teaching, working in schools, mission halls, and all sorts of holy service. That is what you ought to do if you love the Lord; get a good meal once on the Sabbath, and then go and do a good day's work in the rest of the Sunday. Praise God with your mouths and have the two-edged sword in your hands. To war against ignorance, to war against vice, to war against drunkenness, to war against infidelity and sin of every kind, is one of the best ways of praising the Most High. Until the last sinner is saved, see to it that you keep the two-edged sword of God's Word in your hand, and then forever let the high praises of God be in your mouth.

Through the Bible in One Year: Malachi 1–4

Scripture Index

378

383